Love Poems
DANIELLE STEEL

SPHERE BOOKS LIMITED

A Sphere Book

First published in Great Britain by
Sphere Books Limited 1982
Reprinted 1982, 1983 (twice), 1984, 1985,
1986, 1987, 1988, 1989, 1990, 1991

Some of the poems in this book appeared
in *Cosmopolitan*, *The Paraclete*, *McCall's*,
Ladies Home Journal and *Good Housekeeping*

Reproduced, printed and bound in Great Britain by
Cox & Wyman Ltd, Reading

ISBN 0 7221 8240 6

Sphere Books Ltd
A Division of
Macdonald & Co (Publishers) Ltd
Orbit House
1 New Fetter Lane
London EC4A 1AR
A member of Maxwell Macmillan Pergamon Publishing Corporation

This is a special book about special people. People who have loved me, and whom I have loved. People who have brought me joy beyond measure, and sometimes incredible pain. People I have hurt, sometimes more than I can bear to think about. People who have hurt me, sometimes more than they know. Yet each of their gifts has been precious, each moment treasured, each face, each smile, each victory, each defeat, woven into the fiber of my being. In retrospect, all of it is beautiful, because we cared so much. In essence, this book covers fifteen years of my life, and a handful of precious people who mean, and have meant, everything to me. This book is written for them.

But in writing this book, or rather putting together the pieces and poems of so many years of my life, I must also thank the many people who have cheered it on, who have written and asked and encouraged and urged this to happen. To all of you, and especially Anne Lerch, my thanks.

And to Linda Grey and Sandi Gelles-Cole, my thanks for a birthday gift beyond measure.

With much love, d.s.

Contents

1   When Love Is New   9

2   Growing Together   45

3   Growing Apart   65

4   Letting Go   103

5   Lonely Feelings   127

6   Beginning Again   143

7   Love Lost Once More   187

8   And then you love again ...
      carefully this time.   211

9   ... and then love is born again.   235

10   Love   247

1

When Love Is New

First Meeting

Razzle
    dazzle
        snow scene,
my life
    so white
        so bare
            so vast,
and then
    your open
        door,
my heart
    whooshing
        toward
your arms,
    racing
        much
            too fast,
too free,
    as your eyes
waltzed
    slowly
        over me,

the cadence
  yours,
the tempo
  mine,
the music
  poured
    like
      vintage
        wine,
the magic
  of our moment
    so rare,
      so good,
        so new,
as breathlessly,
  I gazed
    at you.

Strangers

Fragments
of two
lives
sifted
through
fine wire,
spread out
like
fans,
added
and
subtracted
and shaken up
like dice,
then rolled
across
a board,
a map,
your life
laid
gently
out

before
me,
mine
tossed
helter
skelter
in your
lap.

Waiting for Your Call

Backing
  and sidling
hurting
  ribs
    within
      my stall,
fighting,
  fleeing,
    running,
      seeing,
hoping,
  dying,
    aching,
      being,
waiting
  for
the soft
  ring
    of your
      call.

Poem to Danny

It doesn't matter
  at all
      if you
          call,
if you care,
   if you dare,
if you
    dream,
if
    you sing
      in a tree.
It doesn't matter
   at all,
       not at all
          ...just
              to me.

Shuffled Papers

Clumsily,
　but gently,
I push
　you
　　from
　　　my head,
as I fumble
　at my desk,
shuffle
　papers,
try to see
　and think
　　and do,
when all
　I find
　　beneath
　　　my hand,
　　　　my eye,
my heart,
　is
　　you.

No Choice

Comfortable
   in my ivory tower,
barren,
   lonely,
     safe,
hidden,
   shrunken,
     tiny,
       small,
and then you,
   suddenly
     peeking
       over my wall,
with firelit eyes
   and dazzling smile,
I flew away,
   I ran a mile,
I hid from you,
   I shoved you back,
     and then you called,
I felt
   my lack,
     my ache,

your eyes,
   your smile,
I turned again,
   I ran a mile,
feeling all
   your charms,
hungering
   for your arms,
wondering if
   I'd come
      to harm
or safe,
   listening for
      your voice...
knowing that I had
   no choice.

El Señor

You take a matador stance,
  I see you do it,
standing very near,
  you let me brush by,
tucking in your soul,
  looking very whole
    and strong and free,
yet never touching,
  reaching out to me,
    but always there,
you carry fire and smiles
  like darts and banners,
your manner
  pulls me closer,
    I brush near once again,
rushing through your cape,
  you smile,
    you watch,
      you know,
        you wait,
and I fly on and on
  again,
    ever closer,

ever faster,
ever more,
and ever farther
from the safety
of the gate.

Your Call

I wait now
  every morning,
    every day,
      for your voice,
your call,
  your smile,
    your hand,
      your eyes...
waiting for the phone
  to ring,
I realize
  how hard
    I hope
for a reason,
  an excuse,
    a word,
      a game,
an anything,
  a joke,
    a song,
      a ring...
I wait
  and then

I hear
your voice
at last...
I smile...
I fly,
I sing!

Party Shoes

Brown galoshes
and red party shoes,
my old life
and my new,
my days alone,
my life with you,
funny funky
old galoshes,
sad and brown and cold,
then you, my love,
smiling, sparkling,
shy yet bold,
changing my life,
my world,
my blues,
to dazzling,
dancing,
party shoes

Zippety Click —
I Love You

Zippety click,
   hop and skip
     from one thing
       to another,
dancing,
   running,
having one sweet
   hell of a good
     time,
zippety click,
   involvement
all those
   lovely causes
     to espouse,
and people
   to be met,
until quite
   suddenly
    today,

everything
   went Pow!
I love you,
   can you even
     start
       to think
of such a silly
   joke
     today?
I love you,
   by golly,
     yes,
       I do.
I do love you
   today.

—From Opposite— Ends

From opposite ends
  of the earth
    we came,
trundling
  our bags,
    our treasures,
our laughter,
  our
    hearts.
From opposite ends
  of the city
    we came,
from different points
  where we
    once stood,
so near,
  yet far apart.
From opposite ends
  of the world
    we came,

silent and cautious,
  unseen.
From opposite ends
  of a lifetime
    we came,
and found
  a breath
    of magic
      hovering
        in between.
From opposite ends
  of a kiss
    we come,
to hold
  each other
    tight
      beneath
        a starry sky.
From opposite ends
  of a heart
    we smile,
two lives
  blended
    into one,
with no more
  opposites
    to approach,

but simply together,
    laughing
        and young,
the beautiful man
    that you are,
        and I.

—Each of Us—

Each of us
  with our
    secret gifts,
magic potions,
  lovely notions,.
    waiting to be
      shared,
waiting to be
  aired,
each of us
  a half,
a whole,
  a mind,
    a soul,
      a heart,
and yet
  a part
of a better
  richer
    more,
      looking for the
door,
  the key,

the you,
        the me,
the we
    growing
        day by day,
looking
    for the way
to find
    what
        I'd always
dreamed
    and never seen,
always tried
    and never been,
always thought
    but never knew,
until at last
    I discovered
        that the gift
I always sought
    was you.

Knots

The rest
   of the world
      sits
         around
            in a knot,
a complicated
   ball
      of strangled
         confusion
and bungled
   hopes
      beyond
         repair.
While we
   in simple
      silence
have our
   private
      miracle
         to share.
O pity
   the poor
      tangled,

strangled
knots,
which we,
thank God,
are
not!

Are You Comfortable?

Are you
  comfortable?
Can you
  breathe?
Two pillows
  or one?
Is my arm
  crushing
    yours?
Is your
  leg
    wedged
      too tight
        under mine?
Are my hipbones
  too pointy?
    My nipples
      too
        small?
Oh, stranger

asleep
  at my side
    here
      tonight,
are you
  warm?
   Am I
    safe?
Could you
  love me
   at all?

Daughter of Love

I've never laughed
  when I made
    love
      before,
never touched
  tenderly
    and kissed,
feeling
  young
    and old,
and then
  rolled
    over
      slowly
with a smile
  of glee,
as looking up,
  you kiss
    my eyes,
and say

something
   silly,
      teasing
         me.
I never knew
   that a bed
      was
         a place,
where
   people
      shared
         their hearts
            with smiles.
I never
   made love
      with
         a giggle
            before,
laughing
   and glowing,
and silently
   knowing
that
   laughter
      is part
         of the art,

like hands
   are to gloves....
I just never knew
   that laughter
      was sweet
and so much
   a daughter
      of love.

Jam

Jam.
  There must be jam,
    you told me
    firmly,
with a half-hidden
  smile
    of satisfaction
and a promise
  I was yet
    to understand.
You were making
  your presence known.
Toast.
  Eggs perhaps.
    Double coffee,
      some milk,
        one sugar,
maybe juice,
  but always,
    always
      jam.
Yes, I understand.
  I think I can

        manage
            that,
monsieur,
    even in my halfstate
        in the morning
And you sat
    watching
        with the smile
            that made me feel,
so bright, so gay,
    so light…
and then I knew
    you'd spend
        the night…
You did, my love,
    and there was
        breakfast
in the morning,
    with birds
        singing,
hearts flying,
    sun streaming
        in over scrambled eggs,
            and ham…
and, oh, yes,
    of course…
        there was jam.

—*Nary a Care*—

You're gone,
　　new lover.
Gone
　　to your day,
　　　　to your life,
　　　　　　to your way
　　　　　　　　of doing things,
whatever it is
　　you do,
　　　　when you are far
　　　　　　from me.
And I,
　　like a child
　　　　with a dream,
gaze
　　starry-eyed
　　　　into the summer
　　　　　　rain,
feeling anguish,
　　gentle
　　　　pain,
fearing
　　you will vanish

from the bright
universe
we created
side by side
last night.
And then,
in bittersweet
despair,
I linger
with a cup of tea,
fearing
you have forgotten me,
feeling foolish,
old with fright,
yet young
with promise
long forgotten
in my distant
dreams....
And suddenly,
you're at
the door,
full of brand-new
schemes
for this path
we choose
to share.

Home from your wars,
　　from your tasks,
　　　from your day,
　　　　with nary a care
and only more love
　　to strew
　　　on my way.
I rush
　　to your arms
with a gurgle
　　of laughter,
　　　a thunder
　　　　of glee.
Dream man
　　come true,
you actually
　　did
　　　come back
　　　　to me!

Moonlit Sunshine

What
  do you
    do
for me
  with me
    to me?
You
  send
    silver
      sparkle
thunder
  moonlit
    sunshine
      shivers
through
  and through
    and through
      me.

2

Growing
Together

Sunshine Dancing

Heavenly, heavenly
    mornings
        unraveling
            our bodies
and then tying them
    in a fresh knot
        with sleepy smiles
            and tender words,
as morning birds
    sing past our window,
        sunshine dancing
            on our life,
and I for the first time
    ever
        feeling like
            a wife,
yet lover, friend,
    making breakfast,
        smiling to myself
as I burn the toast,
    and break the eggs,

still feeling
   your hands
      and kisses
         on my legs...
surely this is what
   life
      always had in store...
oh, darling,
   you make me ache for you,
      always hungry,
         always glad,
            always wanting more...

Ordinary Pleasures

I love our mornings,
  waking,
    finding you there
      next to me,
        smiling,
desperately needing
  that first cigarette
    to start your day,
and then dashing off
  to make you eggs,
seeing visions of
  your face,
    your hands,
      your legs,
your back
  as I juggle coffee,
    butter toast,
and wonder what
  I love the most
    about all that it is
      you are,

brightest star
in my heavens,
answer to all my
unborn dreams
and secret wishes,
I clatter dishes and
arrive
to help you undress
after you have just put
yourself together,
the weather is sublime
and we are fine,
and you are more precious
than you know,
as we both begin to
glow,
it is another perfect day...
and then you're on your way
to work
and I, wife-style,
driving,
thriving on the rich
delights
we share,
the tiny ordinary pleasures,
I come home

and tuck into my heart
like wondrous
sparkling
tiny treasures.

Friend

My house
my car
my bed
my arms
my life
my soul
my smiles
and all
my dreams
are touched
by the magic
of your
sounds,
your
smell,
the perfume
of your life
intertwined
with mine
in a silvery
blend,
so that I can

think
of only
you,
precious
lover,
partner,
friend.

Comfortable

You shout at me
   and I yell
      back,
you push,
   I shove,
and we squabble
   comfortably
over who sleeps
   where,
which side,
   whose spot,
you are,
   I'm not,
you won't,
   I will,
you grouse,
   I'm shrill,
a symphony
   of loving,
a song
   for every day,
a way

to say
"I love you"
in our own
familiar way.

Bill

I love your macho swagger,
   the look in your eye,
     in your smile,
      all the while
       you move toward me.
You always seem to know
   I'm there,
sometimes I sit back
   and stare
     quietly
      for a while,
waiting for you to know
   I'm near.
You sense it,
   see me,
and walk purposefully
   toward where I wait,
as I fall in love
   with you again,
watching your special
   just you
     macho
      gait.

Rainbow Dreams

As evening comes,
  I race,
already hungry
  for your face,
    your hand,
      your touch,
so much you have
  to give,
    and lavish on me
      with such style...
I think of you...
  I see you smile...
my heart dances,
  prances,
    runs, cavorts,
      and preens,
as quickly
  I do my face,
    my hair,
      and wait for you,
        with a myriad
of rainbow dreams.

Ball of Yarn

I have this funny
   ball of yarn
      in the corner
         of my head.
It sits there
   nice and neat
      and then I walk over,
         pick it up,
            look at it,
smile,
   and then I start
      to worry it
         a little,
just because it's
   there,
and then it starts
   to look all
      tangled up
         and messy
and I start
   to trip
      and fall
         in my ball of yarn.

Then you come home
      and gently
          pluck it
              from my hands,
smooth it out
      and make it
          neat
              again,
set it down,
      and smile at it
          with me
and I know
      again
          why I'm so glad
              when you come home.

Dashing
  zigzag
across
  the pattern
    of our life,
playing
  husband,
    mother,
      genius,
        wife,
scholar,
  chauffeur,
    student,
friend,
  then finding
you alone,
  for a fraction
of a moment,
  a sliver
    of a day,
loving
  what you are

and wish
  and try to be
in a very
  very
    special
      way.

—Love's Tango—

In an anthill,
in a tree,
in a crowd
of sixty-three,
I feel
lost
and then
confused,
but smile
at you,
bemused,
you squeeze
my hand,
we swim
for land,
you hold
my arm
and render
harm
a useless thing,
a broken
spear.

With you,
my love,
I know
no fear.
Only
warmth
and sunny skies
that dance
love's
tango
in
your eyes.

Cool

Okay,
　okay
　　so
　　　　I'll be
　　　　　cool.
At least
　I can
　　pretend
　　　to be,
since
　you can't
　　see
　　　me
near
　the phone,
　　or lying
　　　in the bath
　　　　at night,
wondering
　if
　　you'll
　　　marry
　　　　me.

3

Growing Apart

Peeling
Away

I feel you
   peeling
away
   from
     me,
like sticking
   plaster
     tearing
       slowly
from a wound,
   a layer
of my skin
   soldered
     to yours
       until
suddenly
   slowly
infinitely
   painfully,
you began

to pull,
just
   a little
      not
         a lot,
just enough
   to make me
      wonder,
and then
   suddenly
all of it
   being torn
      asunder,
my heart
   with its
      top
         popped,
drunk
   emptied,
      finished,
         gone,
            and now the
rest
   of me
      pried
         loose,
            torn free,

and I tired,
    frightened,
      crying,
          wondering
              why
you can't
    love
        me.

Recapture — *the Dream*

I want to come back
   to you,
want to feel happy
   about you again,
I want to look up
   at your eyes
      and giggle with glee,
not see
   the reflection
      of the pain you've caused me.
I want to feel merry
   and good,
and grateful for your love,
   not distant and remote
      and somewhere
         far
            above.
I want to fly
   to your arms
      like a child

sailing
   off
      a swing.
I want to remember
   the warmth
      your loving can bring.
I'm so tired
   of the chill,
      the winter,
         the snow.
Can't we rekindle
   the fires,
      and bring back the glow?
So much between us,
   So much sorrow
      it would seem...
oh, distant man,
   help me
      recapture
         the dream.

Trying to Pretend

Trying
　to pretend
　　I'm cool,
lying
　in the bed
that is
　absolutely
　　vast
　　　without you.
Trying to pretend
　that I
　　don't
　　　care
how late
　your key
　　plays
　　　chimes
　　　　in my ear
as it turns
　in the lock.

Trying to pretend
   I'm
      free
but stayed
   home
      only
         because
            it rained
and I
   was tired
      tonight.
Trying to pretend
   that I
      don't
         care
but caring
   far
      too
         much.
Trying to pretend
   that I don't
      give
         a damn
            about you,
my one
   and only
      man.

So go out.
   Go ahead.
Don't come home.
   Stay out.
      Get drunk.
         Get laid.
            Fly free.
I'll be here
   all night tonight,
trying to pretend
   I am
      the super splendid
         lady cool
I can't
   even
      begin
         to pretend
            to be.

Regret

Someday I will learn,
  I will stand stately,
    proud,
      noble, dear,
        as you expect.
And reluctantly
  relinquish
    the unpredictable,
uncontrollable child
  you have known.
That look of dark despair,
  of fear,
suspicion,
    of "oh...what now?"
      that you glaze me with
      in darker hours.
Fierce frown,
  flashing eyes,
brows so tightly knit,
  they bristle
    to discourage
      girlish prattle,

that prattle is the last shout
   of those baby days
      you long to know.
Sometimes mere girlish glee,
   harmless,
      yet unwanted.
Someday it will fade
   slowly, unnoticed.
Till it is gone,
   and I will have become
      the woman,
         and not the girl.
The girl will vanish
   if you wish it so.
Will you be proud?
   I don't believe you will.
Too late, my love,
   too late,
      and we shall share
         Regret.

Peekaboo

You run
in and out
of my simple
life,
as though
it were
a game,
a child's sport,
a sort of
forest
where you can
dart
among
the trees.
Now I see
you,
now I
don't.
Perhaps you
will,
perhaps
you won't.

The phone lies
   still.
It means
   you're happy
      somewhere
         else.
The phone
   then comes
      alive again.
It means
   you're tired
      of the world
         of men.
You come,
   you go,
      you flit,
         you fly,
You run into
   my arms,
you lie.
   You disappear.
And then I see
   you,
      standing there,
playing
   peekaboo

behind
a tree.
Oh, no.
No more.
This time
I score.
Farewell,
poor childish man.
Have your fun.
Live your life.
Play all your games.
But not
with me.

Where do you go
   when you go out
      for milk
         and come back
            seven hours later?
What happens
   when you park
      the car
         and go home
            somewhere else?
Whose cigarettes
   are you buying
      when you go out
         for mine
and come back
   with the wrong brand?
Whose name do you
   mutter
      in your sleep?
What heart do you
   keep
      in your pocket,
         hidden from my eyes?

What lies will you
    concoct next,
        my dear,
while I pretend
    that I don't fear
        the end
which came so long ago
    while I pretended
        not to hear
its deathlike
    footstep
        on my heart?

Noise

Motorcycle,
  airplane
    noises,
hot rock
  on the stereo
    in your car,
swift step
  and static
    always
      in the air.
Ever quicker
  pace
    hastening
      away
from peace
  toward
    noise,
playing
  volleyball
    amidst
      the people
        in your life.

Run faster
    faster
        still
midst
    your self-created
        noise
that will never
    kill
        the angry
            whispers
                of your soul.

A thousand dreams
   we shared,
     a thousand tears
      we shed,
a thousand days,
   a thousand nights,
     a thousand joys,
      a thousand fights,
a thousand episodes,
   a thousand epithets,
     a thousand hopes
      you shattered
       at my feet,
a thousand hearts
   you scattered
     and then mine,
and all the time
   I thought
     you cared,
how rare
   the joke,
     how sweet the gag,

how much I thought
    you loved
        this hag
a thousand years
    ago,
        my dear,
a thousand moments
    strung like tears,
        icicles across
            my soul,
a thousand ways
    of letting love,
        once oh so warm,
            die softly,
and then grow
    very
        very
            cold.

Only Violets

Only violets,
   I only wanted
      violets,
not masses of
   red roses,
      and vulgar ribbons,
         and finery,
            and lies.
I only wanted
   violets,
just two
   or three,
      or scribbles
         in the sand,
a trinket,
   some small
      thought,
a warm hand
   in the rain,
a smile,
   an apple,
      or some trifling

imperfection
 I could love.
Too much,
 and much too little.
A turtle,
 yes, a turtle
  would be nice too,
three-leaf clovers
 and fading leaves,
not stifling vulgarity
 and expensive emptiness.
But now I know how
 costly are the trifles,
how dear
 and almost
  unattainable.
Just violets,
 my love,
just that,
 remember it
  next year.

Carved
in Stone

You carve me
  in stone now
with your
  lazy
    finger
      sculpting
        me,
etching
  the icy
    nooks
you once made
  soft
    and warm,
you carve me
  in stone
    now
with the plastic
  passion
    of your
      torch,

shooting
tinfoil
sparks
at my flinching
marble.
You carved me
differently
before,
turned
my wood
to bark,
bearing leaves,
giving birth
to flowers
with the powers
of your
burning
love,
which secretly,
we both know
burns
no
more,
as your lukewarm,
too weak,
too quick
to chill,

fraying magic
    forces me
        to speak,
when once
    silence
        was
            enough.
Now,
    after you are
        rough,
you ask
    "happy?"
        just before
            you go,
and silently
    I nod
        my head,
whispering
    softly
        "no."

Dread

I dread you
   now,
dread
   your touch
and the smile
   that doesn't
      warm
         me
            anymore.
I dread you
   now,
your hand
   that frightens,
      makes me
         flinch
and hurts me
   to
      the
         core.
I dread
   you
      now,

your anger
quicker
than
the laughter
that
we
knew.
I dread you
now,
dread
the sight
of all
that
I
no longer
see
in
you.

─── *Nothingness* ───

A man
   touched me
      today,
and covered me
   with
      nothing,
a man
   I used to
      love,
the one
   I cared
      about
         so much,
but this time
   as he
      touched me
         with his nothingness,
there was only
   shock
      to realize
how far
   behind
      I'd left
         him.

The Year of the Bears

Side by side
   through the winter,
    tucked in
     like bears,
we snuggled
   and hugged
    and shared
     all our cares,
we teased
   and we talked,
and we whispered
   a lot,
until suddenly
   spring
    and at once
     you were
      not…
not mine
   and not there,
not here
   and nowhere,

your eyes
empty
in mine,
your lies
never
on time,
until finally,
grieving,
I knew
from your trend,
that our
magical,
mystical,
marvelous
year of the bears
had come
to
an
end.

Desperation

In desperation
  I counted
    on my fingers
      whom to call,
to turn to,
  reach out for,
    cling to.
Seven, eight,
  nine
    people
      to hold
        close…
nine,
  seven,
    four,
      none.
Mistaken
  I had been
    in desperation,

finding that
    others wouldn't
       do.
I only
    wanted
      him.

I can't bear it
   anymore,
      I can't...
too much anger,
   too much pain,
      too much sorrow,
         too much rain,
no matter how madly
   we once
      loved
         each other,
I can't trudge
   another
      step
on this lonely
   journey
      by myself...
left here
   on the shelf
where you put me
   for safekeeping,
I sit here,
   always weeping,
      waiting

for your return,
while deep inside
    I burn
        with slow despair...
I care...
    oh, darling,
        yes, I care...
but now I can't,
    I won't,
I will not sit here
    dying,
        fading,
            crying,
loving,
    hating,
        waiting
            for the fates
to deposit you
    in my arms
        once more
with your smile
    so rich and slow...
oh, no, my love,
    I can't
        love you or not,
            this time...
                I go.

Silence on the Stair

I watch
   the top
      of his head
as he travels
   quickly
      downward
into the vortex
   of the spiral
      staircase,
running
   down,
lightly
   like water
      down a mountainside,
his feet
   barely touching
      one step
before they rush
   headlong
      toward
         another...

he waves
　　his hand,
　　　then looks
　　　　up,
sunlight
　　dancing
　　　on his face.
It is
　　a moment
　　　filled
　　　　with grace...
and then
　　despair.
Before
　　I gave
　　　my heart
　　　　its head
to tell
　　its tale,
I let him
　　go,
I let him
　　flee,
to dance
　　his freedom
　　　dance
　　　　so far from me.

Gone now.
Gone.
And only
silence
on the
stair.

4

Letting Go

Free

Setting the bird free,
   raven haired,
      soaring high above my head,
watching him,
   wings stretched out,
with only a brief last look
   back,
circling high,
   wider now,
pride swooping low
   in my heart,
and coursing through
   my veins,
pride
   because I set him
      free,
only to remember
   all too quickly
      that it was not
         I,
      but he,
and with a last tender
      look

at my now empty
    horizon,
I know that he was
    always
      free.
Gone now,
    raven bird,
      gone to your own sun,
far from mine,
    far from here now,
much beloved bird,
    fly well,
      soar high,
        go free.

Bereft

What is it like for you right now?
   Is the snow as grayish
      as the world you left behind?
Is it all as filled
   with being busy,
is it as much effort
   to laugh harder than the crowd?
Have you told as many
   funny stories?
Have you almost cried
   as many times?
Or are you really having fun,
   the very best of times,
and feeling much relieved
   to be cavorting
      in the snow,
and very far away at last,
   feeling that you have
      escaped
before the time could come
   when people don't turn back?
Or worse,

have you just forgotten
     everything that passed?
Are you being happy?
   Or feeling quite bereft
     the way I do?

Crash into My Life

Did you mean
  to crash
    into my life
      this way,
leaving everything
  so topsy-turvy
    as you left?
Do you mean
  to tell me
    that you
      didn't know
        I'd care?
Did you really
  think I'd laugh
    and walk
      away?
How small you must have
  thought me,
if even
  for a moment
    you believed

I could
    smell roses
        in the air
and taste
    champagne
        again,
and walk
    away
        at midnight
to rake
    my leaves
        and give up
            life again.

How do I find my way back
    from the place
        where you
            led me?
The arbor,
    the swing,
        the lilac,
            the ring,
the promises, the dawn,
    the dreams
        that they spawned.
I understand.
    It is all different now,
        you aren't a boy,
            you're a man.
But show me, my love,
    the way back
        from it all,
and I'll follow the path
    if I can.

Sketch

That sketch of you
   so perfect
     at the time,
so endearing
   because you smiled
     above it
as we stared at it
   together,
     pleased.
Now it stares
   at me,
     alone,
and hangs coldly
   on my wall,
no longer part
   of you,
     or us,
no longer anyone
   I even
     once
       remotely knew.

It is but
    a strong man's
      face,
your kind
    of eyes.
A man
    in a beret.
Someone
    born here
      on my wall.
It could be
    anyone
      but you,
in fact
    it is
      no one
        at all.

Fingering
Our Sand

Going back
   to tender places,
      full of you,
touching
   once warm
      moments,
         looking at
our sun,
   standing
      twixt
         our sea
            and sky,
and fingering
   our sand,
      looking at
         the places
we both
   once wore
      like hats,

I wondered where
the moments
went,
flying past
my head
like cranes
and darting
through
my feet
like rats.

Silence

Your silence hurts,
   it weighs heavily,
      dammit,
I cared so bloody much,
   I hurt, I gave,
      I cried,
         I wanted,
needed,
   hoped,
      the scope
         of it all
            still overwhelms me
as I paint portraits
   in the sky,
      seeing you
         in my life's eye,
            painting in
your presence
   for a thousand years
      to come,
wanting, wishing,
   hoping,
      seeing,

yet frightened
   that
      you'll
         fade away...
and then,
   trembling,
      I realize
         once more...
there was no call
   from you
      today.

No One There

I offer him
  silence
    and take back
      despair.
I look
  for a rainbow
    and find
      only dust.
I wish
  for a dream
    and wake up
      in a trance.
I cling
  to a smile
    and choke
      on a sob.
I tender
  my hand
    and bring back
      the air.

I reach
for the man
and find
no one
there.

Soaring Silver Bird

Soaring silver bird
  in the noonday
    sky,
weighted
  with the man
    who chose
      to leave me.
I wish
  for safety,
pray
  for flame,
knowing hotly,
  in the midst
    of my confusion
      that
        flame
or no
  he will be
    dead
      to me
        now.

—Fear Not —

Farewell

Fear not,
   sweet love,
the hands
   of time,
for poems
   do not
     always
       rhyme,
fate runs
   its course
     and plays
       its tricks
and in the
   last
     and final
       mix,
one wins
   it
     all
       and loses
        naught,

if love
   was good
      and battles
         fought
to their
   very
      final
         end,
good-bye,
   sweet love,
farewell,
   my friend.

Fragile Moments

Shock.
Blast.
Zap.
Gone.
Gone?
Gone.
He's gone
now.
Dead.
Finished.
Over.
Yes,
gone.
And strange
how it
all works,
how it
happens,
what lasts
in one's
mind.

Only the
    tiny
        fragile
            moments,
                the unlikely
gems,
    the morsels,
        and not
            the cake,
the taste
    of the whole
        forgotten,
and only
    the faint
        perfume
            of unreality
                remains...
his whims...
    his smile,
        the guileless
            way he looked
only once
    or twice,
        and in a thrice
            he's gone,

the tale
     too brief
        to tell,
and you remember
       nothing
          very long
             or
                very well.

5

Lonely
Feelings

Couples

Couples.
  Happy couples,
clinging close,
  hugging tight,
    dancing fast,
      being one,
laughing loud,
  singing high,
    giggling shrill,
      showing off,
loving love,
  living hard,
    and making
      my heart
break
  and
    snap
      and
die
  as
    I
      watch
        them

from
  this
    spot
      where
        I
still
  stand
    alone.

Two Thirds

Two thirds
  and two thirds,
Two apartments,
  two separate
    homes,
      neighbors.
Together
  we make
    four thirds,
one
  too
    much
and twice
  one
    short.
You have
  your
    man,
      neighbor woman,
and I
  my child,
and as your husband

trotted
down
the
stairs
today
with his dog
and my child,
I watched
his legs,
the sway
of his hips,
the way
his haircut
ended,
and you watched
my small girl's
bright red
sneakers,
starlit hair
and tiny hand
clasped
in his
larger
one.

Two thirds
we are
in either
house,
and neither
of us
whole.

Woman
Laughing
in the Night

Shrilly,
  a voice
    in the night
caw caws
  raven-fashion,
it is a cactus
  sound,
it prickles me,
  and, curious,
    I rise,
stealthily
  pulling back
    lace curtains
that have
  come to me
    too soon.
Silently
  I watch...

a taxi
   giving birth
      to a man,
         and then
            a woman.
She laughs again.
   She gropes
      for him,
throwing back
   her head,
hurling
   laughter
      from her mouth
again
   like sparks
      this time,
         staccato,
            sharp,
he fondles her,
   the cab leaves,
      I watch.
She laughs again
   and he silences
      her,
         but only for an instant,
            with a kiss.

She laughs
   she holds his hand
      she leads him
         home,
her prey
   into her laughter lair.
while I,
   too soon old
      while still
         so young,
watch,
   bereft,
      alone,
         unseen.

On the Riverbank

Two men once
  found
    me
naked
  on the riverbank
    at different
        times,
and then
  a third
    came by.
All brothers,
  all the same,
    seeking
only
  naked
    maidens
near a
  body
    of cool
      water

to quench
   their many
      thirsts.
Two men
   left me
      on that
         riverbank,
the third
   left
      me
         for dead,
and if
   a fourth
      should
         happen
            by,
he'll not
   find me
      on the
         riverbank
listening
   for his
      tread.
He'll find
   me
      armed
         and shielded,

hidden
near
a strong,
stone wall,
if a fourth
should even
happen
to find me
there
at all.

Boat Come In, Tide Go Out

I sat and watched
  a boat
    come in,
the tide
  go out,
a bird
  fly by,
a man
  swim past,
a life
  go by.
The sun
  had set,
the man
  had gone,
the tide
  was out,

the day
　　was done,
the life
　　gone by
was mine.

—Princes, Toads —

Princes,
   toads,
     and butterflies,
sugar cookies,
   bitter apple tarts,
     and frosty lemonades,
circus tents,
   and puppy dogs,
     and hayrides,
icy midnight
   swimming
     in a lake,
muddy roads,
   woodsy smells,
     fresh grass,
and dandelions,
   and oranges,
     and wine,
faded denims,
   musty silks,
     and faded memories
of princes
   turned
     to toads.

6

Beginning Again

—Now I Want—
the Have

I've faced it then,
   have I?
     I suppose I have.
—The magical
   answer
     to the cannonball
     question
  "what do you
   really
    want?"
I have want,
   now I want
    the have,
the touch,
   the hand,
    the real,
the feel
   of the same
    leg
cast easily

over mine
   for a decade
      of winter
         mornings...
for two decades...
   or three...
that same leg
   flung
      over
         me,
the same smile.
   A sameness.
Oh, God, yes,
   I'd love that.
I've tasted
   the hors
      d'oeuvres,
nibbled
   at the cakes,
      the pies,
tasted
   all the lies
      of liberty
         and free.
Who sold me
   that?

I want mine
back,
the savage sweet
of same
and same
and same again
the same sweet man
to share
a life
of love
and have and same
with me.

Matador

I play
   a matador's game
     with life,
face it
   squarely,
     deceive
       its sharp
         horns,
wave
   embroidered
     glitter
       in its face,
I flaunt
   who
     I am,
and proudly,
   in the noonday
     sun,
I dance
   for no
     audience,
save
   my own

soul,
I lust not
  for blood,
    merely
      for life.
I stand
  here
    alone,
with the
  cape
    in my hand,
I flee
  not
    from battle,
I laugh
  when
    I can.
Ha! Toro!
  See me here,
    see me
      now!
See me, Life!
  I am
    a Woman!
I am
  no man's
    wife.

Are You Still There?

Leafing through
   the pages of my address book.
Looking for you,
   your name
     scribbled
       somewhere,
stuffed
   in my back pocket
     lo those many years
       ago.
Groping
   for you
     in the attic
       of my memory,
never
   lost,
     but put away.
Strange time
   to call perhaps,
     your name
       and face

retrieved
  so late
    after time
      has tossed us
both
  from here
    to there.
But now
  I'm here
    again.
        Are you?
Seven numbers
  and a long
    thin
      ring
        ringing on.
You must be
  gone.
    And then your voice
      again.
Surprising
  in its nowness
    right here
      in my room,

as I wonder how
  you look
    these days,

after such a lot
of years
pressed between
the pages
of a frayed
red leather book.

Snow in Your Hair

Snow
in your
hair,
not age,
warmth
in your
heart,
not rage,
a smile
in your
eyes
just for me,
I lean
gently back
and you
are my tree.
Your heart
has been
farther
than mine,

You love
  your cognac,
    your cigars,
      your white wine.
There's no
  haste
    in your
      pace,
you
  no longer
    must
      race,
no more
  do you flee
    or break
      dates,
no need
  to rush
    past,
      dodging fates.
You give me
  the sun
    and the moon
      in your palm,
you need me,
  you love me,

you make me
feel calm.
You gave me
the woman
I wanted
to be,
you hold me
so gently
and let me
feel free,
we stand
close together
and smile
at our truth.
You gave me
the sun,
now I give you
my youth.

Pretend
Forever

Devastating,
  debonair,
    delightful
      man,
and I,
  the dazzling
    darling,
as face to face
  we dance,
    we waltz,
we do a minuet
  of hope
    on our desert isle,
I laugh,
  you smile,
    we float
      with glee,
Together
  hand in hand,
    so free,
then suddenly

I see
   the narrow
      band
of gold
   that holds
      you fast,
         and at last
you see
   that I am
      fettered
         by the same,
and now
   it is
      a kind of game,
         as you hold
            my arm,
I touch
   your sleeve,
      enjoying
         the pretend
            forever
magic
   of our
      cinderella
         eve.

For a Year, For a Day

Music and singing
   and laughter
      and bringing
daffodils
   to toss
      in the air
and nary
   a care,
and a river
   to wear
and a sky
   to put on
      like
         a cloak,
and Coke
   to drink
      and then
         champagne

and carriage
    rides
        at midnight
            in the park,
and all
    a lark
        until
the gingerbread
    begins
        to crumble,
and at last
    you stand there,
        broken,
            foolish,
                humble.
Go ahead,
    sing.
        Don't wait
            for a ring.
Laugh
    while you may,
        for a year,
            for a day,
smile,
    and never look
        harried,

if the man
you insist
that you
love
is
already
married.

Peacocks
and Frogs

Peacocks
  and frogs.
Princes
  and pickles.
Gingham
  and mustard
    and giggles
      and tickles.
Onions
  and daisies
and raindrops
  and stars.
Cheap wine
  and fine wine
    and love
      sold in jars.

— *Sacred Papers* —

Front page,
  back page,
    sports page
and financial
  section
    all a jumble?...
Oh, no,
  it is
    not I
      who'll make
        you mumble
in despair,
  wondering
    precisely
      where
the page one
  news
    has fled,
as you
  lie
    cozily
      abed,

sipping tea
   and smoking,
while
   exasperatedly
      and in secret
         choking
wondering
   where
      in hell
         the Dow Jones
            might be...
Oh, no...
   no sacred
      rite
to be
   defiled
      by me.
Separate
   papers,
      separate
         baths,
united joys
   delighted
      laughs,
the meeting
   of two

very
   independent
     sorts,
while above us
   one big
     bright star
       cavorts
and tall trees
   which gently
     flow and bend,
and in our laps,
   two morning
     papers,
sacred
   till the
     very
       end.

—— Too Much ——

Silence today...
   too busy?
      You couldn't
         get through?
What does it mean?
   Are you already bored?
      Does it matter?
         Is the telephone
            out of order?
I check my watch
   again
      and fiddle with
         the border
            on the bed,
running reasons
   through my head,
      thinking
         of all the possibilities,
why perhaps you
   couldn't call
      last night...

but still
   a chill
      of fright....
         Does it matter?
            Has he fled?
And slowly,
   I go back
      to bed,
heavy hearted,
   lonely,
      and a little bit afraid...
Have I played it wrong
   this time?
Too open?
   Too much too soon?
      Or is it something
         that I've said?
Or have I quickly become
   just anyone,
a someone to take
   for granted,
      an old shoe?
Or is it that I am
   already
      much too much
         in love
            with you?

Open Hand

Oh, such an open hand
  I hold out to you,
    so wide open,
      filled with my heart,
my soul,
  my life,
    my sins
      and pleasures
       and despairs.
It used to be
  that I held it all
    hidden
deep inside
  my pockets,
    for none to see,
no one to hurt
  or touch
    or tell,
yet already I know you
  so well,
    trust you so much,
that I hold it all
  out for you to touch

and see...
knowing that
you won't
hurt me,
oh, treasured,
gentle,
much loved man
to whom I hold out
my open hand.

— *Only Close* —

Yes, love,
   I know,
      it's hard
         for both of us...
my wanting,
   needing,
      hoping,
         waiting,
almost
   seeming
      to be baiting
as I reach
   out
      in a way
that fills
   you
      with
         fear...
it's
   all right,
      runner man,
it's okay,

yes
I know
you'll stay
while
you can
then you'll
go
and I'll
grow,
and I'll
cry
for a while...
ssshhh...
it's all right,
darling,
smile.
I shan't
get you
lost
in a life
that you dread.
as visions
of wedding rings
dance
in your head.
Fear not,
don't flee.

I only
want you
close
to me.

Fondly

I care about you.
  I like you.
I relate to you.
  I understand you.
I feel for you.
  I'm fond of you.
    You're dear.
Oh, no, my dear.
  You're not even
    here,
nor barely
  there
    with your "fond"
      words
that relate
  to like
    and care.
      You are nowhere.
I need you,
  want you,
    love you.

That's what's
really there,
but do you
dare?

The Inside
of Your Arm

You make love to me
   as though
      you wore
         the manual
            on the inside of your arm.
You touch,
   you feel,
      you reel,
you slide
   along the inside
      of my thigh...
         you sigh,
you smile,
   you keep yourself aloof,
      you arch sharply
         toward the roof,
you moan,
   and then you glance
      to see if by chance

I am as transported
    as you want me
        to think you are...
but no,
    no different
        than the backseat of a car
            a century ago,
                and then as well
there's one tiny tender thing
    that you, m'friend,
        forgot
with all your ravishing,
    ravaging,
        macho, sexy, free!...
You never even kissed me.

You Too?

Good-bye
  hello
     good-bye
     good-bye
hello.
  Hello
     once more.
        Yet again.
And then
  good-bye
     another
thousand
  times
     and
        more.
From
  the end
     to
        the beginning,
and then
  back
     again,

starting
  new,
    no longer
      starting
        fresh,
no
  fresh
    left.
And each
  hello
    has
      the echo
        of good-bye
hidden
  in
    its heart,
ah, yes,
  my friend,
    I know.
      Hello?
Yes.
  For a while.
    And then
      you too
        will
          go?

Twinkles and Sparkles

Twinkles
    and sparkles
        and horrible
            shakes,
shivers
    and giggles
        and frivolous
            quakes.
Vague looks
    and dark looks,
        odd thoughts
            and green eyes.
Yesterday's
    wonders.
        Tomorrow's
            good-byes?

First Hello

First hello
  on a bright
    spring day,
fresh green
  splashed
    on all
      the trees,
flowers
  everywhere,
    in my hair,
our hands,
  your voice,
a ferry boat
  ride,
    laughter,
      songs,
and ice cream
  cones
    on a newly
      painted
        bench.
Then summer
  was ours,

we held it
tight,
grew
brown
and strong
and gay,
sailing days,
and waterfalls,
and woods,
picnics
and promises
and time
always
wanting
to stand
still.
And after
all that,
autumn
came
as a surprise,
crept up,
unfurled
its golden
hair
and scarlet
wares,

it grew chilly,
    leaves fell
        as we began
            to drift,
we had
    no picnics
        left
            to share,
barely time
    it seemed
to remember
    spring
        and salute
            our first
                hello
before
    we said
        our last
            good-bye.

Count

I used
  to count
    my men
but it
  embarrassed
    me,
well
  bred,
    well
      fed,
well
  led
    on a proper
      path
for one
  or two,
perhaps
  secretly
    a third,
      but not
        a fourth.

A fifth?
    Good
        God!
            A sixth,
                disgrace,
and the
    seventh
        could
            only
make
    me know
        I was
            a whore.
Now
    I don't
        count
            my men
ever
    any
        more.

Friend

We compare notes,
  my friend and I...
    shyly, nervously,
      but strangely
willing to tell
  the truth
    about our youth,
      about our then,
        about our now....
How many have you had?
  Did you care
    about them all?
Were they young?
  old?
    splendid?
      tall?
You mean you had one too
  whose name
    you never did
      quite
        know?
All right, all right,
  I understand.

I had one too.
       It made me grow.
And a man you clearly
    didn't love,
        the kind that made
        you feel
            a whore?...
I had one too...
    yes.
        What a bore...
            and degrading.
It chewed a nibble
    from my soul.
        Oh, and one so old.
        And two so young.
            I've come unsprung.
I'm telling you all this?
    about them all?
        right up to the very end?
But you tell me too,
    and I feel good,
        loved, accepted,
            understood,
sharing my victories
    and disgraces,
tragedies
    and comedies,

bruises and how they mend...
with one single, very special,
treasured
friend.

7

Love Last Once More

— *Sing Softly* —

Sing softly
  sadly
    hollow
songs
  of bygone
    days
and yearning
  dreams
    of once upon
      an almost time.
Sing gently,
  love,
    at eventide,
on wintry
  nights
    and summer
      days.
Sing to
  your other
    love,
      my love,
and if our time

should come
again,
come softly
to my door
by night.
You'll find me
waiting
for you
there.

Come Back

Funny
  that they all
    come back.
      They always
        do.
Back
  they come
    with a change
      of heart,
long after
  they had
    gone.
Back
  they come
    with all
      the words
        I wanted
once
  to hear.
    But they come
back
  too late.

Ears
go deaf,
hearts
die,
moments
pass
and time
ceases
to be
of much
importance.
This time
make it
different.
Bring him
back
while I
still
care.

—Broken Day—

I bought
  groceries,
    forgot
      to wash
        my hair,
picked up
  a pack
    of cigarettes,
and
  eighteen
    nails,
I had
  a project,
    forgot
      a lunch,
I think
  it rained
    all
      day,
all year,
  all life
    gone
      gray.

Someone
said
that
you
got
married
yesterday.

No Man, Our Man

Was he a man
   the man
     who was
       my man?
You know,
   that man...
     the man...
       my man...
         ...her man.
The man
   who was
     her man,
       was mine,
         I thought,
and I hear
   she thought
     so too.
Foolish
   to think
     the man
       was ours.

No man,
   our man,
      her man,
         my man,
and I only
   wonder
      now and then
         who is his
woman now?

Scoundrel Love

You ask me if I loved the man,
    unworthy as you say he was,
      it seems to me I did,
      my friend,
        without much reason,
          or a good "because."
What a wretch he is now,
    in my ever-clearing brain,
what a dandy, what a scoundrel,
    and, oh, my friend,
    how much pain
      he inflicted on my heart
        without ever looking back.
O alack!
    Plague take the rogue
    and curse his soul,
      what a devil was that man,
      what an evil sort of troll!
But was he really all those things?

Was he quite as vile as that?
Then why is it that I love him,
    sitting here
        and looking back?

He Calls

And now,
  at last,
    he calls,
in tears,
  in fears,
    in dread,
instead
  of having
    loved me
    then.
He calls me
  now,
  in pain,
    in grief,
      in guilt,
with endless sorrow
  for the old cruelties
    he once enjoyed
      so much.
I remember...
  and now
    I answer him
      with caution,

with a sigh...
  a distant
    something
     in my eye,
not quite a tear,
  no longer love,
    almost anger,
yet
  not
    quite
     hate,
      too late...
he asks
  if I will see him
    and I answer,
     cowardly,
      vague,
muttering
  "don't think I can"
    to this
pitiful,
  not quite,
    too late,
     guilty
      man.

Octopus
Hectopus

Octopus
  Hectopus
    Hexagon
      Round
        Lovers
who cheat
  make their own
    wailing sound,
shrieking
  like banshees
    explaining their ways,
breaking
  all hearts
    till the end
      of their days.

Someday

Someday
   is a place,
     a time,
       a dream,
a blade of summer
   grass,
     dried out,
and reminiscent
   of a day
     when someday
was reality
   and filled
     with hope.
Someday
   was a word
     we used
       to taunt
         each other,
a distant spot
   we hungered for,
     but were anxious
       not to find
         too soon.

Someday
    was a yearning,
        a man I knew
and loved,
    in a someday
        sort of way,
because today
    was never quite
        his style.
Someday
    was a child
        we would have
        had,
            but didn't,
a time I knew
    would come,
        but never has.

To Clo:
Christmas
Remembered

The Christmas most dear to me?
   The one we danced beside the
   tree,
   The Christmas you lay next
   to me.
The year we shared each other's
hearts,
   The Christmas we were one.
Ah, dancing man of long ago,
   Come back to me again,
The tree is lit, my stocking's hung,
   I wait now as I have since then,
For but one more Christmas Eve,
   In the brilliance of our midnight
   sun.

Father,
Daughter,
Friend

Extraordinary moments
   stand out now,
special days,
   the big events,
     the times I can't forget...
my wedding day,
   riding in the car
     bathed in a cloud
      of white,
hidden by my veil,
   my hand clutched in yours,
and then you suddenly
   so pale
     as we walked
      up
       the aisle...
and then I smile,
   another time, another day,

while still a child,
wearing something ghastly,
   wild,
and you pretending that
   I looked okay,
      beautiful, in fact,
         divine…
do you remember
   that funny time?
And then the times
   you came to camp,
the day I broke your
   favorite lamp,
the bookcase
   I destroyed,
the absurdity of meeting
   boys,
      and bringing them to you…
the memories a kind
   of glue
      between my then
         and now,
I see you with a furrowed brow
   poring over
      what I wrote,
scribbling, writing,
   making notes,

and in later years,
  only your voice
    in the midnight hours,
as silently I dialed,
  so relieved to find you there,
    so good to know you cared,
how much we said,
  how rich the gifts,
how lucky we both were
  to have been father,
    daughter, friend...
and even now, that you are
  gone,
    the joy of that will never end.

Crying Rainbows

Crying rainbows,
  dripping tears,
    reminding me
      of what you were
       to them,
I listen to your friends,
  I read the notes,
  I nod my head,
    I hold my pen,
I try to say
  the things
    they need
      to hear....
But what of me?
  Where will you be
    next week
      when I'm alone,
or when I want to send
  my book,
    who will look

at my work
the way you did?
Who will speak
the truth,
who will remind me
of my youth?
Must I be a grown-up
now
that you have fled?
Who will tuck me
into bed
if I wish to be
a child again
of one
or two
or three?
Who will take
care
of me
as you used to do?
Oh, Daddy, is it
true
that you are gone,
and I am grown?...
Yes, you are,
I am,

as I sit here,
all alone,
crying rainbows
of my own.

8

And then
you
love again . . .
carefully
this time.

Hurray for the Legalized Lover

Were they so wrong
the madwomen
of the fifties
who endowed
each lover
with the gift
of wedlock?
Are we so much
better off
with bedlock?
Am I so free
because
I wear no ring,
and carry only
my brave name
after all
these scars?

Ah, no,
   really,
      I think by now
I ought to
   have a medal
      or two,
a name or three
   or four
      or five.
After all
   is said
      and done
who will know
   that in fact
I was once
   very much
      in love, alive?
And with all
   our lively
      seventies games,
I begin
   to yearn
      for an endless
         fifties
            list of names.

If we're so free
    why should
      we be
        so very undercover?
Next time
  I think
    I'll find me
a name-throwing
  legalized
    lover.

Champagne in *My Shoe*

Sitting here,
   with early
      morning coffee,
wondering
   where you are
      right now,
I still feel good,
   like well-polished wood,
well-oiled springs,
   waiting to see
      if the morning
         brings
you back,
   or will you wait
      till noon?
         So soon?
Or not until...
   tonight...
      and then a shaft
         of fright...

like sunbeams
    at my feet...
so sweet
    our hours
        before the dawn,
the dreams
    they spawned,
        the pains
            they stilled,
the tears they dried
    from years ago,
        oh, let it grow
all this bright
    new love
        I need so much,
your gentle touch
    like champagne
        in my shoe...
oh, dear new man,
    come back,
        come back,
I promise I'll be
    good
        to you....

Attic

Over the years,
   I have carried
boxes,
   treasures,
     objects,
       beds,
old shreds
   of people
     who had hurt
       or cared,
people I had pared
   down
     in memories
      and dreams,
people who had shrunk
   and grown,
     those who had left me
     all alone,
I carried them along,
   I sang their song,
I kept their faces
   in sacred places
     in my mind,

a kind of album of my life,
   my years as child,
      my days as wife,
         my broken toys,
            my shattered joys,
lying in a myriad pieces
   near my feet,
      swept into piles
         with all the smiles
that faded all too soon,
   as I sat,
      woven into the cocoon
         you quietly unwound,
where somewhere
   deep within
      you found me
         hidden,
playing with a doll,
   a bear,
      how much I care,
how good you've been
   as I notice
      what I should have seen
         an eternity before...
the debris beneath the bed,
   the brittle chaos in my head,
      the wilted flowers,

forgotten hours,
the whispers and the taste
of ash
buried in the attic
of my not so many years,
and suddenly the tears
seem to have mattered not at all,
it is no longer fall
but spring
as you bring
me all this joy
to have and hold
and keep,
and I,
laughing,
pull aside the blinds,
let in the sun,
hitch up my skirts,
pick up the broom,
and finally,
begin
to sweep.

Brand-new Now

Let us not
   confuse
      the actors
         in the play.
He hurt me,
   she broke
      your heart.
He left me,
   and she was
      a rotten cheat.
Let us instead
   see only
      each other.
You took
   my pencil,
I failed
   to wash
      the tub out,
         dry your razor,
we forgot
   to buy

a loaf of bread
    for lunch.
Those are
    our only
        griefs
            to cry for.
So if he
    left me
        long before
            you came along,
I bid him now
    adieu,
        and if she left
            you broken,
I'll help you
    to begin anew.
And tomorrow
    you'll give
        back
            my pencil,
I'll dry
    your razor,
        wash the tub out,
            and we will buy
                the bread
                    together,

and start
a solid
you-me-now
life.
Only me
and you.

Loving You

Childlike,
 I hear
  the echoes
   in the halls,
the footfalls
 that never came,
I hear the silence
 in the night,
I taste
 the fright,
and yet,
 I am a grown-up
  now,
   or so they say,
a mesh of gray
 woven into my hair,
  too old to care
   if the footsteps
    ever come again...
and yet,
 last night,
  I felt my heart

listen,
   tremble,
      wait,
fearful
   that I shan't find
      you
         waiting at the gate,
fearful that you'll
   cross
      the fields
         and vanish in the night...
too old
   for this fright,
it should not matter
   quite so much...
and yet
   it does...
      it does...
         you do....
The world
   would be
      my tomb
         again
were it not
   for the joy
      of loving you.

Matching the Pairs

The roof
   brought down
   around
      our ears,
the curtains
   wrapped
   around our
      heads,
all our apples
   so carefully
      stacked,
so instantly
   scattered,
      the patter
         of every day
halted
   as we sat there
suddenly
   lame,
suddenly tamed
   by life

and anger,
            fear,
                    and despair,
dismay,
    as we glared
        from
                opposite
                    corners,
throwing rocks
    tossing dreams
like used socks
    somewhere
        behind us
into a place
    we would never
        find
            again,
and then scurrying
    about,
clutching
    our accusations
        in our arms,
the charms of each
    forgotten
        until the magic
            clock
began to chime

the hour...
  not quite midnight
   yet,
 still time,
  a moment or two,
   in which to run
and dash and hurry,
 scurry about
  again,
   finding the socks,
    washing them clean,
asking each other
 "what did you mean,"
  matching the pairs,
   saying "I care,"
and just enough
 time
  to run
   from doom,
and meet once again,
 in the heart
  of the room,
holding out hope,
 baring our souls,
feeling my insides
 no longer cold,
  but slowly warm,

slowly glad,
slowly good,
slowly new,
and you with that
smile,
the same
much loved
you.

Morning Friends

Quickly
   I pitter-pattered
      up the stairs,
knowing what I'd see
   as I juggled
      your usual breakfast
      order,
more or less,
   but never did I
      guess
that the scene
   I'd meet
would warm my soul
   and mist my eyes,
      and make me realize
      again
how much I care,
   how good you are,
      how sweet the scene
      I saw,

as I heard her whisper
   gently
      "please,"
seeing my daughter,
   her best doll,
      and her teddy bear
perched
   on your knees,
your sleepy face
   peeking between
      the mob
thronging
   in your arms
      as she held your hand
         and you his paw...
how much I loved
   all that
      I saw.

Joy

Joy
   in the morning,
     in our
dawn,
   in your
     sun,
joy
   in the morning,
being
   two,
     feeling
      one.
Your head
   on my pillow,
     my heart
      in your
       hand.
new life
   in our
     loving,
in our
   own
     magic
     land.

The Gift
of Love

Ever hopeful,
  filled with dreams,
    bright new,
     brand-new,
      hopeful schemes,
pastel shades
  and Wedgwood skies,
    first light
     of loving
      in your eyes,
soon to dim
  and then you flee,
    leaving me
     alone
      with me,
the things I fear,
  the things you said
    burning rivers
     in my head,
bereft of all
  we shared,

my soul
    so old,
        so young,
            so bare,
afraid of you,
    of me,
        of life,
            of men...
until
    the bright new
        dreams
            begin again.
The landscape never
    quite the same,
        eventually
            a different game,
aware at last
    of what I know,
        and think,
            and am,
                and feel,
the gift of love
    at
        long
            last
                real.

9

...and then love is born again.

Tomorrow's Child

Small and warm,
tiny hands reach up
to touch and prod,
small toes stretch
and something deep inside
feels like the ripple
of a giggle,
as our tiny
precious
unborn child
begins
to laugh
and dance
and wiggle.

Moonbeam

How proud I am
    of all you are
        and all you do,
how rich I feel
    when meshed
        with you,
how strong
    I know
        our love to be,
how lovely
    to be us,
        yet free,
and how delicious
    this new gift,
        this moonbeam
            in my soul,
this gift of you,
    this part of me,
how very loved
    our child
        will be.

Come Soon

Waiting for you,
  little one,
    getting ready
a steady
  flow
    of rainbows
dancing through
  my head,
    the single thread,
      the constant theme,
        the tender dream
of you
  in our midst
    at last,
the planning
  and the hope,
    the gingham
and the little boat
  we bought you
    at a fair...
      ...oh, yes, we care...

we dream,
   we scheme,
      we wait,
we've found the house,
   the home,
      the room...
now, hurry, child,
   come to these
      waiting arms,
who long for you,
   come home,
      come now,
         come soon....

New Life

Silently, I watch you grow,
   magically planted inside of me...
      But soon I'll set you free,
         sweet soul.
You are so small,
   so big, so young, so old...
      you push so hard
         as though to shove me aside...
and soon my heart
   will open wide
      as the magic of your new life
         is unfurled.
And you push yourself
   into your world.
      Go ahead, little one,
I wait here, to cheer you on....

Arrived!

You have arrived
  and safely,
    long awaited miracle,
precious bundle
  lying in my arms,
your eyes staring
    into mine
      as though asking
what took <u>me</u> so long
    to get here,
and I, laughing
    and crying all at once,
      hold you tighter,
        press you near,
feeling you
    so infinitely dear,
      so mine, so ours,
        sweet gift of joy...
the prince!
    The heir!
      Our baby boy!

The Joy
of You

Yes, she was lovely too,
   your sister...
      she came with tissue paper
translucence,
   all white and pink
     and frail,
like porcelain lit from
   within,
      a child to dress in silks
        and pink ribbons,
so perfect,
   and delicate
     in her beauty...
while you, robust fellow,
   lie here,
      beautiful and rosy cheeked,
bright eyed,
   and looking as though
     you should be
       in a swing,

or chasing puppies,
    counting guppies,
or picking flowers in a field,
    eating candied apples,
or cookies,
    dripping crumbs,
        not sucking on my thumb,
as I eye you once again,
    wondering who you are,
        will be,
if you are like her
    or him
        or me,
if your eyes will be
    brown
        or blue,
and then I laugh again,
    overwhelmed
        by the sheer joy
            of you

—Welcome Home—

I have waited a lifetime for this,
  climbed mountains,
    counted dreams,
schemed and prayed
  and danced
    and would have,
      if I'd had to,
        drunk witches' brew...
I would have done all that,
  beloved babe...
    and more...
      just to have you...
I have waited,
  I have pined,
    sometimes cried,
      and never whined,
in silence and in darkness
  I have often prayed,
I have tried to forget the hoping,
  yet never ceasing to muse
    about this day...
wondering if...

wishing that…
  aching, longing,
and then finally knowing,
  growing,
    glowing,
overwhelmed with joy
  and gratitude…
and now this moment,
  you are here…
you've come at last,
  after waiting all these years…
    second child of my heart,
      sweet babe of my dreams,
holding fast to one finger,
  your eyes locked in mine,
your heart already sewn to my own…
  welcome, my darling…
    welcome at last,
      welcome, sweet babe…
Welcome home.

10

Love

Life with its odd endings
   and beginnings,
its occasionally
   very painful
      middles,
its riddles,
   its surprise hellos,
      and at times
         astonishing
         adieus,
its greens, its grays,
   its reds, its blues,
      its flowers which come
like sunbursts
   on a gloomy day,
      given by a man
         you barely know,
and its birthdays
   forgotten
      by the men
         you love…
Life, with its rare gifts,

its strange charm,
　　its strong arm,
its vast sass,
　　its more than occasional
　　　boot in the ass,
its blunt pain,
　　its bleak rain,
　　　its sorrow
　　　　and its grief...
is somehow all too brief,
　　like a cinderella ball,
so deck the halls,
　　put on your pumps,
　　　your furs,
　　　　your minks,
　　　　　don't shrink,
put your tiara on,
　　step out,
　　　prance high,
　　　chin up,
dance nigh
　　the flame
　　with eyes aglow,
and above all, dear friends,
　　before you go,
before it ends,
　　and there remains

no further tale to tell,
dare once...twice...
often if you choose,
but dare,
yes, dare to love,
and if you do,
make sure that you
love well.
For love is worth it all,
is worth a call,
a dream,
a scheme,
a sleepless night,
a carriage ride,
or crossing
half the world,
for a glimpse, a touch,
a truth...
for love is youth,
is fun,
is grand...
a carnival...
an opera ball.....
For truth to tell,
Love is Life...
and Life is Love...
and Love is All.

A captivating bestseller . . .

WANDERLUST
Danielle Steel

At 21 Annabelle Driscoll was the acknowledged beauty, but it was her sister Audrey – four years older – who had the spine and spirit. She had talent as a photographer; she had the restless urge of a born wanderer.

Inevitably it was Annabelle who was the first to marry, leaving Audrey to wonder if life were passing her by. The men she met in California were dull, worldly. Even in New York, they failed to spark her. Only when she boarded the *Orient Express* did she realise she was beginning a journey that would take her farther than she had ever dreamed possible . . .

0 7221 8307 0
GENERAL FICTION

KALEIDOSCOPE

Danielle Steel

THREE SISTERS, BONDED BY BLOOD,
SEPARATED BY FATE . . . COULD THEY EVER
FIND EACH OTHER AGAIN?

When Sam Walker returned from the front lines of
World War II, bringing with him his exquisite French
bride, no one could have imagined that their fairy-tale
love would end in such shattering tragedy . . .

And, at the age of nine, Hilary, the eldest of the Walker
children, clung desperately to her two sisters – five-year-
old Alexandra and baby Magan. However, before the
year was out, they too would be painfully wrenched from
her tender arms. Cut off from every loving warmth,
Hilary swore she would one day track down the man who
had destroyed her family and find her beloved sisters
again. But could they risk everything to confront a dark,
forgotten past?

John Chapman – lawyer, prestigious private investigator
– chosen to find the sisters, embarks on a labyrinthine
trail which leads him to Paris, New York, Boston and
Connecticut, knowing that, at some time in their lives,
the three sisters must face each other and the final, most
devastating secret of all . . .

0 7221 8314 3
GENERAL FICTION

'*Dark Pines* is deliciously menacing, with a gutsy and intelligent heroine in Tuva. I can't wait to meet her again. Never has beautiful countryside felt quite so hostile!'
Elizabeth Haynes, author of *Into the Darkest Corner*

'#DarkPines is definitely dark, but it's also terrifyingly beautiful, and I LOVED it.'
Joanna Cannon, author of *The Trouble with Goats and Sheep*

'Engaging Scandi noir with more interest in characters than body-count, and an oppressively atmospheric sense of place. Recommended!'
Francesca Haig, author of *The Fire Sermon*

'I was instantly engrossed in the mossy, rotting, claustrophobic Swedish forest. All this plus a deaf, bisexual protagonist – I loved it.'
Kirsty Logan, author of *The Gracekeepers*

'Great work. Creepy cast, terrifying trolls, sinister setting… Those pines are dark!'
S.R. Masters, author of *The Killer You Know*

'Compulsive Scandi noir! Highly recommended.'
Syd Moore, author of *Strange Magic*

'*Dark Pines* is the kind of thriller I've been waiting to read for a long time. Claustrophobic, creepy and completely compelling, it feels both classic and fresh at once. I adore Tuva – a gorgeously drawn character I want to see more adventures with. I loved it!'
Miranda Dickinson, author of *Fairytale of New York*

'A brilliant, gripping read! Beautifully written and atmospheric. Highly recommended.'
Claire Douglas, author of *Last Seen Alive*

'I loved *Dark Pines* and highly recommend this gorgeous slice of Nordic noir.'
Holly Seddon, author of *Try Not To Breathe*

'Terrific thriller, vivid imagery and characters. My heart was pounding at the end – really great read!'
Mary Torjussen, author of *Gone Without A Trace*

'Ace! Tuva is a fascinating character in a sinister world. Highly recommended.'
Adam Hamdy, author of *Pendulum*

'Claustrophobically atmospheric and spine-tingly tense, *Dark Pines* kept me enthralled to the very last page. A stunning debut from a major new talent.'
Steph Broadribb, author of *Deep Down Dead*

'I think this is an astounding and confident debut. Superbly plotted and beautifully written. The characters jump from the page in perfect 3D. The tension builds exquisitely all the way through to the dramatic end. From the first page you know you're in the hands of a major new talent.'
Imran Mahmood, author of *You Don't Know Me*

'It's incredible. Exceptionally well written, thought provoking and deeply unsettling. Bravo.'
Rebecca Tinnelly, author of *Never Go There*

DARK PINES

DARK PINES

WILL DEAN

A Point Blank Book

First published in Great Britain and the Commonwealth by Point Blank,
an imprint of Oneworld Publications, 2018

This mass market paperback edition published 2018

ISBN 978-1-78607-385-3
ISBN 978-1-78607-249-8 (ebook)

Typeset in Janson MT 11.5/15pt by
Palimpsest Book Production Limited, Falkirk, Stirlingshire
Printed and bound in Great Britain by Clays Ltd, St Ives plc

Oneworld Publications
10 Bloomsbury Street
London WC1B 3SR
England

Stay up to date with the latest books,
special offers, and exclusive content from
Oneworld with our newsletter

Sign up on our website
oneworld-publications.com

For VP. Always.

1

Gavrik, Sweden

An elk emerges from the overgrown pines and it is monstrous. Half a ton, maybe more. I stamp the brake, my truck juddering as the winter tyres bite into gravel, and then I nudge my ponytail and switch on my hearing aids. I get the manufacturer's jingle and then I can hear. The elk's thirty metres away from me and he's just standing there; grey and shaggy and big as hell.

My engine's idling. I think of Dad's accident twelve years ago, about his car, what was left of it, and then I punch the horn with my fist. Noise floods my head, but it's not the real sound, not like you'd hear. I get a noise amplified by the plastic curls behind my ears. The horn does its job and the bull elk trots away down the track with his balls hanging low between his skinny grey legs.

I speed up a little and follow him and my heart's beating too hard and too fast. The elk walks into a patch of dappled sun up ahead and then stops. He's prehistoric, a giant, completely wild, ancient and taller than my rented pickup. I brake and thump the horn again but he doesn't look scared. I'm panting now, sweat beading on my brow. Not enough air in the truck. There are no police here; no headlights behind me and none in front.

The fur that coats his antlers glows in the sun and then he swings his heavy head around to face me. His posture changes. Utgard forest darkens all around me and he stamps his hoof down and breaks a thin veneer of ice covering a pothole. My headlights pick out a splash of dirty water hitting his fur and then he looks straight at me and he drops his head and he charges.

I brake and pull the gearstick to reverse and slam the thick rubber sole of my boot down on the accelerator. My scream sounds alien. The truck pushes backwards and opens up a clear space between me and the bull elk; between my face and his face, between my threaded eyebrows and his rock-hard antlers.

I lift my phone out of my pocket and place it on my lap even though everybody knows there's no reception in Utgard forest. My eyes flit between the windscreen and the rear-view mirror. I'm trying to look in front and behind at the same time, and there's a flash of movement in the trees, something grey, a person maybe, but then it's gone. This is all my fault. I should never have driven after this elk. I see dull sky through his antlers and somewhere inside I reach out for Dad. I hit potholes and fallen branches and those black eyes are still there in my headlights. Thirty kilometres an hour in reverse gear. My phone falls off my lap and rattles around in the footwell. I reverse faster. The light levels are dropping and the elk's still coming straight at me. My left tyre gets caught by the edge of a ditch and I have to turn hard to jump out of it, and then his antlers touch my bumper, metallic scratches piercing my ears, and I can't see a damn thing. I feel a stick of lip balm digging into my thigh and then my mirrors flash and it's someone else's headlights.

Behind me in the distance there's a truck or a tractor, something driving straight at me. It should be a welcome sight but it's not. This track's only wide enough for one of us. The antlers scrape my bonnet again and I wince at the screech. My mouth's dry and I'm hot in my sweater. I'm reversing into a crash with an elk in my face.

And that's when I hear the gunshot.

The elk bolts to the trees and he jumps a ditch and flees into the darkness of the woods. The last thing I see are his rear legs as Utgard forest takes him back.

My palms are sweaty and the steering wheel feels damp and slick.

I brake but keep the engine ticking over. The vehicle behind me, perhaps a quad used by a hunt team to haul out a fresh kill, has turned off into the pines.

'Breathe,' I tell myself. 'Breathe.'

I've been saved by a rifle shot on the first day of the elk hunt. Three years ago, in London, that sound would have been a headline and it would have been horrific. Now, here in Värmland, in this life, it's normal. Safe, even.

I pull my sweater over my head and it gets tangled in the seat-belt. I fight with it for a while, hot and flustered, before pulling it loose. Strands of fine blonde hair float up from the fabric on a breeze of static.

I push the gearstick forward and drive. Not as fast as before, and not as fast as I'd like, but carefully, headlights on full beam, eyes glancing into the dark places at the side of the track. And then I'm swinging the truck up and onto the asphalt road and back towards Gavrik town. The traffic on the E16 is still gridlocked but from now on I'll stay on the motorway. No more shortcuts. No more parallel forest roads.

I'm tired and hungry and the adrenaline in my blood is starting to thin. I've got thirty-two hours to write up eight leading stories before we go to print on Thursday night. I dip my headlights and I can still hear the sound of antlers scraping my bonnet. I pass the sign for Gavrik and the streetlights begin. Civilisation returns in layers. First cat's eyes and lines down the centre of the road, now municipal lighting. Unlit forests can keep their fucking distance. I want pavements and cafes and cinemas and fast food and libraries and bars and parking meters. I want predictable and I want man-made.

I pass between the drive-thru McDonald's and the ICA Maxi supermarket and head onto *Storgatan*, the main street in town. My pulse is slowing down but I keep getting flashbacks to Dad's crash. And I wasn't even there. My memories are lies, the images solidifying over the years. I drive on. The twin chimneys of the liquorice factory loom in the background like the spires of a cathedral. Shops are closing and staff are saying goodnight in as few words as possible before they shuffle off, collars raised, to their Volvos and their homes and their underfloor heating and their big-screen TVs.

My parking space is marked with my name, but if it wasn't it wouldn't matter. The town is over-catered with parking facilities. It's future-proofed, but nobody knows if and when that future, the future where Gavrik grows by fifty per cent, will ever happen. Why would it? Those who grow up here, leave. Those who visit don't seem to return.

I lock my truck and open the door to *Gavrik Posten*, the town's newspaper and my place of work. Weekly circulation: 6,000 copies. I didn't expect to end up here, but I did. I interviewed at four decent papers all within a three-hour radius of Mum and I got four offers. My mother lives in Karlstad and her family consists of yours truly so when she got sick I moved back from London. It's not easy, *she* is not easy. But, she's my mum. Gavrik's close to Karlstad but it's not too close and Lena, the half-Nigerian editor of the *Posten,* is someone I can learn from. The reception is two chairs and a dusty houseplant in a plastic pot, and a counter with a brass bell and an honesty box.

Lars, our veteran part-time reporter, isn't in. I flip the counter – a slice of pine on a squeaky hinge – and hang up my coat. My fingers are still shaking. I kick off my boots and slip on my indoor shoes. The front office is two desks, one for me and one for Lars. Then there are two back offices, one for Lena, and one for Nils, our pea-brained ad salesman. Altogether, it's a shithole of an office but we turn out a pretty decent community paper each and every Friday.

I don't want to live in Gavrik. But I do. Mum needs me although she's never said as much, not even close. It's spread to her bones and her blood and if I can do tiny things – bring her the rose-scented hand cream she loves, read to her from her favourite recipe books now that she finds it too tiring, bring in fresh cinnamon rolls for her to taste – then I will. I'm not good at all this, it doesn't come naturally to me just like it never came naturally to her. But I do what I can. And then one day, one sad-happy day, I'll return to the real world, to a city – any city, the bigger the better.

'Tuva Moodyson,' Nils says, stepping out from his office. His hair's spiked with gel like a teenage boy's and his shirt's so thin I can see his nipples. 'What happened to you? Go home for a quick roll between the sheets, did you?'

I sit down and realise my T-shirt's still sticking to my skin with sweat and my hair's all over the place, strands plastered to my face, my ponytail falling apart. I'm a mess.

'Just a quick threesome,' I say. 'Would have invited you to join us, but there were criteria, so . . .'

He looks a little confused and slowly closes his door, returning to his office which is actually the staff kitchen.

I wake my PC from its slumber and find the articles I've written and those I've just titled and outlined. I hear a beep in my left hearing aid, a battery warning, the first of three before it'll cut out and leave me with the ten per cent hearing I have remaining in that ear.

Behind my PC's anti-glare screen, I have eight Word documents stacked one behind the other. A local nursery is expanding, creating three more childcare places and one new job. The facade cladding of a block of apartments near mine is being rebuilt because the original wasn't fit for Värmland weather and it's coming off in chunks like flakes from a scab. The local council, *Gavrik Kommun*, has decided we can make do with one less snowplough this winter. It's keeping two extra farmers on standby. The contest for the 2015 Lucia is underway and applications need to be sent to the Lutheran church on *Eriksgatan* by the end of the month. There's a Kommun-wide tick warning because of a spike in Lyme disease and encephalitis cases. The critters will be frozen dead soon but thanks to a mild September we still have a few more weeks of their company. Björnmossen's, the largest gun and ammunition store in town, will stay open two hours later than usual for the first week of October so hunters not taking time off work can still buy their supplies. There will be a handicraft fair in Munkfors town on October 21st. Finally, the story I've been working on today, the unveiling of a new bleaching plant at the local pulp mill, the second largest employer in the area after the Grimberg liquorice factory.

That's my news. That's it. Derived from rumour and council minutes and eavesdropping in the local pharmacy. It may sound pedestrian but it's what my readers want. How many times have you torn out an article from a national paper and stuck it to your fridge? How many times have you cut out a piece from your local paper, maybe your daughter scoring in a hockey match or your neighbour growing the town's longest carrot, and stuck that to your fridge? My readers give a shit and because of that, so do I.

Lars walks in and the bell tinkles and he starts to peel off his old-man coat.

I'm writing so I switch off my aids to concentrate. The fabric of my T-shirt is loosening from my skin and I'm starting to feel normal again. I can smell my own sweat but my deodorant masks most of it. If I was still interning at *The Guardian*, I'd have freshened up, but here, no. It's okay. Not a priority.

Lena's door opens.

She's standing there. Diana Ross in jeans and a fleece. Her eyes are wide and she's saying nothing.

'What?' I ask.

She holds her hand over her mouth. She's shaking her head and speaking but I can't see her lips. I can't read them.

'What?' I say, fumbling to switch on my hearing aids. 'What's happened?'

Lena takes her hand away from her face.

'They've found a body.'

2

'Put the news on,' says Lena, pointing at the old TV attached to the wall.

My aids come to life and the jingle plays in my ears.

'I knew it,' says Nils, as he joins us in the main office. He looks excited like a schoolboy. 'Didn't I say, Lena? Them woods are cursed. My brother reckons the body's down in Utgard forest, that's what he reckons. His mate down at the ambulance station got the call. Didn't I say it'd happen again in them woods? Yes I did.'

I switch on the local news.

'What did you hear, Nils?' I ask. 'What exactly did your brother say?'

Nils looks at Lena. 'You reckon it's Medusa again?' Then he turns to me. 'Before your time, Tuva.' And then he looks to Lars. 'What year was Medusa?'

'The last body was found in 1994,' says Lars. 'But this won't be . . .' He scratches his bald patch. 'That was twenty ago, this'll just be some hunting accident.'

'Yeah, right,' Nils says. 'Just an accident. In Utgard forest. Sure. My brother reckons they found the body in Mossen village.'

I take my coat.

Nils looks at Lena. 'You gonna let her go to Utgard all on her own?'

I pull on my boots and nod to her. 'Call me if you get details.'

'Take the camera,' she says.

Of course I'm going to take the fucking camera. 'Sure,' I say, and then I grab it from Lars' desk, where it's recharging and step out into the dark empty street.

It's not raining but a damp haze drifts through the air in waves. Was the gunshot that scared my elk the same one that killed somebody? I shiver and jog to my parking space.

I drive thirty kilometres straight out of town and under the motorway. Utgard forest is everything I can see on the right-hand side of the road. I pass a signpost covered in bindweed and approach the mouth of the woods, a barely visible gap in a thick barrier of spruce. I skirted Utgard earlier on my way south from the pulp mill to avoid traffic, but now I have to drive deep inside it. Radio Värmland interrupts a folk song to tell me that the police have sealed off an area of Mossen village due to the discovery of a body. They ask hunters and dog-walkers to stay away until further notice.

The radio starts to break up as I leave the asphalt behind and turn onto the grey gravel track. It's wide enough for two cars to pass if both nudge the open ditches. It's as dark as crushed velvet out here so I switch my beams to full and squint into the floating mists. In spring the forest is okay if you're inside a truck. It's all light green spruce growth and wild-flowers. Driving my Hilux pickup, I can handle it. But this is October and the pine needles are dark and sodden and the moss is brown and the birches are naked. My dash reads two degrees above zero. I'm driving up a dark alley with pine walls as tall as lighthouses.

The radio comes back on intermittently but it's just a weather forecast. More rain. My GPS map shows a thin track that enters a featureless green area from the south and then stops right at its core. There are five houses dotted along the track so I just need to find the one with a cop car parked outside. I scratch my left ear and touch my hearing aid, partly because it's unavoidable, and partly because it's reassuring when I'm somewhere like this.

The Medusa murders were twenty years before I arrived. They're a kind of local legend with a few facts and then plenty of bullshit piled on top. Three shootings in four years. The police never charged anyone and then the killings just stopped. The bodies were all found out in the woods and they were mutilated in some way, and that's about all I know. Local people don't like to talk about it. And the ones that do aren't worth listening to.

I approach the first house of the village with my radio on low in case there's more news. I slow down to ten kilometres an hour. The place looks run down. The wooden clapboards need painting and ivy covers some of the windows. The only thing I can really see is a garden, lit dimly by barely functioning solar lights, the cheap kind that this far north work a little in summer and barely at all in October. The houselights are off. Nobody home. As I accelerate away, I look in my mirrors and notice a light I didn't see before, but it's not in the house. Then it goes off as quick as it came on.

My phone battery's low so I plug the adapter into the truck's cigarette lighter. The music on the radio changes from harmonicas to banjos but the signal's weak and there's lots of white noise. I drive slower now. The track gradually gets narrower and narrower and on each side of it are scratched cliffs of granite and boulders piled on top of each other in clusters. The pines lean in towards each other, meeting in some places over the centre of the track, so that it's almost enclosed. Looks like an awkward reverse to me.

The next house looks normal. It's lit up with pendulum lamps hanging in all the windows and outdoor lights attached to the walls. One-storey high, it's a *torp*, a traditional dark red cottage. I slow down again and let the truck amble with no pressure on the accelerator pedal. I switch on my wipers to clear the windscreen and stare out of the passenger-side window. Through a cloud of bugs I can see a *Taxi Gavrik* Volvo in the driveway. There are dead plants in the window boxes, some kind of geranium. I think I see a face look back from a window; a child's face, low at the sill. But now I'm past the house and approaching a steep hill. I rev the Toyota and pick up speed. Heated seat to low. The hill has been recently gritted

9

and my truck sounds noisy, winter tyres chewing up the stone chips as I climb. At the top, the track bends sharply to the right so I brake and my wheels skid on a slick of fallen leaves.

Each side of the track is marsh now, not ditches. The gravel track, elevated a few centimetres, slices through boggy land with reeds and murky water reflecting the sky.

The next house is on the right side of the road and I smell it before I see it. My lips are dry from the car heat so I take the lip balm out of my jeans pocket. I can smell fire, woodsmoke, and it's reassuring in a way. Like a home. But this place doesn't look like a home, it looks like some kind of workshop. I don't slow down because inside there are faces lit by fluorescent strip lights. A one-storey workshop, open on one side with a wood burner in the centre and two, maybe three men in overalls – maybe three carpenters, carving and sanding. Next to the workshop is a modest house painted yellow with a couple of dead birds hanging from a hook outside the front door. Pheasants, maybe? Partridges? There's a row of five numbered post boxes screwed to a metal bar.

The road narrows even further so I have to focus to stay on the level. The ditches either side look steep and full. They're October full, just like the lakes and the reservoir outside town and the wells in local gardens. I think I see a flashing light in the distance but then the trees obscure it.

My phone has 22% battery. I pull it from the adapter and throw it down next to the camera. The windscreen starts to fog and I switch on the fan and crack open the window. The forest smells earthy like soil underneath an upturned stone. It smells of woodlice and rotten apples and slugs and wet carpet. I turn a corner and swerve past a fallen birch branch. There are lights up ahead: flashing blue roof-lights on three cars and an ambulance, and I'm happy because they're protection and they show me where my story's at, but also I'm happy for the powerful lights on their roofs, flashing up and bouncing off the wet pine branches like blue strobes at a rave.

I park and switch off my engine. The rain's stronger now so I pull off my hearing aids and tuck them into my jacket pocket. If they get wet, they won't work and I can't afford to replace them. Each aid is a month's salary. If I wear them with a hat I get crackling and feedback. I take my camera and my phone and pull up my hood and step out onto the track. The air smells even more pungent than before. Mulch. Old leaves and sitting water.

The house is quite nice, actually. It looks more expensive than the others, two storeys with large windows and a first-floor veranda wrapping round the entire building. A TV's on upstairs. The room's flashing.

I sense a voice somewhere but can't hear the words or see anyone. I reach under my hood and slip my left aid over my ear.

'Tuvs,' says a voice from the veranda above me.

I look up.

'You took your time.'

It's Constable Thord Petterson, number two in command of Gavrik's two-man police force.

'It's the middle of nowhere,' I say. 'Can I come inside?'

He shakes his head and smiles, rain dripping from the gutter above his head. He points to himself and then points down to me.

I keep the camera in my bag and wait by the front door. The veranda above protects me from the rain so I place my right hearing aid back in and switch it on.

The front door opens but something else seizes my attention. To my right, behind the house, I see two paramedics carrying a stretcher out of the woods escorted by Gavrik's police chief. Soaked through and covered in mud to their knees, they step carefully over a derelict stone wall and through a thick patch of brambles. Then I see the other one. There's a man walking behind the police chief and he's wearing a bright orange baseball cap and he's carrying a rifle.

3

But it's not a man, it's a tall, athletic woman with her hair swept up in the cap and the collar of her jacket zipped up to her nose. I can see her eyelashes.

The body the paramedics are carrying has a grey sheet laid over it. There's a dark smudge in the centre of the sheet above the torso of whoever is underneath. The smudge is shiny. I can see a limp hand and a gold wedding ring. I lift my camera to my eye but the cops, Thord and Chief Björn, shake their heads at me as they walk past to the ambulance. The back doors are open and the paramedics carry the stretcher inside. Björn climbs in after them and the doors close and the ambulance drives off towards the motorway.

The woman with the rifle walks towards me and then Thord joins us. Together we stand there in the middle of Utgard forest under the shadow of a veranda. We say nothing for a full minute.

'I can't tell you much tonight, Tuva,' Thord says. 'Best to call the station in the morning.'

'ID of the victim?'

'Let's leave all that till tomorrow.'

He turns to the woman in the cap.

'Can I give you a lift back home, Frida? I think Hannes would want me to. You've had a hell of a day and I bet you've had just about enough of this weather.'

'I can do it,' I say, desperate for information, a lead, a source, a quote. 'Where do you live?'

'Who are you?' Frida asks.

'Tuva Moodyson, I'm a reporter at the *Posten*. Sorry, I should have said.'

She holds out a strong hand and it's red with cold.

'Frida Carlsson,' she says. 'I'll take you up on that lift. I live at the end of the track, it's just a few kilometres deeper.'

Thord nods to us both.

'Earlier today,' I say to him. 'When the traffic was bad, I heard a gunshot in these woods. I was on the track parallel to the E16. About 3pm.'

Thord wipes rain from his face. 'Gunshots everywhere this week. You see anything, anyone?'

I shake my head.

'About three o'clock, you say?'

I nod.

He nods and walks towards his flashing car. As he opens the driver's side door, he turns and looks up and waves to someone.

I step out from under the veranda and into the rain to see who he's waving at but the windows are blank and the veranda's empty.

'I'm parked up there,' I tell Frida.

We jog to my truck and get in. Frida puts her rifle down on the back seat and I notice a leaf motif on the butt of the gun. I think it's a shamrock. I turn the heat up high and hand Frida a small towel I keep in the central console to wipe condensation from the windows.

'Who was Thord waving to?' I ask.

Frida looks at me while she's patting the towel over her dyed blonde hair.

'David, I expect. Old friend of Thord's, I think they went to school together. He's a ghostwriter.'

I switch the headlights to full and focus on the track.

'Just one house left?'

'Just one,' Frida says. 'My husband and I live at the end of the road.'

The track's been relatively straight until now but suddenly it turns twisty, climbing up and over boulders and around old Scots pine trees with ferns sprouting from their trunks.

'This must be fun in winter,' I say to her.

'It's okay if you've got your head screwed on right,' she says, and that makes me think of Mum, she used to use the same expression. 'You got the right clothes, the right car, then it's fine. You have to be practical. It's not like town.'

I see her house through a glossy tangle of wet pine branches. It's like I'm driving a rally car in a video game, lurching from left to right, spinning the wheel and skirting toadstools as big as kittens. I turn into a clearing and up a long gravel driveway. The house is large and well lit.

'Nice place,' I tell her. 'I didn't expect a house like this here.'

'Nobody ever does.'

There's a flagpole in the garden and the house is pale grey with white trim. A mansard roof slopes down at different angles. It's dated but well maintained. There are security lights outside and there are lights in every window except one upstairs room.

'I think you've saved me from a cold,' she says. 'And to tell you the truth, I'd rather not be alone just now. Can I get you a coffee before you head back?'

I leap at the chance.

'Sure.'

We park next to a grey timber garage with a weathervane on the roof. We walk towards the house and Frida looks pale. I've left my truck unlocked. Mosquitoes and midges buzz around the porch lights; they're big fuckers this time of year, fat on blood and bold as hell, but the snows will soon fix all that. Frida opens the front door and slips off her boots and coat. I do the same. She shuts her rifle in a metal gun cabinet under the stairs. She seems tired now. The house is dry and clean and it smells of furniture polish. The floors are parquet wood and they're warm, underfloor heating on high. I need more material, Lena needs more material. As I follow Frida, I take in the rooms and snatch a glimpse into her world. These details are the colour that will bring my articles to life – Lena taught me that. It's all about the personal details: armchairs and blankets and bookshelves stuffed with well-read romance novels, and travel guides to Spain and Portugal. There's an expensive stereo and a fireplace made up with sticks and birch logs. I spot last week's *Posten* scrunched beneath the logs ready to light. Then I smell garlic, and my mouth waters.

'You have a lovely home.'

'Oh, it isn't usually this tidy. I've been cleaning up. It's never my mess but it's always me cleaning.'

We walk into the kitchen and it's like something out of a magazine. Not grand, but stylish and cosy. I've gone from murder forest to sanctuary in ten minutes and that's fine by me. The tiled floor is warm under my damp socks; warm to the point where it would be too much for me to live with, but right now it's good. I smell something like a stew and my stomach rumbles. The sound's like a tube train coming out of a tunnel, but I'm not sure if that's my aids or if hearing people feel the same when their stomachs growl.

'You hungry?' Frida says. 'I have zero appetite after today, but I've got a kalops beef stew in the oven, just a thing I threw together. Made enough for the Gavrik hockey team. No bother if you'd like a quick bowlful and a chunk of bread. No bother at all.'

It smells amazing but feels wrong to eat a stranger's food. Especially on a day like this.

'Thanks, but I don't want to intrude. A quick coffee would be lovely though ... and do you mind if I ask you a couple of questions about, well, about what you found today.'

'I don't know,' she says, her face apologetic and torn.

I smile and wait.

'I suppose I can tell you what I know,' Frida says, shaking a foil bag of ground coffee into a pot with a plunger. 'It's such a dreadful business.'

She joins me at the table with fresh coffee, a small plate of cardamom shortbread biscuits, a jug of milk, and a sugar bowl, all arranged on a vintage-style tray. On the table is a silk-lined box of silver teaspoons, eleven lying there in a box made for twelve. The silk lining has what looks like a family insignia printed on it, the letters in fancy script, white on grey.

'That coffee smells good. Do you mind if I record this on my phone? My hearing's not great.' I point to my ears. 'And I don't want to miss your words.'

'Okay, sweetie. Go right ahead.'

And suddenly I like her for not asking me about my deafness or my hearing aids. She hands me a spoon from the box and takes one for herself. I stir sugar into my coffee and turn the phone to record mode.

'What happened tonight, what did you find?'

Frida looks down at her hands, and sighs.

'Well, I was out picking ceps in the woods, they're Hannes's favourite. It's been raining a bit and I thought they might have popped up so I grabbed a basket and ...'

She pauses. I nod for her to continue and then I take a sip of from my cup and it is excellent coffee.

'And I have my usual spots where the ceps come back year after year so I picked a few good handfuls and then I saw something next to a fallen beech tree. I thought it was a coat someone had left behind so I walked closer.'

She looks up at me.

'I could smell it.' She sips her coffee. 'Like a fresh deer kill. So I stopped in my tracks and I ran back home, I didn't have my mobile with me and it wouldn't work out there anyway, so I ran back here and called the police station. I wasn't half as scared as I should've been. Björn asked me to meet him at David Holmqvist's place.' She pauses. 'He's the ghostwriter whose house we just came from. So I took my husband's gun and walked straight there and took them through the woods to the body. And that's it.'

'Did you recognise the body?'

Frida shakes her head. 'Reckon it was a man but can't be sure. It's just awful. He was lying face down. I just saw a red stain on his jacket so I checked his pulse on his neck and he was completely cold. Been dead a while, I'd say.'

'Could you see if he'd been shot? Stabbed? Attacked by an animal?'

'He was bleeding through his coat, that's all I know. Expect the police can help you with the rest.'

I turn off the recorder on my phone and slip it into my pocket.

'I'm sorry you had to see that.'

'It's not nice, but that's nature's way. Life and death out here, you get to see enough of it over the years. Don't know if this was an accident or what it was, but I am sure Björn will get to the bottom of it. Björn Andersson's a damn good police chief, you ask anyone in Gavrik Kommun. Him and Hannes have been best friends since they were your age. Chief looks after his own – always has done, always will.'

4

Frida hands me my coat and pulls out a chair from the wall so I can put my boots on. She passes me a brown paper bag with a Tupperware carton of her kalops stew and to be honest I don't argue too much, because it must be better than a frozen microwave ping meal for one. Along with the stew there's a tiny loaf of bread in a clear plastic freezer-bag with a green clip, and a small pot of something with strips of Sellotape securing the lid.

'Thanks for this. I may be in touch if I have more questions, if that's okay.'

'Okay,' she says, smiling. 'Think I'll fix myself a proper drink now, think I need one. You make sure you drive carefully, okay. The track can be tricksy this time of year.'

I pull up my hood and head out to my truck and I can almost taste Frida's 'proper drink' on my tongue. My pulse quickens. I drag my hand over the bonnet and it's scratched up pretty bad from those antlers. It'll need a repaint. I hear wind in the trees and then my hearing aid beeps another battery warning. As I drive out of the clearing, I spot Frida in my rear-view mirror. She's lit from behind, waving goodbye from her front doorstep.

The steering wheel's cold. I set out from the centre of the forest, from Frida's place, and the track feels much shorter than when I drove in. I keep to about thirty kilometres an hour and drive past the ghost-writer's house and it's all dark. The police and ambulance are gone. I continue past the carpenters' workshop. All dark, except for the smouldering fire. Then I drive through the bog and down the long, steep hill and past the torp where I saw the child's face at the window. When I reach the first house I notice the light I saw earlier comes from a caravan parked in the garden. I approach the main road and accelerate and the road widens and I bump up onto the smooth asphalt and I'm pleased to leave that dark village behind in my mirrors.

I get home just before midnight. First thing I do is email Lena and tell her what I saw and what Frida Carlsson told me. Then I bolt my door, and change into a pair of tracksuit bottoms and a cotton lumberjack shirt. I plop the glutinous kalops stew into a small saucepan, my only saucepan, and slide it onto the hob. I take out the bread, it's a small rye loaf, home-made, with a cracked crust along its top. I tear off the Sellotape from the other small pot Frida gave me and sniff the pale contents. Some kind of sour cream thing with lemon and parsley. When it's hot, I pour the stew into a bowl and take a spoon and a chunk of the bread and move over to the sofa. No ping meal tonight. Meaty steam hits my face and the tension in my shoulders disappears. I take off both hearing aids and place them on my table.

Silence.

Blissful, natural, personal, silence.

I spoon the food into my mouth and it is good. Home-made, slow-cooked, family food, and it tastes like Frida Carlsson's made it a thousand times before, like she's unknowingly improved her recipe on every attempt. I made all our meals growing up and let's just say I don't have a gift for it, but this is bloody delicious. The meat falls apart as I spoon it up and then it melts on my tongue; the carrots are as sweet as candies. I dip the bread into the dark, viscous sauce and chew it, and feel my stomach start to fill.

I'm finally warm inside now from the stew. From that hellhole of a forest, not even a proper village, back to Gavrik town and to my rented, fully-furnished apartment, and to my sofa, and now to this. I'm nourished and I feel at home and I've never really felt like that here, not really. Home could be a proper newspaper in London or Chicago, but not here, not in Toytown. But Gavrik, especially after today, needs a decent reporter and I'm it. At least Frida's food makes it all better for a moment. No hearing aids, no rain, no cold inside my chest.

I take my iPad and walk over to my unmade bed. On the bedside table sits a photo of Mum and Dad, from before, from when Mum still managed, from when I didn't worry about her, from when we weren't completely failing each other. I focus on Dad, on his easy smile and oversize ears. I never really look properly at her because it's unnerving. She's me but with green eyes. Lazy journalists knocked the life out of Mum and they'll never even know it. Lies about Dad, rumours and gossip, misquotes and bullshit. He was never drunk that night, he'd stopped by then. So when I write, I always focus on the people hurting because that was Mum and me. I wish I could visit her right now, a midweek impromptu surprise thing, but those days are long gone. She falls asleep early now, a side effect of all the medication. It's weekends only and that doesn't feel like enough. I rub my eyes and force myself to glance at her side of the photo. Mum's the reason I can't imagine having kids of my own.

I collapse face first onto my duvet. I'm too full to move and too tired to game; I just want to read a little and then sleep. I browse the websites of two nationals and then turn to *Wermlands Tidningen*, the regional paper. They all have the story but none of the local specifics. It's all just filler and historical crimes and speculation and geographical details. One of the nationals has spelt Utgard forest wrong and that really irritates me. I google 'Medusa murders' and get a Wikipedia article as the first search result. Three murders just like I remembered. 1991, 1993 and 1994. A paper mill worker, a technician, and the assistant manager of the local hotel. Three men, all mid-thirties, all shot in the torso. And then I see it, the thing that connects them all. The Medusa nickname is misleading. The name, it makes little logical sense. In fact, it makes no fucking sense whatsoever, but that's nicknames for you, they stick.

The corpses. They'd all had their eyes removed.

Wikipedia says that all three victims had their eyes taken after being shot dead. 'A neat job' the then-district coroner is quoted as saying in a press conference in '94, much to the outrage of relatives and local councillors. I find no photographs of the bodies or of the injuries, just of the woods. I load a map of the murders and they're pretty well spread throughout Utgard forest, kilometres apart from each other, in every direction from Mossen, the string village running through the woods. Half the town was questioned in the early '90s. An eighteen-year-old from the area, Martin Farsberg, was arrested, but then released without charge.

I pick up my aids and open the battery compartments and drop them into a jar of desiccant to dry out overnight. Then I take my wand from the bedside drawer. I think about a girl I studied with in London. I come. I close my eyes to sleep, but see the image of an eyeless man in my head, each socket pale and empty to the bone.

5

My pillow alarm shakes me awake at six.

The room lacks air and I need to change my sheets. I hook on my hearing aids and get up to open a window, and the chilled air slaps me in the face. I retreat back to warmth.

My iPad's almost dead so I plug it in and scan the Swedish print news and TV. Most of the interesting chat's on social media, and the hashtag *#MedusaMan* is starting to trend.

Shower. Clothes. Change battery in left aid. There's lint in the transparent tubing connecting the earpiece to the aid itself so I take off the tube and blow down it and wash it under the tap and wait for it to dry and then I push it back on. When I open a box of Coco Pops and pour them into a bowl, a bat falls into the centre of the cereal and makes me jump. Was the gunshot that scared away that elk the one that killed someone?

I drive the five-minute walk to the office – which is ridiculous, especially here, where locals cycle everywhere – but I'll need the truck later.

Lena's Saab is parked outside the office in her spot. She's the 'first in, last out' type. I walk into *Gavrik Posten* and the bell chime rings above my head. It sounds like glass breaking.

'I'm gonna put Lars on your usual work, on the articles for tonight's print,' says Lena, appearing as soon as I walk into the office. 'So you can concentrate on the murder. You're okay with that, aren't you?'

I nod.

'Reckon the nationals will be here in force by lunch and then it'll be a shitshow deluxe so do as much as you can before then.'

I nod. 'I'll talk to the cops this morning, then head back to Mossen village to interview the other residents.'

'This could be the thing that I was telling you about,' Lena says. 'This could be *your* story. Medusa, if this is Medusa, could be the making of you, so keep your head down and your ears open and your wits about you, you hear me?'

She doesn't think of me as a deaf person or she wouldn't have said the last three words and I love her for that.

'This my Pulitzer?'

'You'd like that now, wouldn't you?' she says with one hand on her hip. 'You wanna leave me up here all alone with Tweedledee and Tweedledum? Not yet, you don't. You get any stick from them about your Medusa assignment, just send them my way. I'll be fixing for the print, but you need me, you got me.'

She's why I'm here. Lena's an award-winning reporter who ended up specialising in embezzlement and organised crime cases on the US east coast, and then had the misfortune to fall in love with Johan, a hydro-electric engineer from a small Swedish town. *This* small Swedish town. Still, she seems content enough to live here although she's never said as much.

I sit down and email all my stories over to Lars. There's a body lying in a morgue someplace near here. What if Nils is right and Medusa has come back? Or we have a new Medusa? What if the new body doesn't have any eyeballs? How the hell do you take the eyes from a corpse? I look at my screen and the headlines about faulty apartment facades look plain ridiculous.

I call the police station over the road. Nobody picks up. My phone has an octagonal stick-on pad to minimise feedback and it works pretty well. I keep hitting redial as I google Mossen village to get the names and details of the five households. That's the peachy thing about Sweden: tax records, addresses, telephone numbers – they're all public information.

Redial. The first house is owned by a Bengt Gustavsson, the man with the caravan. Redial. Second house, Viggo Svensson, the local taxi driver, I recognise the name. Third house, the carpenters' work-shop, but I just get two female residents, Alice and Cornelia Sørlie, a Norwegian surname. Redial. It's engaged now, someone else trying to get through, some other hack with wet hair and a triple-shot morning latte. Redial. Then the ghostwriter, David Holmqvist. And then Frida and her husband, Hannes. Redial. I add their numbers to my phone's contacts list. Redial.

'Gavrik Police department, Thord Petterson speaking.'

'Hej Thord, it's Tuva. Morning. It's not too early to ask you a few questions, is it?'

'It is. Chief wants to hold a press conference at noon. Some of your colleagues from Karlstad and Stockholm are driving up. Can't do anything much until then, I'm sorry to tell you.'

'Fair enough,' I say in a disappointed voice. 'Was the victim a local guy? Would I know him?'

'You'll find out plenty about him at noon.'

So now I know it's a 'him'.

'I read online that no gun's been found yet, that right?'

'I ain't falling for that one, Tuvs, and I don't appreciate you trying to play me. Now, you do your job and I'll do mine. I'll see you at lunch.'

He hangs up.

Lars walks in fifteen minutes late. It is the most important news day in Toytown since 1994 and he's fifteen minutes late.

'You're taking over my stories today, I've been told to focus on this shooting. They're all in your inbox, any questions just ask Lena.'

'I knew it,' says Lars, with a smile that shows too much gum and not enough teeth. 'Fine with me. Old news, slow news, that's my speciality, has been for thirty years.'

He hangs up his coat and unzips his boots like a glacier stuck in neutral. He puts on his unbranded sneakers and Velcroes them up and then he walks to Nils's office-slash-kitchen.

I join him.

'What were the last murders like? Medusa. In the '90s. From your perspective.'

Lars turns around as he fills the old percolator from the tap next to Nils's yuppie Rolodex.

'You looking for an exclusive?'

I perch on the edge of the desk.

'It was godawful, that's what I remember. That's number one. Small town like this lost three good men and that's the main thing to keep in mind here, Tuva. Three good men died. They had mothers and neighbours and friends and if I remember correctly, they all had wives and kids too. They all read this very newspaper every Friday and they all walked these very streets. It was a sad thing and it's still a stain on our town.'

'I know,' I say. 'But what should I be prepared for in the coming days?'

'Stay human, that's what's really important if you ask me. Let the victim's family and friends have their say in their own time and in their own words. Don't rush them, they'll get enough of that from the nationals and, God forbid, the TV leeches. Those parasites have got manpower and they've got sway. We haven't. I remember back in the '90s, some of them pulled strings in Karlstad with the politicians and even with the coroner. They might have got the scoops back then, but we had the local angle. Remember that. We're on the inside, and we know everybody and how they all connect up. That also means that we have to stay here in Gavrik once this has all blown over, whereas the Stockholm clowns will just up and leave. They leave, we stay, and we have to shop next to the families and park next to the relatives and that's another reason why we have to report this in the proper way.'

Nils walks in and stands in the doorway to his office.

'What's this, then?' His spiked hair glistens with wet-look gel. 'You two think I could get to my desk? Some of us got work to do.'

I move and take his place in the doorway, but Lars carries on making his coffee at his own speed.

'What you heard?' Nils asks me. 'What you find out?'

'So far, not much. I suspect the victim is male but that's about it. Heading back to Mossen village in a while, then we've got the cop show over the road at noon.'

'And you call yourself a professional reporter,' he says, reclining his leather office chair and grinning. Through his pale yellow shirt, I can see halos of wispy chest hair circling each nipple. He turns his head to Lars. 'What about you, old-timer? You know who met his maker yesterday?'

We both stare at Nils.

'Oh, wait, but I'm just the ad man around here. I just pull in all the money so you two no-hopers can get paid a pretty penny each month, that's all, no big deal, I'm just a dumb salesman, what the hell would I know?'

Lars takes his coffee and walks out back to his desk in the main office.

'Talk,' I say, focussing on Nils's thin, chapped lips.

'Freddy Malmström, at least that's what they're all saying. Lotta's badminton partner lives next door to the Malmströms down by the cross-country ski trail. Freddy's a nice guy, teaches maths, I think, maybe science. Well, he didn't come home last night, did he? Went out hunting with his dog but he never made it back home. Him or the dog. So I reckon it must be him.'

'Shit,' I say. 'A schoolteacher?'

'You gonna quote me on that, Little Miss Hotshot? That's on the record just for you that is, it is on the record.'

I walk out and knock on Lena's door. 'You got a sec?'

She's seated at her computer, arranging obituary and birth captions for tomorrow's paper. Symbols of flowers and angels that we use for either type of notice.

'Freddy Malmström?' I ask.

'Name rings a bell. Phil Malmström's boy?'

I adjust the volume on my right hearing aid. 'Dunno.'

'Used to be talk that Phil Malmström was in the local poker game. Died a few years before I came to town, but people still talked about him. Head of the council or something, must have been important to get a seat at that table. The poker game ended years ago but maybe this Freddy is his son.'

'I'm gonna drive into Mossen village and see who's around. I'll ask the locals about Freddy and see what I can get.'

'Watch your back up there, okay?'

'Cos there's a murderer on the loose? Thanks, I know.'

'I remember going to that forest to pick mushrooms a few years back with Johan,' Lena says. 'It's well known for foraging, and professional pickers use it this time of year. It was September when we went, lighter than it is now, and not so wet. Well, we drove all the way in and then we drove all the way the hell back out and we never even got out of the car.'

6

The display on my dash reads three degrees above zero. I pass between McDonald's and ICA Maxi, the two landmarks signalling the start and end of Gavrik town, and take the exit. I drive under the E16 motorway, under the lorries feeding paper mills and the towns further north. There are no longer any other cars around, and there are no longer any cat's eyes in the asphalt.

The sky's as white as printer paper. In the distance I can see the wall of spruce trees marking the edge of Utgard forest. There is no fence, they're enough on their own.

It's just after 10am when I make out the weed-covered signpost to Mossen village and take the right turn onto the gravel track. It's less weird in the daylight, at least this section is, the wide part where two trucks can just about pass each other. After a few kilometres I see the first house in the village and hope Mr Bengt Gustavsson, sixty-nine, retired, is at home. The house is clad in vertical white boards and they're frosted with something green. I think it's pollen but it might be some kind of mould or rot. Ivy curls up from the ground, from between uneven concrete paving slabs, some of them cracked, and up each side of the house. I stay in the truck for a while and eat the three wine gums left in the packet, two orange and one yellow, not bad, and then shove my phone down into my jacket pocket. From my driver's seat, I look the place over. Can't see anyone. To my left, the ivy-smothered entrance has a set of wind chimes hanging from a porch roof. To my right, a caravan on bricks, a henhouse, and a neat, fenced-off vegetable patch. The chickens look like they live better than their owner. The vegetables are immaculate and thriving. Ahead is a woodshed or a potting shed or something, a hut with a heart carved into its door.

I hop down from my truck and land in mud, the splash coating the bottom of my jeans. The air is more damp than cold, and it is completely still here in the woods; there is no breeze whatsoever.

'Hello,' I call out. 'Mr Gustavsson?'

My hearing aid echoes so I adjust it. There's no answer apart from the jagged caw of a crow, so I approach the front door. The chimes are just dangling there, vertical metal rods hanging motionless in damp air. I guess it's some kind of doorbell so I jangle it. The noise is ungodly. Sharp dings and resonating gongs attack my hearing aids and hurt the inside of my head. The door's open, well it's not open, but it's not locked. I knock on it and then push it, but it stops. I can just about squeeze my boot through the gap and that's all. I push the door and there's something heavy on the other side resisting me. Something's pushing back. It's open enough for me to stick my head through the gap, so I do.

It's dim inside and there are no lights on. The windows are so dirty they may as well be walls. But I can see *things*. My head is indoors and the rest of me is outdoors. There are *things* everywhere. Piles of newspapers tied up with string; the piles are highest by the walls, some reaching the ceiling like pillars holding it all up. In the centre of the room there are some floorboards visible but only in patches like stepping stones weaving through chaos.

The door still won't give any further and I can't see what's behind it, so I walk back out to the truck and get my camera. I'm a little worried the old man may have passed out behind the door. Or, even, you know ... I've covered stories like that, pensioners found weeks after death, slumped and emaciated, piles of post and junk mail, neighbours disturbed by the smell. At least there's no smell in there, other than damp and dust. I stick my camera through the gap of the front door and arch my arm around it and take a photo. I see the flash light up the room like lightning, and it's even worse than I thought. There's a whole town's worth of crap in here.

Just as I pull the camera back to look at its screen, a hand pushes past my face from behind me and grabs hold of the door handle, pulling the door shut.

I turn on my heels.

He's scowling. Way too close to me.

'God, Mr Gustavsson?' Stay calm, it's just an old man. 'I'm sorry, the door was open. I thought ... Hello, I'm Tuva Moodyson from the *Gavrik Posten.*'

He licks his lips and holds out a hand. It's clean and sinewy and covered in liver spots.

'Nice to meet you, Tuva Moodyson. You see all that, did you? Get a good look, did you? It's a life's work in there, but it's not ordered, not ordered at all. I still have a lot of sorting to do inside the house.'

I swallow and slow my breathing and move off the porch into the garden for some space because the doorway suddenly feels too small, and I don't want to be close to the ivy or close to the chimes in case they jangle.

'I'm writing an article about the body found last night in the woods. I was hoping to talk with villagers to get the local perspective.'

He nods and then his nod morphs into a shake. His ears are as big as pork chops. He pushes his long grey hair behind them and pinches the tip of his nose.

'It's a bad business. I don't condone the killing of any living creature but then I expect you already know that.'

He stares at me like he's waiting for a reaction.

'I think you recognise me, don't you? I recognise you, Tuva Moodyson.'

I open my eyes wide even though I don't want to. I don't think I've seen him before.

He walks away to the caravan wearing white socks and black sandals and then he pulls out a banner on the end of a wooden stick. Ah, okay, right, now I recognise him. The banner shows a colour photograph of a rabbit being injected with something into its eyes. Bengt Gustavsson is the local animal rights guy.

'I'm pretty well known in these parts, I'd say. I got a crusade, well, that's what I call it anyhow, and that's why I don't have time to sort out the archives in the house, not just yet anyway. Maybe this coming winter. The archives are important, but helping defenceless animals takes priority, wouldn't you say?'

I nod and smile.

'Cup of tea?'

I don't mean to frown, but one escapes.

'Ha,' he laughs loudly and scratches his ear. 'I didn't mean in there. I live in the caravan for the time being, come on.'

I follow him towards the fibreglass caravan; placards and banners are stuffed under the base between the brick supports, and I take a peek at the camera screen to see what the hell is stuck behind that door. The image is blurry but I can see a brown leather sofa topped with piles of yellow *National Geographic* magazines and copies of *Greenpeace Quarterly*. Each stack's bound with garden twine.

'How do you take it?' His head pops out of the caravan.

'Black, please. No sugar.' I take it white but I don't trust his milk.

As I look inside the cramped caravan I relax a little. It's as orderly as a naval officer's cabin. The single bed's made and the fleece blanket covering it is pulled so tight I could spin a coin on top. The caravan's small but everything seems to be in its place.

'This is where I'm living until I sort out the archives in the house. I've got plans for winter and spring next year, it's all good material, some of it even important, just need to get it organised. I need to develop some kind of system.'

31

He hands me a chipped white mug, steam rising from it.

'I got plans,' he says.

I nod and smile and thank him for the tea and then I notice half a grapefruit on the sink drainer with a curved serrated knife sunk into it. Clear pinkish liquid is pooling around the grapefruit like juice from a hot roast chicken.

'Take a seat,' he says, pointing to the only available option, a collapsible camping chair with integrated cup holder. He sits on the bed. 'Ask away, I'm not shy.'

'How long have you lived here, Mr Gustavsson?'

'Call me Bengt. Twenty-two years, ever since I left the service.'

I click my phone on to record, and place it in the cup holder of the chair.

'I was in the army for twenty-six years and they were the best years of my whole life. Then I came out here. This is my uncle's place since way back.'

'So you lived here during the '90s, when the other bodies were found?'

'Place was like a circus back then. When young Karlsson was found, he was the last of them, we had twenty-two vehicles up here in one day, I counted all of them in and I counted all of them out. Twenty-two. Did you ever hear such a thing? And that was October too, they all were, so they carved up the track pretty bad. It's a wet time of year, but you probably know that. Hunting season, murder season more like it. All them tyres ain't good for a loose track like this, just ain't designed for it. We had to resurface a fair amount. Yeah, I remember them three bodies and I hope we're not heading back to them bad old days. There's enough bloodshed as it is around here.'

'Do you know who was found yesterday?'

'Some hunter,' he says, and I notice his lower lip's covered in an outbreak of cold-sore blisters. 'Some hunter out to kill something

32

that ain't carrying a loaded gun like he was. Some bloodthirsty hunter who didn't see it coming, I suppose.'

I take a sip of tea and notice a bunch of carrots in a basket hanging from the caravan ceiling.

'Good-looking vegetables you're growing out there.' This is part of my job. I have to relate to the locals on some level. I have to keep them talking.

He smiles and licks his lips. 'You noticed my veggie patch, did you? I use an organic fertiliser I make myself. If I was to enter a competition in Gavrik or Munkfors or someplace, I dare say I'd come back with most of the trophies if that ain't boasting.'

'What's in your fertiliser, Bengt?'

He brushes his cold sore with a fingertip. 'I can't tell you that, can I? Trade secret.'

'Okay, then,' I say. 'Have there been any changes in Mossen since the three '90s murders? How has the village evolved?'

'Well, let's see. The pines are taller now, they're over seventy years old so it's about time to harvest. Hannes and Frida owns most of it, most of Utgard forest, most of the timber. Kind of an investment for them I guess, they've got a pretty good economy that pair.'

That phrase takes me back to London for a minute, back to my studies at UCL. I used to say 'so-and-so have a good economy' and people would look at me like I was stupid, and I'd say it means 'well off' and they'd tell me it doesn't translate too well.

'Have there been any new residents?' I ask.

'Residents?' He smiles. 'Residents is a fancy name for us lot. Well, back then it was me, then Viggo's old dad as my nearest neighbour, may he rest in peace. Viggo drives the taxi cab, you probably seen him around. He's got a boy who I babysit every now and then, whenever Viggo gets night work or weekend jobs. At least I used to, reckon he's found someone else to help him now. Then there's the sisters, the wood-carving sisters, you bumped into them yet?'

I shake my head.

'Well, good for you, Tuva Moodyson. You won't get much from that pair, that's for sure. Why don't you ask them why they left Norway in a big hurry, eh? You won't get a mug of fresh-brewed tea from those two.'

'What about the ghostwriter, David Holmqvist?'

'Davey's been here the whole time,' Bengt says, his finger picking at his lip. 'He was born in that house, and his parents passed when he was about seventeen or eighteen. Car accident, may they both rest in peace.'

I get a flashback to Dad's crash, and then I notice the crucifix on the wall by Bengt's bed and the small engraving of Jesus resting near the sink.

'Do you have any idea who may have been responsible for the '90s murders, Bengt? Any personal theories?'

'Well, there's lots of rumours cos people talk and people think they know things they don't, especially in a small place like this. But the people in the know reckons it was one man who did it. There were similarities, you see.'

This is nothing new to me but I try to feign interest.

'I won't go into the details, but it was the ...' He points to his eyes. 'And they was all shot in the back. Lung shots, all of 'em, so I'd say it was another hunter that killed them.'

'A hunter?'

'Yep, which covers just about the whole population around here except me.'

Convenient theory. But maybe a man who shoots hunters in the name of animal rights wouldn't call himself a hunter. A protester? Guardian?

'Do you know who it could be?'

'Well, people talk about Davey all the time, speculating about his books and hobbies and whatnot, rumours about what he did as a kid. Most of it's nonsense, people jealous and all sorts, you know, bigots and fools looking for trouble. But, I don't know. He's a bit different, that's true enough, I never said he was normal. He's a book writer, you just gotta look at his hands, they're smoother than yours. But he ain't no hunter. Davey sure ain't no Hannes Carlsson.'

7

When I arrive back in Gavrik, the clouds are thinning and occasional beams of warm light are falling on the liquorice factory, the one building that dominates the town.

I park outside my office and walk over. There are a couple of extra cop cars outside the station, detectives and specialists from Karlstad, but most of the vehicles are vans with satellite dishes on their roofs.

The ticket-queue machine thing has been moved out of reception, and Thord's manning the front desk. He'd be handsome if it wasn't for his horse teeth.

'I kept a seat at the front for you, Tuvs, front and centre.' He emphasises the word 'centre'. 'You're just in time.'

I thank him and walk past the bolted-down chairs and through to the conference room, which I know as the place where school kids get taught road safety and cycling proficiency. It's heaving. Half a dozen sitting on chairs, and ten more standing up. Cameras on tripods. Laptops open and ready. Nobody notices me because they're all focussed on the man at the podium, Chief Björn Andersson. Björn looks at me and then he looks away. I reach inside my handbag and take out my digital Dictaphone and a pad and pen. Then I place the Dictaphone in front of Björn, alongside the microphones of TV4, SVT and *Aftonbladet*.

As soon as I take my seat, Thord walks in to introduce his chief and then he stands beside him like a soldier at ease on day two of basic training. Björn has a pair of glasses that split into two, each part connected by a cord around his neck. He brings each half to his eyes and they snap shut on the bridge of his nose.

'Ladies and gentlemen, welcome, thanks for coming. Yesterday, at 17:08, a call was placed to the Gavrik district police station by a female resident of Mossen village. Said female informed us that a body had been discovered in Utgard forest, some thirty or so kilometres from here. When officers arrived at the scene they discovered a deceased male in his fifties suffering from an apparent gunshot wound. A rifle was also recovered which had not been fired. This investigation is being handled by Gavrik police with guidance and support from Karlstad specialist homicide unit, and the National Forensic Centre. We have not yet identified a suspect or suspects pertaining to this incident. Because of the nature of this investigation there may be some questions I am unable to answer at this point. That's it. Questions, please.'

The room doesn't burst into shouts like you see in the movies. Nobody's hustling here. Hands go up. Someone calls out the Chief by his first name and I smile. *Big mistake, boyo.* I focus on Björn's gold tiepin, I've never seen him wear one, and raise my hand.

'Tuva,' he says as a flashbulb goes off at the side of the room.

'Chief Andersson, have you identified the deceased male?'

The Chief moves on his heels and looks at Thord standing next to him. He coughs and nods.

'The victim has been formally identified as a Mr Fredrik Erik Malmström. Some of you will know Mr Malmström. He's been a pillar of this community for many years and a very well-respected teacher at Gavrik Gymnasium school. Our thoughts are with the Malmström family.'

I put my hand up again but he points to someone behind me.

'Was the victim's body intact when it was discovered?'

Björn scowls. 'I can't comment on that at this time.'

He points to someone else.

'Are you connecting this murder to the Medusa murders of the 1990s?'

Björn removes his glasses. 'I will not comment on that at this time.'

His voice is strained and although his police uniform shirt is dark blue, I notice sweat rings growing from his armpits. I can see the faded edge of a tattoo on his wrist: it's a red love heart, or a diamond, but most of it's hidden.

The questions are coming fast now.

'Where was the victim shot, Chief Andersson?' asks a man standing behind me. 'With what kind of weapon?'

'We understand that the murder weapon was a rifle. As we speak, we have investigators combing the forest to locate it. The victim was shot in the general torso area.'

'Is it true that the army may be called up to help you search the woods?'

Björn frowns at the woman asking the question, as though she's arrived this morning from a different planet.

'No,' he says. A moment later, he adds, 'The terrain is extremely challenging, even for us local officers. But, no.'

I throw my hand up again.

'Tuva.'

'Is there any evidence that this was a hunting accident? Were there any hunting parties in the area at the time of the murder?'

Björn waits a while before answering. He snaps his glasses back together and takes a sip from a plastic cup of water and I see that red tattoo again.

'There was a hunting party in Utgard forest at the approximate time of the incident. However, that party was operational in a different quadrant of the woods. At the present time, we are keeping an open mind and following up on all leads and all lines of enquiry.'

Thord coughs.

'Okay, I'm going to wrap this up now, but before I do I want to appeal to your viewers and readers. If you know anything about this incident, any detail, no matter how small, any suspicion, please contact Gavrik police immediately.'

Björn steps away from the podium as a flurry of further questions are yelled out, the loudest being, 'Is this a mass murderer, Chief Andersson?' and, 'Is it safe to go back into the woods?'

Thord opens a door to the private office behind the front counter and Björn walks through it. As soon as they've left, I hear multiple cheeping sounds through my hearing aids. High-pitched squeals. My peers are sending their tweets in a race to be the first to report.

The journos are babbling to each other, some talking to me, some over me, but it's a jumble and I can't understand a word, so I take my Dictaphone and walk over to the front desk and then back out onto the street.

Two people follow me out, a tabloid Stockholm guy with slicked-back hair and a beard, and a TV woman with a really bad fake tan. There's a white taxi parked across the street with its engine idling.

'You're local?' asks the woman as she lights a cigarette and holds it palm facing the sky.

'I am not local,' I say.

'But you work for the local paper?'

'I work for the town paper.'

She exhales. A breath and a frown and a bitch-smile all in one.

'Listen, Tuva,' the man says, waiting for me to be impressed that he remembers my name from the conference. 'Where's a good place to eat around here? And,' a truck passes by at speed, 'the best?'

I would read him but his beard is in need of a trim and I can't see his lips clearly.

'What? Best what, sorry?'

'Hotel,' he says. 'Not too stuffy, but nice rooms and good food.'

I laugh internally but it bursts out.

'You've got a choice of one. If you turn to your left, you'll see it. It's really stuffy and the food is twenty-four-carat horseshit.'

He looks around to the half-brick, half-timber building back-dropped by the lorry exit gate of the liquorice factory. The sign says Hotel Gavrik and it isn't broken or anything, but it's not quite positioned at the centre of the front of the building.

'Lunch, then?' asks the orange woman with the white neck. 'Where for lunch, just something simple?'

'Head out towards the E16, first place on the right. I recommend the nuggets and the double cheeseburger. Best food in town. Now if you'll excuse me, I gotta get back to work. Guess I'll see you around.'

I walk ten metres and open the door to *Gavrik Posten*. The bell above it rings and I close it and walk inside.

8

I save my work, grab my coat and leave the office. My belly's full of microwaved noodles and Korean hot sauce, and my taste buds are swollen and grateful for flavour. For the last hour, I've felt as if someone was watching me through the window from the street, but there's nobody there. I'm paranoid. Understandable. Lena's secured me an exclusive interview with the victim's sister tomorrow morning. Her name's Esther, and apparently Lena knows her from yoga class. I've met her before. She used to work the drive-thru window at McDonald's the year I arrived here in Toytown.

So I have an open remit. The locals are whispering on street corners and in the newsagent, excited about having national TV crews and reporters here, maybe even a few faces they recognise. I know many of the Gavrik people and I know some of the local ways, so I have that on my side, but I'm no celebrity journo. I'll escape here someday, and I'll need a portfolio that'll get me into meetings. No gaps in my résumé. I want a story that will open doors and get me fast-tracked. I've been here for three years and I'll stay for as long as Mum needs me. After I moved here she got a little better but then it spread. The doc says she's got one year, but I can't even think about that, I can't even begin to cope with that. One year, four seasons or maybe less, to say all the things I need to say and hear all the things I need to hear.

It takes me all of five minutes to reach the gas station. I fill up the tank and buy a small shovel and a chocolate bar but I doubt they'll do more than provide some background sense of reassurance. I'm going to be in that forest a lot. A forest the size of an English county, bigger than New York City, the area of an inland fucking sea. Utgard forest is thirty kilometres by twenty-eight. From the air, it's almost eight hundred square kilometres of dark green. I hate the size of it. Doesn't need to be that big.

As I drive under the motorway I switch on the radio so I can catch the three o'clock news. We're the first story up; a snippet from the press conference. Björn's voice now has a gravitas that comes from being recorded and played back and broadcast, that it didn't have when I was sitting there right in front of him and his shiny tiepin. It starts to rain so I put on the wipers. Then it stops for a moment and hail starts to fall. As I turn onto the gravel track into Mossen village, tiny white bombs hit the truck. I switch off both aids when the tapping on the roof becomes unbearable. Now I can only *feel* the hail. Vibrations, like a sardine trapped inside a can being hit by machine-gun fire. And then it stops.

I pass Hoarder's house. He's not Medusa, I didn't get that vibe from him. But do you ever get that vibe? I drive on, the track narrowing and sprinkled with a fine coating of what look like mint imperials. The taxi driver's house comes into view. No taxi. There's a kid's plastic car, taller than it's broad, bright red and yellow, lying next to the front door at a jaunty angle with its tiny door wedged open in the dirt.

I accelerate as I approach the hill. The Toyota takes it with ease and this is why I rented it. It's early October. This is nothing. For me, living somewhere like this, I need a great vehicle. I can't do nature, it scares the crap out of me, so I need the best that man has made to be able to skirt it and pass through it without actually ever having to face it. That's the deal. If I live here, I need great boots, an all-wheel drive truck, a Gore-Tex ski jacket, a brand new phone, GPS, the whole caboodle.

At the top of the hill there are less hailstones on the ground like this is a different place up here, a slightly different weather system at this altitude. The track narrows, and although it's only mid-afternoon, it's dark and my headlights are doing their thing. I pass the swamp and there's a little more light here, albeit filtered through a million identical spruce trunks, and I drive on. There are no passing places this far in. It occurs to me that I have no idea what Mossen really is. Is it a village? It has no church, no store, and no bus stop that I can see. And if it is a village, then where is it exactly? Where's the core?

I pull up by the carpenters' house and check the notes on my phone for names so that I can introduce myself to them. Cornelia and Alice Sørlie. I switch my aids back on.

As I open the truck door, my nostrils fill with woodsmoke and it smells good, like a childhood Christmas, a cosy one, not like mine, but one from a book. I decide to leave my camera in the truck for now and walk over to the open-fronted workshop.

I see two women, both about fifty years old, working at heavy pine benches with sawdust all over the floor. The one on the left is almost bald and the one on the right has shaggy home-cut grey hair. The one on the left looks up from her bench and nods without smiling. The one on the right licks her lips and says, 'You lost, girl?'

I smile. 'Hi, I'm Tuva Moodyson, I work for the *Gavrik Posten* in town. Sorry to bother you unannounced.'

'We was bothered already before you turned up.'

'Can I come in, just for a few minutes?' I look up at the grey sky, an appeal for shelter if nothing else.

'Don't know what good it'll be, do you Alice?'

'Nope,' the other woman says.

I step under the roof and walk towards the log-burning stove in the centre of the rectangular shed. The walls are timber but the roof's corrugated iron.

'Well,' says Cornelia.

'What are you making?' I ask. 'It looks very ... intricate.'

'Craft fair next weekend in Munkfors, ain't there, Alice?'

'Yep,' says the other woman.

'So we're getting stock ready. This here,' she holds up a smooth pine cylinder, 'will be a troll, just a standard type. That one,' she nods towards her sister. 'That'll be a special, won't it Alice.'

'Yep,' Alice says, as she threads something through a small piece of fabric with a needle.

Both women have large silver crosses hanging from their necks on chains.

'Special?' I ask.

'Made to order,' Cornelia says. 'They take quite some time.'

'Can I see a finished one?'

Both sisters look at me and tut.

'You don't think we're busy enough as it is?' Cornelia says. 'We don't look busy to you out here, our fingers all cold and calloused. We don't look occupied, girl?'

I start to apologise but Alice is walking towards me holding her made-to-order troll. She hands it to me like it's a newborn baby. I look down at it and everything about the doll-sized thing feels wrong. It's too heavy for its size. It feels, not alive exactly, but animal, its features are too, I don't know ... I pass it back.

'That *is* special,' I say to Alice. 'What's it made out of?'

Cornelia points to the little thing in her sister's hands. Alice is wearing woollen gloves with the fingertips cut off.

'Best Utgard spruce, that there's the heartwood. We use real materials, so much as we can get hold of them. This one's not done yet but it'll have fingernails and toenails just like you and me. You can see Alice has started threading through the hair on that special.' She touches her head. 'This one got yours or mine?' she asks, looking at Alice, but her sister only shrugs. 'We used to get teeth from the local dentist but that all stopped a few years back, some nonsense about privacy and consent, they were just a few rotten old teeth for goodness sake. The men trolls get a little hair on their chests. They get real eyebrows, lashes, ear hair. We have one client who orders toe hair on his specials. They're like little hobbits, ain't they Alice?'

'Yep,' Alice says, walking back to her workbench.

'It's what the local council, the Kommun, it's what they call "artisanal industry": traditional local-folk products and ours is the best. We got prizes.' She points to a not quite horizontal shelf behind her. 'We take pride in our work.'

'Those are your tools?' I ask, pointing to a rack of antique chisels and files.

'We do everything on site. We use machines, and then we use them hand tools that belonged to our Grandpop. We use carvers and mallets and fishtail gougers and coping saws and small chisels for every single one. Keep 'em all perfect sharp with the stones and the belts.'

I stare at the gougers, each one clean and razor sharp. They look like surgical instruments.

'How much would a troll cost, if I was to order one?'

Cornelia snorts. 'You want one or not, girl?'

'I don't know,' I say. 'How much?'

'One of mine, one of the standards, about two thousand kronor. One of hers, well that's a whole different world, girl. She's an artist, ain't you Alice?'

'Yep,' Alice says, threading God-knows-whose hair to the padded skull of her half-finished troll.

'All depends on what the client asks for. You want one of Alice's, you tell me what you want and we'll work out a price, okay, girl? We have some quite remarkable clients I can tell you, people from all over the country, but we never reveal names, do we Alice?'

'Nope.'

'I think they're amazing,' I say to Cornelia, and I do, just not in the way they think. 'Really, amazing.'

'You done here, girl?' Cornelia asks.

I hadn't noticed, but Alice had placed a black, cast iron kettle on top of the log-burning stove on her way back to her bench. It starts to whistle and I touch my ears defensively.

Cornelia frowns and I see that her eyebrows are thin and sparse, and her left eye has no lashes at all.

I show her the aid in my ear. Cornelia nods. I point to the kettle. Cornelia smiles, then walks over to it and takes it off the stove.

'It's four o'clock,' Cornelia says, her voice noticeably louder than before. 'We take a ten-minute tea break at four, never longer, never shorter. Looks like you're in luck, girl. You can ask us your questions but I can't say for sure you'll like what you hear.'

She pours hot water into two tea-stained enamel mugs and passes one to her sister. They sit down on dark green plastic patio chairs. They don't offer me a tea and I'm almost more taken aback by this than their hideous troll dolls.

'Okay,' I say. 'Yesterday, the murder. Did you hear the gunshot?'

'Don't be stupid, girl,' Cornelia says, blowing into the enamel mug clasped in her calloused hand. 'We hear gunshots all day long this time of the year. It sounds like the Wild West most days this deep in the woods. They're still out hunting today, even with all this going on. Anything south of the hill, anything west of the track, is still okay. Three-quarters of the wood, still okay to hunt.'

'Did you notice anyone strange drive or bike up the track yesterday before your four o'clock tea break?'

Cornelia turns to her sister. 'Did we, Alice?'

'Nope.'

Cornelia drinks from her mug in noisy slurps and then moves her tongue between her lips and her teeth.

'Listen, girl. This is the woods and sometimes people just die in the woods. The only people in these woods with any right to be here is woods people. If you meet us or people like us in this wood, we'll be carrying a rifle or a shotgun and we'll have a gutting knife and we'll have a plan to do some killing and that's about all I know.'

46

'Do you two hunt elk?'

Cornelia takes Alice's empty mug. 'Girl wants to know if we hunt elk, Alice.'

'Nope,' says Alice. 'We make trolls.'

9

I get back to the office just before six and Lars has already gone. He's done a great job. The stories are all written and they look fine but the subjects seem ridiculous now. Like news from some kid's picture book. The real local news is as far away from this stuff it as it could possibly be.

Lena's in her office, door ajar, fact-checking and perfecting the layouts. I'll write for two hours solid to get copy to her in time for the deadline. I nudge the tiny buttons behind my ears and switch off the world. This is a benefit of being deaf. I'm not hearing impaired. Fuck, no. I am not impaired at all. You can't do this, can you? I can shut out almost all noise when I want to focus or relax. I don't need noise-cancelling headphones on a long flight. My flatmates in Bethnal Green used to stockpile earplugs to counter the traffic noise. Not me.

I've got a 500g chunk of Marabou chocolate in the top drawer of my desk. Each individual square has a raised *M* letter on the top. By the time I've drafted what will fill the first four pages of tomorrow's paper, I have two rows left and I feel sick, but it's done. I rub my eyes and hit print and walk over to Lars's tidy corner desk. I pull out his chair, and with a red rollerball pen secure between my teeth, I read the warm pages. Has to be accurate, as accurate as I can get it. Dad's death was misreported in three different papers; stupid, careless, heartless errors about his seatbelt and the speed he was driving. Errors that made people whisper and gave Mum a push when she was already standing right on the edge. One paper even wrote about his drinking, about his blood alcohol levels, which was bullshit, ancient history, and we only got an apology weeks later in the middle of the goddam paper. Another got his age wrong by two years. Details are important, they can have consequences. I edit and rewrite and double-check, and then I email it to Lena.

'Thanks,' she shouts from her office. I don't hear the actual word, just a noise, but I know what she said because she always shouts 'thanks' from her desk on Thursday evenings. I click my aids back on and put the chocolate squares back in my desk drawer. I'm full of sugar but hungry as hell.

I open Lena's door. 'You need anything before I go?'

'No,' she says. 'I'll call you if I need you.'

I crack my knuckles and sniff. 'Night then.'

The truck's cold and when I start the engine the dash shows zero degrees. I see a cloud of breath form between my nose and the windscreen, and I realise that the flipchart of seasons has turned a new page. We're still officially in autumn for another month or so but for me, zero means winter. We've had the leaves fall off and we've had the mushrooms and the gales and now it's time for the white months.

I switch the heat to max and wipe condensation from my windscreen and edge away from the kerb and then someone knocks on my window.

'Tuva, it's me, Ola, *Aftonbladet.*'

'Hi,' I say, opening my window a crack.

'I'm going shit crazy in this town. Jesus, I don't know how you manage living here full-time. You want to get out for a coffee?'

I smile and shake my head and mouth no thanks and wind up the window and drive off. I'm too tired for what I know will come and have no interest in the bearded slick-back or his opinions on his life or my life. Window up, gone.

It's a six-minute drive from my office to Tammy's takeout van, accounting for the three sets of speed bumps and two sets of lights. Tammy Yamnim's parents moved to Sweden a few years before she was born. Her dad was a prick and ran off with a Barbie lookalike back in the '90s, or so Tammy says. Her mum moved back to Bangkok. Tammy is probably the main reason I've endured three years here. Her and Lena.

She's serving a young guy with a mountain bike when I arrive. Looks like Thai green curry, the one on the menu without the spice or the Thai basil that she automatically adds to mine. Liberally. Her curry, the right way, is a thing of wonder. It's silky and rich and fragrant and fresh and it almost blows my knickers off. This guy's getting the PG13 version, for Swedes who've been to Phuket twice on holiday and enjoyed the all-inclusive hotel food. She winks at me and I wink back.

Mountain-bike guy pays and leaves and I breathe in the scent steaming up from her six menu options. How she manages to cook and serve this stuff from what is essentially an old camper van is beyond me. She is a marvel.

'Steamed rice with plain curry sauce, easy on the curry sauce?' she says, pointing to the vat of mustard-coloured gloop that is her number one bestselling dish and that has nothing whatsoever to do with Thai cuisine.

'You hungry?' I ask her.

'What do you think? Hang on a minute and I'll shut down this money machine and then I'll take you out for a fine-dining experience, how's that sound? My treat. Gimme ten.'

She clangs and bangs and turns things off, cleaning up and packing away as I stand outside shivering, eating unsold prawn crackers out of a brown paper bag. Tammy's van is at the far end of Gavrik's ICA Maxi supermarket car park and it backs onto farmland. I'm staring out into a field. It's black. The night is clear and the stars are shimmery, greedy for attention. But the land, the world at my level, is so dark that I may as well be blind. It's a field and there could be a wolf fifty metres away or a mass-murderer fifteen metres away or both and I'd never even know it. It's not even wild nature and still I hate it. I want to asphalt it and fence it and light it up from every angle.

'All done,' she says, stepping down from the van to greet me. My chin sits on her head as we hug and then she pulls back and punches me affectionately on the shoulder and starts walking. I race to catch her up.

We walk side by side back towards town. There isn't another human being on the street, just Tammy and me.

'Fifth Avenue, baby,' she says as we pass the wild boar sign outside Björnmossen's gun shop. It has ammunition displayed in the window along with a poorly-stuffed brown bear. There's a light on upstairs and I can hear music and men laughing and jeering. We pass a cross-country ski store and a fishing supply shop before walking past my office, the lights still on, Lena still working. On the other side of the street, business isn't so good. There's Mrs Björkén's dusty haberdashery store which is my sanctuary, and next to it stands Ronnie's bar, boarded up, awaiting refurbishment.

We walk briskly. Tammy hasn't got the best boots on and I can tell she's starting to shiver.

'I'm tired of delicious Asian food,' she says, opening the door to McDonald's. 'I'm twenty-two years old and cute as a bee. I live in Shitsville, Värmland, and right this actual moment, life's okay. Let's get some grease.'

We sit down and I devour my Big Mac as Tammy picks at her two hamburgers. The problem with cooking for a living is that she's always tasting, always grazing.

'How's your mamma?' she asks.

'Same,' I say. 'They're managing the pain but there's no new treatment. The last round of chemo didn't work. She's coping, I guess.' I feel my stomach hardening, my guts tight and twisted. 'I'm going down there this weekend.'

Tammy nods and pulls out the gherkins from her second hamburger and wipes her fingers on a paper napkin.

'A good daughter would be there twice a week mopping her brow but Mum makes it so damn hard. I just . . . She's impenetrable. Has been for ever.'

'What do the docs say?'

'They say they're doing what they can. They say she's comfortable. But their eyes tell me everything I need to know. I look at their eyes and they say prepare yourself, be strong for her.'

Tammy puts her hand on mine.

'I feel like time's running out and the closer we get to it, the harder it is for me to visit her. I'm terrified she'll have changed. Or gone, just an empty bed. I should be there more than ever and I'm too scared to go.'

'I'll go with you. Anytime. I'll wait outside if you like, but you'll know I'm there. Don't say yes or no, just think about it.'

I squeeze her hand and change the subject. 'What do you think about the shooting?'

She cringes and folds a long, limp fry into her mouth.

'You know everyone in Toytown,' I tell her. 'What's your theory, Holmes?'

'I got two,' she says. 'One: it's the same crazy dude as in the '90s. Two: we've got ourselves a copycat killer. Number one's scary cos it means he's been here all along, ordering my food and shopping in ICA and walking down *Storgatan*. Number two's scary cos how can we have two crazies like that in little old Shitsville? So, either way, I don't plan to start foraging in the woods again anytime soon. I got customers who reckon this one's a hunting accident but that's bullshit. Doesn't happen.' She looks up at me. 'Were Freddy Malmström's eyes gone? Like the Medusa bodies?'

'I don't know, the police haven't said. Gunshot wound, that's all I know. I'm meeting Esther, Freddy's sister, in the morning. Not looking forward to that one bit.'

'I heard,' Tammy says, leaning in closer to me over the Formica table. 'I heard Hannes Carlsson and his buddies are going out in Utgard forest. I heard they're taking it in shifts to hunt the killer down. Cops have told them to stay out of the area where Freddy was found but do you reckon for one minute that Hannes Carlsson will listen to that? The man's treated like a king around here.'

'Well,' I say. 'It's not like the killer will be wandering around the forest with a sign and a pocketful of eyeballs is it? Could even be one of Hannes's team for all he knows.'

Tammy wipes her mouth with a paper napkin.

'You ever hear anything about a poker club in this town?' I ask.

She shakes her head.

'That stuff's all online these days,' she says, screwing her hamburger wrappers into a ball. 'Rumour is – Nils's sister told me this earlier when she picked up her panang curry – that they're stationed in all the Utgard elk towers with walkie-talkies, to get him. Freddy's been in Hannes's hunting team for a good few years now. Anyone not in the team will be warned, and then, well, y'know . . .'

I tear off the end of my furnace-hot apple pie. 'What could possibly go wrong?'

I drive Tammy back to her flat, kiss her goodbye and head back home. I remove my hearing aids, take a shower, pull on a robe, and fall onto the bed with my iPad. I research the '90s killings, the 'Medusa' murders, and dig deeper into the articles and speculation around the killer's identity. I scan forums and chatrooms. He killed three men in four years, all in elk-hunting season, all by rifle shot to the back or chest. There were rumours that at least one of the victims was gay and that the killer was either a homophobic maniac or else a jilted lover. Sweden is one of the most liberal countries on planet earth but browsing some of these chatrooms you wouldn't think so. Up here the white hetero caveman still thrives in his natural habitat. I read that the eyes were removed neatly and cleanly on all three corpses, prompting the police back then to question surgeons and nurses and butchers registered in the Kommun.

They never found any good tracks. The police chief twenty years ago was Thord's late father. He was Björn's boss back then and he reckoned the killer was a woodsman because he used the rocks and the trees and the ditches so that no boot prints could be traced back to any particular car or house. He was smart. The killer probably moved around in circles, concentric circles of increasing radius, before finding the direction that suited him. He was very familiar with Utgard forest. Thord's father suspected the killer had an accomplice, someone actively helping him to evade police. No fingerprints or hair fibres were ever found.

It's almost 2am. I switch on my PlayStation 3. I just need fifteen minutes of *Grand Theft Auto* to get serial killers out of my head before I can fall asleep. Just fifteen minutes.

At 4:15am I turn it off and go to sleep.

10

My pillow alarm shakes at 7am. I stare at my face in the mirror and it's a puffy mess. Eye drops. The bottle says one to two drops in each eye but I use half the bottle.

Breakfast is five digestive biscuits and a mug of tea. I need to go shopping. I shower and clean my aids and dress and then plug in my aids and grab my bag. I slam the door shut on my way out.

I googled Freddy's sister's address yesterday. Even in a small town of 9,000 people, I don't know every street yet, not like the locals do. I drive past identical semi-detached wooden houses with small, well-maintained gardens. Number 43.

A woman answers the door and I know it's her before she even opens her mouth. Her make-up is on and it's pretty good but it can't hide her eyes or the effort it takes for her to smile. She looks like she's been punched in the stomach a hundred times.

'Tuva, come in, I'm Esther Malmström.'

We step inside. Shoes off.

The house is quiet and there are too many flowers. I can see she's run out of vases. Some of the bouquets are identical because there's only one proper florist in Gavrik town. Bunches of lilies sit in buckets, and by the stairs there are long-stemmed white roses leaning unceremoniously in a deep saucepan.

'Please, let's sit in here. Thanks for coming to talk to me.'

She leads me into the living room. IKEA sofa, big wall-mounted TV, log-burner, monochrome wallpaper on one feature wall.

'I'm sorry for your loss,' I say. 'I'll try to keep this brief.'

'It's all right,' she says. 'I want to talk to you. I want them to find the bastard who did this. Small town like Gavrik, we have to pull together and find out who did this to Freddy.' Her smile cracks. 'I'm ready and I want to help.'

'Okay, I appreciate it. Esther ... did your brother ever mention to you that he was afraid or that someone had threatened him?'

'Cops already asked that,' she says, stroking her palm against the arm of the sofa. 'Not that I know of. He was a friendly guy, a school teacher. Everyone liked Freddy. He was a saint, really. I was always the bad one.'

I frown.

'When we were kids, I mean. Freddy was a goody-two-shoes.'

'Has he ever been attacked before? Any fights that you know of?'

'No.'

'People are linking this murder with the '90s killings. Do you think they're connected?'

'Are you serious? Of course they're connected. You think there are two freaks out there who take people's eyes out? Cops didn't find the killer back then and now he's come out again and,' she looks up at the ceiling and lowers her voice, 'of course it's the same guy.'

I'm quiet for a second.

'I'm sorry, I didn't know about that.'

'I had to identify him, didn't I. Thought it'd be a curtain pulled back and all, thought I'd be able to say goodbye to him properly.' She sniffs. 'But it was just a photo. And they'd covered up his eyes so I think that tells you everything you need to know.'

'I'm sorry.'

'Yeah, me too.'

I pause.

'Esther, did Freddy have any friends that you considered to be dangerous? Anyone you didn't like?'

She stops stroking her palm against the armrest and looks at it. Then she looks at me.

'Well.' She goes back to staring at her palm as if waiting for it to take over. 'Perhaps.'

My stomach rumbles and I squirm in the armchair to try to stifle the sound, but it carries on. It's a preposterous noise and obscene in the circumstances.

She rubs her eyes, and with her hands covering much of her face, continues to talk. I can't get the words. No lips to read, no clear speech.

'I'm really sorry,' I say. 'I'm deaf and I didn't quite catch your last words.'

'You're deaf?' she says, eyebrows high on her forehead. 'But, you can hear me?'

I point to my ears.

'I can hear pretty good with hearing aids, and I lip-read as well, as a back up.'

'You talk really well for a deaf person.'

She says this with kindness but my gut tightens anyway. It's like saying to a man with a prosthetic leg, 'Hey, you walk pretty well for a cripple.' It's not a compliment. It's just not.

'You were talking about Freddy's friends, maybe one that you didn't like or trust?'

'Can you sign?' she asks.

I shake my head.

'What's it like?'

I sniff. 'You mean, being deaf?'

She nods and moves forward slightly on her sofa.

'It's like being you, but not being able to hear. It's no big deal, I've been deaf since I was a little kid.'

'Why? I mean, how did it happen?'

'Meningitis.' I have flashbacks to the things I remember hearing: a birthday party, an ice-cream van, the sound of Dad laughing. 'I don't mean to sound rude, but I really want to write a good story for you, so we can have people call us or write in with information about Freddy. Can you tell me about his friends, please?'

She sits back in the sofa and slides one hand down between the cushions.

'Freddy and I were always very close, we told each other everything. There were two of his friends I didn't like and he knew it. One was Hannes, his hunting buddy.'

'Hannes Carlsson from Utgard forest?'

'Yeah, he owns most of it. Him and his wife have a very good economy.'

There's that phrase again.

'They're some of the richest in the Kommun,' she continues. 'But, he's a bully and he bullied my friend's husband when he worked up at the pulp mill. I reckon, he's the hunt leader you know, I reckon he bullies his whole team.'

'Do you think he's responsible for Freddy's death?'

She shrugs. 'I don't know. I told the cops to talk to him, to check his guns, but you know . . . they're all real good mates with Hannes. He's the big fish and they all want to be friends with the big fish and hunt his woods. I told them but I don't know.'

'Who is the second person you were unsure of?'

'Don't know her name, not her real name. "Candy" is what she goes by, works up at the strip club on the E16, you know the one stuck out in the middle of nowhere, little way south of the SPT pulp mill. That place used to be a brothel, did you know that?'

'I didn't.'

'Well, you do now and I reckon it still might be some kind of brothel . . . unofficially somehow. You know what strippers are like.'

Actually, I don't.

'Fred and Candy were . . .' I pause and look down at my Dictaphone for a split second, 'friends?'

'They weren't friends, no. He was paying her. They were not

friends. He told me he couldn't afford it, but he couldn't stop going either. Reckoned he was in love with her. I told him he was being a drip, falling in love with a goddam stripper but that was what happened. He spent two, maybe three nights a week up at that dive, drinking Diet Cokes and watching her dance.' She wipes a tear from her eye, or it could have been an eyelash. 'Not much of a life was it, really.'

I chew on my lip and look around the room. Photos in white wooden frames, a low bookshelf half-filled with board games and jigsaw puzzles.

'Must be hard being a divorced man in his fifties in this town,' I say.

She nods. 'His boy's upstairs, you know. He's upstairs playing his damn computer games right now. Won't come down. Doesn't want to talk about it.'

'How old is your nephew?'

'He's fourteen going on twenty-one. Won't let anybody in, won't talk to no one. I have to leave his food outside his door like he's a monk or a prisoner or something. His mum's in Florida and he's heading off there at Christmas time. I think that should do him some good, although he don't like her much.' She looks up to the ceiling and lowers her voice. 'I can't blame him for that.'

'If you want, I can try to talk to your nephew? I'm only twelve years older than him after all and I know all about video games.'

'I don't know . . .'

I say nothing. One of Lena's many tricks.

'Well, I guess you could try,' she says. 'Can't do any harm, just for a minute.'

She leads me upstairs and knocks on the boy's door.

'You decent, Martin?' she says.

No response.

'You decent in there, Martin?'

'No,' he shouts back.

'Okay, he's decent. I'll be out here.'

I push the bedroom door open and see a lanky kid lying on the floor playing *Call of Duty* on his PlayStation. I glance at him but then focus solely on the screen.

'You wanna upgrade to the RPG,' I tell him. 'And you wanna watch your back.'

He looks up at me for a moment, console in hand, then turns back to the TV. His eyes are red. I'm not sure if that's from tears or gaming.

'You a journalist?'

'I'm Tuva ... Watch your back, I get ambushed just here every fucking time.'

He looks at me and sniffs and then he pauses the game.

'You gonna write about my pappa?'

I nod.

He swallows hard. 'You know they scooped out his eyes. And his eyes looked just like my eyes, too. Blue-grey. Mum says we have the same eyes. Exactly the same. That's what she says. None of this feels right, it's like he might come back home anytime, just walk back in. But that's bullshit, I know that. And I've got the same eyes as him. The exact same colour. I might be next.'

He points to his eyes.

'No,' I say, louder than I'd intended. 'No, that's not going to happen, Martin. You'll be safe here.'

'Mum's not here and Dad's gone,' he says. 'All my mates think that writer did it.'

'Which writer?'

'Freak who lives in the woods. My mate's big sister works in ICA. Freak comes in every week, same day, same time. Freak always comes to her till, she reckons he fancies her. Freak always buys a load of the weirdest stuff. He doesn't get nachos and potatoes and ham and normal shit. This writer freak buys pigs' feet. He buys the tails too, even the ears. Who buys pigs' ears?'

'Well,' I say. 'I'm sure the police will be talking to everyone in the village so they'll be speaking to him. But some people do cook offal and the cheap cuts. Not me, but it's not as uncommon as you might think.'

'He's a freak,' he says. 'Put that in your paper.'

Esther Malmström steps to the doorframe.

'You hungry, Martin? Want me to fix you a sandwich?'

He nods at her.

'Thanks for talking to me, Martin,' I say, and I feel like the police-woman that spoke to me on the night Dad died. 'I'm going to finish my chat with your aunty now. I'm sorry about your pappa, I really am. I want to help get to the bottom of this. I promise you I'll do whatever I can.'

He unpauses the game and I close the door.

Esther leans in towards me at the bottom of the stairs and talks softly into my hearing aid.

'He can't talk about it with his mates because they're all fourteen years old,' she says. 'And he can't talk about it with me or any other grown-up because he's fourteen years old. You think he's got a point about that writer?'

The smell of lilies hangs in the air. Do we have one killer in this town or a copycat? Why the hell is there a twenty-year pause?

'I don't know if he's got a point. But I've been assigned to write about this and it's the only thing I'm working on. I'll try to help find out who did this so you can all get some justice and some closure. What Martin said, well, kids say some weird things, but I'll certainly check it out. I'm heading over to Mossen village this afternoon.'

11

After my sandwich, a cling-filmed margarine crime from the news-agent's fridge, I check in with Lena.

'It's post-mortem day,' she says. 'Bumped into Chief Björn out on the street. His people have been tracing the last movements of Malmström, checking if anyone noticed anything unusual.' She leans back in her chair. 'Reckons the forensics guys found very little in Utgard, what with the rain and all the boot prints from police and paramedics. It was a muddy mess.'

'Any physical evidence? Fibres?'

'Björn wouldn't say but I could tell by his face it's not looking good. If Freddy was shot by a hunting rifle, the killer could have been hundreds of metres away. They'll do the bullet analysis, try to fix the direction it came from, but it's not like a city-centre murder with CCTV and witnesses, nothing like that.'

She looks up at me.

'I got some good material from the sister and a list of rumours as long as my arm.'

She nods. 'Okay.'

'And two more houses to visit in Mossen.'

She nods again and I leave.

On the drive to Utgard forest, I notice a few features that I missed before. In the underpass beneath the E16 motorway, someone's hung a piece of knotted string, threaded through CDs. Some kind of scarecrow, I guess. Orange plastic poles are dotted along each side of the road to mark the edge of the ditch for when the winter snows come. I pass dozens of them. And then I turn right and I'm in Mossen.

I drive past Hoarder's place and see nothing. When I look into the woods I realise I may as well be looking at Alaska right now, or Siberia a thousand years ago, or Norway in a hundred years' time. There is no evidence of time. No markers or guides. It's stark and vast and I cannot see past it. I look up through the windscreen and think of Dad and wonder again if the bullet that scared off my elk was the same one that killed Freddy Malmström. Will *Call of Duty* kid be okay with his dad gone and his mum so distant? Is he going to be me at that age: isolated, throwing every waking hour into studying and gaming?

The taxi driver's house is still empty, no Volvo in the drive. I speed up the hill and notice some of the potholes have been filled with gravel, light grey pebbles humped where the holes used to be like fresh graves. I pass the sisters, both hard at work, the fire burning in between them, and pull up at the ghostwriter's house.

The day is bright, on-and-off sunshine with a gentle breeze, and his house is one of the least foreboding in the village. It's modern, '80s maybe. The veranda wraps the building in its entirety and partially obscures the windows, which all appear to be mirrored. Something about the place suggests it's well built, more expensive than most homes in the area. In Gavrik Kommun, most houses are built by one of two companies so they tend to look roughly the same. This one stands out.

I ring the doorbell and wait. I can hear classical music of some kind from the other side of the door so it must be loud inside. I wait some more, checking for messages on my phone. No reception. I ring the doorbell again and then knock twice. The music turns off.

I think I hear a man shout 'hello' from the other side of the door but it's unclear to me so I shout, 'Hello Mr Holmqvist, I'm Tuva Moodyson from the *Gavrik Posten*. I wondered if I could talk to you for a moment, please? I'm deaf so can't hear you through this door.'

There's a long pause. I hear a gunshot in the distance, then another.

I hear bolts being clicked and then the door opens a little. A green eye and half a face, neat, clean-shaven, pale, with a faint scar above his lip.

'Hello,' he says.

'Sorry to bother you Mr Holmqvist. I work for the local paper and I'm reporting on the Freddy Malmström shooting. Can I ask you some general questions about the village, please?'

'Did you say you are deaf?'

I point to my ears.

The door opens. He's soft-bodied and he's wearing pressed chinos and brown leather deck shoes and a tucked-in polo-shirt. His forearms are extraordinarily hairy and he has transparent latex gloves on, the thin sort that doctors wear. He's holding his hands up loosely, palms towards the ceiling.

'I'm cooking,' he says. '*Tête de veau*. It's a convoluted business, but absolutely worth it.'

'I'm sure,' I say. 'Good food's always worth the effort.'

'Quite,' he says, nodding. 'Quite. Please, come in. Excuse the mess, I don't get many visitors.'

I walk inside. The house is impressive and there is no mess. Designer pieces of furniture carefully arranged in a large open-plan room with a stainless steel kitchen at one end. Classical music's playing low on the stereo.

'Shoes off just here if you don't mind.' He points to an empty rack. 'Then take a seat just there.' He points to a tan leather armchair. 'I'll get cleaned up, back in a moment.'

I take a seat on the armchair and look at the room. The ceilings are quite high and the floor's a mixture of black ceramic tiles in some areas, and dark mahogany planks in others. There are no photographs, nothing at all on the walls, no art and no clocks. I watch David remove something from the oven, it looks like a roast leg of lamb or something, but much paler. It's almost white. He probes it with a spike, perhaps an oven thermometer, then places it back. It doesn't look appetising, whatever it is. He walks past a gleaming industrial-looking espresso machine and takes two glasses from a wall cabinet and fills them from a bottle of mineral water and then he places them on a small tray and walks over to me.

'Water?'

I take a glass and feel uncomfortable.

'You'd like to know something about this village? What exactly?'

'How long have you lived here?'

'Years.'

'Do you know your neighbours well?'

'Oh, reasonably.'

'Does everyone in the village own a rifle?'

He smiles a painful-looking smile, his lips curving up at one side, and uncrosses his legs.

'What a very insightful question. Tell me, is this little chat you've instigated on the record or off the record?'

'That's up to you, Mr Holmqvist.'

He crosses his legs again the other way and I glimpse a thin strip of pale, hairy skin between the top of his sock and the bottom of his chino roll-ups. He has a dark mole on the apex of his Adam's apple and it moves up and down when he swallows his water.

'Either is fine. To my knowledge, everyone residing in this village owns a rifle with the exception of yours truly.'

'You don't feel the need for a gun? For protection against elk or bears or whatever's out there?'

'I'm rather an indoors person,' he says. 'I write with every moment I have, and when I'm not writing I'm cooking or I'm researching or I'm thinking or I'm reading. I read three books per week. Three, sometimes four. To me, the idea of straying through forestland looking for a wild creature to shoot is preposterous so I leave that sort of thing to the unthinking people. Don't misunderstand me, I'm very grateful to them. I enjoy preparing and cooking and eating wild game very much indeed. I take great pleasure from it. But I'm not the sort to bring it to market. I'm the sort to bring it to table, and for that I require no firearm.'

I glance down at my notebook. 'So, Bengt Gustavsson owns a gun?'

'Our vegetarian hoarder? Oh God, yes, he's an army veteran and for all I know he's the best shot in the Kommun. Ex-sniper I believe, although he ended his career as an army medic. He is, however, strictly non-meat, so I believe his gun has been locked away in his personal museum for some years now.'

'I know Mr Carlsson is a hunter but what about the wood-carving sisters, your nearest neighbours?'

'Tell me, have you met them?' he says, the pained smile back on his face.

I nod.

'Honestly, I could not have concocted such a pair of siblings even if I'd tried. I mean, please.' He sighs and sips his water. 'The ugly sisters are paranoid that someone will steal their, you know . . . They believe their models, their models of those dreadful little men, are valuable and therefore they need protection. I've seen their rifles leaning against their workbenches as I've driven past, but I have no idea if either one of them can shoot for toffee.'

I finish my water.

'And the taxi driver? Mr Svensson?'

'Svensson has a gun, but it may not be a rifle, I'm not absolutely sure. I've used his services many times when I can't bear to drive – when I need to think and focus on a project. He shoots at a range, I believe, part of some sort of club or society.'

'Do you have any information about who shot Freddy Malmström?'

'I do not.'

'Do you have any theories, then? Who do you think is capable of such a thing?'

'Oh, they are all capable. Any of them and all of them. Such is the human condition. Do you know, I've never written a deaf character.'

'Oh? What kind of books do you write?'

'Well, it's difficult to generalise such a thing. I offer a rather bespoke service. Writers who can't actually write but who have *names* send me their ideas and sometimes I write for them for a fee. Then they publish the work in their name. They get the plaudits but I retain my blissful anonymity. What is it like to be deaf, and by that of course, I mean what is it really like?'

'It's . . .' I pause, caught off guard. 'It's all I've ever—'

'All you've ever known, yes, of course, I knew you'd say that, but you see that's not good enough, you're not really *thinking* about my question. Take your time. What, in your experience, does being deaf *feel* like?'

So I pause and close my eyes for a moment. For some reason I want to give a proper answer, an answer that might impress him. But while I'm thinking about what being me feels like I'm also thinking why the fuck am I appeasing this guy? I open my eyes.

'I feel a little detached all the time, a little further away from life than I imagine a hearing person does.'

'Exactly!' he says, slapping his knee. 'That is it exactly. Now, please, more, carry on.'

I smile even though I don't want to.

'I'm relieved for the silence when I need it.' He looks impatient, like he could have said this himself. 'Because it's not a silence that you will ever know.'

He licks his lips, a strange movement that starts at the scar in the centre of his upper lip and swipes to the left. Then his tongue returns to the scar and swipes to the right.

'It's as silent as death is final. It's thick and deep and I can lay in it. It's all around me if I need it to be. I have the option to switch that on and off, and you don't.'

'Good!' he says, staring at me. The mole on his Adam's apple rises and falls. 'Really, I mean it. Well done. Excellent.'

My skin's itching. I have a compulsion to run away yet for some reason I want to answer his questions and impress him. If this guy shot Freddy Malmström, why would he do it so close to his own house?

'Now, this has been more fruitful than I'd expected,' says Holmqvist. 'But I need to get back to my veal if I'm to eat tonight. And eat I must. Please, feel free to pop by if you need to know anything else. But, if I am writing, the door will stay locked. If I am writing, then I'm in a world just as silent as yours can be. If I'm up there,' he points to the ceiling with his hairy hand, 'then my front door will not open for you.'

12

I leave the ghostwriter's house and get back into my truck and lock the doors. I look up at the sliver of sky visible between the trees, and the thick blanket of cloud that's formed while I was indoors. I'm staring through a veil of mosquito corpses on the windscreen. Then my focus extends past it, to the perimeter wall of David Holmqvist's land. It's a collection of moss-encrusted stones stacked on top of each other up to about hip height. It's not a proper wall because it couldn't keep out an elk and it's not a proper wall because it's alive with ferns and reindeer lichen and alder saplings.

I turn my head to the left and Frida Carlsson's standing right there, her face coated with sweat, her skin red and flushed. I can't wind down my window because the engine's not on so I have to open my door.

'Frida, you okay?'

She smiles at me. 'I'm just out for a power walk before the next rainstorms come in. Recognised your truck so thought I'd say hi.'

I open my door wider, seeing her black Lycra leggings and T-shirt. She's in great shape.

'I was thinking,' she says, wiping her face on her running shirt. 'About the dreadful business. About your newspaper. Maybe we should talk some more, what with Hannes being the hunt master and all. I know a lot of the guys who use Utgard.'

'Yes,' I say. 'That sounds great ... Now?'

She looks at her watch, it's one of those big digital pedometer things.

'You want to walk back with me? I've done thirteen kilometres, just got two left. If it rains, I'll drive you back here to your truck after we're done. Deal?'

Before I say anything I'm climbing down from my driver's seat and pulling my waterproof jacket back on. I lock the Toyota and I'm walking away from it, side by side with Frida, not power walking, just strolling down the track and past Ghostwriter's wall.

'You talked to David?' she asks, not looking at his house.

'Just now,' I say. 'Are you friends?'

Frida smiles and then chuckles. She's still using her Nordic walking sticks like she's cross-country skiing with invisible skis on invisible snow.

We're clear of David Holmqvist's drystone wall before she starts to talk again.

'David's unusual,' she says. 'He thinks he's a gifted author, but none of us have ever read any of his books because he doesn't write in his own name. So, maybe we have read him and maybe we haven't, but we have no way of knowing. One time I mentioned the books I enjoy, the classic romance literature of the fifties and sixties, and he raised his eyebrows and made a kind of 'o' shape with his mouth like they were dumb things to read. He's a book snob, you know the kind, and we're all in the dark because we don't have a clue what he writes himself. He's just not our sort, you know? And Hannes and him are practically opposites, so ...'

I stop walking because I've realised that I'm in a forest, a fucking murder forest, with no truck and no gun and no fucking clue what to do.

'I'm going back,' I say, my arms outstretched as if to help me keep my balance. 'Back to my truck. Let's just drive to your place instead.'

'Nonsense,' says Frida. 'Look, I know Utgard seems scary right now, but we're perfectly safe here. Whoever is shooting people is shooting male hunters. Look, let me.'

She straps a fluorescent orange band around my forearm over my jacket sleeve.

'Now, there's no risk to us whatsoever. I give you my word.'

And I believe her. With this shiny bit of plastic fixed to my jacket, I feel reassured.

'Ten minutes, then we're there.'

The track has a thick Mohican of dying grass running up its centre. The woods are quiet apart from our footsteps and the occasional buzz of a horsefly or bee. I try to look straight ahead, to where there's a view, a line of sight. To my left and right are solid barriers fifteen times as tall as I am; organic walls of darkness and they are too close to me so I just keep looking forward.

And there's the house. I see filtered glimpses of the angled mansard roof through copper beech leaves. If I sprint I reckon I could make it to the house in three minutes and that thought's a real comfort. If an elk bursts out of the treeline or a hornet attacks from an overhead nest, at least I can run *to* something now.

'You've researched the '90s murders?'

'Yes,' I say. 'Not as much as I'd like, I've been too busy, but I know the general timeline.'

'You know someone was arrested and then released without charge after the last body was discovered in '94.'

'Yeah. Martin, something? I read on the unsolved crime forums that it was all rumour and gossip, not a shred of physical evidence.'

'Maybe,' Frida says, turning her face to look at me as we enter her driveway. 'I was up in Norrland that autumn taking care of my old dad but Hannes remembers the arrest. Martin something,' she says, 'is now called David something.'

I stop walking.

'Holmqvist?' I say, my voice a little louder than I'd expected. 'He was arrested for the old murders?'

71

'Local people don't like to talk about it. Not good for the town's reputation.' Frida looks at her house and at the Volvo SUV parked outside. 'Hannes is home, I'll introduce you to him.'

We walk inside and Frida shouts Hannes's name. I hear a blurry, deep response from above but can't make out the words.

Frida takes a tall glass and fills it up from the kitchen tap with tea-coloured well water and drinks it.

'I'm going to take a quick shower, I'll just be a jiffy. You want to wait in here with a cup of coffee? Or do you want to meet Hannes?'

'It would be good to meet your husband, if you don't think he'll mind. Just for a quick chat about the story.'

'Follow me.'

We walk back to the front door and up a white-painted staircase. Frida must be in her mid-fifties but her body is so much fitter than mine. I'm walking right behind her and she's lean and taut like a gymnast.

There are black-and-white movie prints on the walls up here, photos of Ingrid Bergman and Cary Grant, golden-age Hollywood stuff.

'You like the movies?' I ask.

'Love them,' she smiles. 'Unfortunately, my husband doesn't share my passion.'

Frida knocks on a door and I hear a grunt, then the clicks and scrapes of a key in a lock. She waits for the lock mechanism to click, then opens the door, slips inside for a moment, then comes out again, beckoning me over with her manicured fingernail.

'Tuva,' she says as I walk into the room, 'I'd like you to meet Hannes Carlsson. Hannes, meet my friend, Tuva Moodyson. Tuva works at the *Posten*.'

He's almost handsome. Old and grey, but his eyes are still bright blue. He looks like one of those republican senators you see on TV, all cheekbones and tan and charm. But as he stands behind his desk and extends his hand to me I see that he's no Mitt Romney. His eyes are ever so slightly too close together. He's a little too short and a little too broad. Frida and him are the same height.

He offers me a seat in front of his desk and Frida excuses herself.

'My wife told me about you, thinks you've got potential in the newspaper business, maybe even big-city work one day.'

I'm simultaneously happy and irritated.

'Thanks. Sorry to bother you when you just got home from work. I'm writing about the awful murder of Freddy Malmström. I understand he was a man you hunted with? I'm sorry.'

'Hunting's not a sport,' he says, rolling an expensive-looking fountain pen between his thumb and index finger. 'We hunt animals for a reason. It's a cull. There are too many elk one year, and what happens? They graze on the new spruce saplings and devastate the crop. We control numbers. Hunters do an important job in keeping balance in the forest, always has been that way and always will be. And you got too many elk wandering around, you got more car accidents.'

I bite the inside of my mouth.

'Now someone comes into my woods and starts killing my hunters. And he's killed four so far. But I don't want you to worry, my team are going to flush him out.'

'Who's in your hunting team?' I take out my phone. 'Mind if I record this?'

He thinks for a long moment, staring at my phone before looking up at me. Behind him I can see maps of the world and engraved sporting cups and shields. Then I see a smile and a shake of his head.

'I don't mind you taping this, but I won't give you all the names, it'd take too long. I have important local people in my team, it's the best elk forest in the Kommun, you can ask anyone. I have local politicians from the Kommun, shop owners, the boss of the factory, police, two firemen, owner of the local hotel, all the key individuals. If you hunt and you live around here, then you'll want to be in my team.'

'What about the other villagers?'

'No, they wouldn't fit. I reckon Viggo can shoot pretty good, he's the fella that drives the taxi and lives down the hill. But hunting, there's a code, it's hard to explain, it's a social thing, too. It's the only time some of us friends get to see each other, so we keep it tight. It's a good group so we keep it how we like it.'

'So you know a lot of the people around here?'

He scrunches his nose and sniffs.

'Do you know the man who owns the strip club on the E16? He in your team?'

He smiles. 'I've driven past that place, but no.'

On his desk, next to a box of man-size tissues, sits his phone. It's flashing and vibrating. He points his finger up in the air and takes the call, spinning in his executive chair to face the painting immediately behind him. It's a painting of a thick pine forest.

I look around the room. On the far side is a wall full of trophies. I don't mean diving competitions or soccer medals, these are corpses. There's a bearskin next to the sofa, an antelope head mounted over the fireplace, and an elephant leg in the corner with a heavy, crystal ashtray poised on top of it like the most hideous thing in the whole world.

He spins back round and ends the call and smiles.

'Where were we?'

'Hunting,' I say, pointing up to the antelope. 'You didn't shoot that in Utgard.'

He smiles and I see that his teeth are sharp and they've been whitened. They're gleaming at me.

'Africa is my heart,' he says with as much asshole pretension as he can muster. 'The big five. Every year I go big-game hunting, have done since I was thirty. These are a sample of my souvenirs. I always bring back a little keepsake from my kills, a memento. Something to get me through the rest of the year until the next hunt.'

I hear a knock at the door and it opens. Frida is standing there looking radiant with the kind of glowing skin you can only get through sweating. She has a towel wrapped around her hair and she's wearing jeans and a white T-shirt.

'Tuva, tea?'

I smile, stand up, and follow her out, thanking Hannes for his time.

She leads me to a conservatory. It's blocky and ugly, a lean-to extension at the back of the house. There are two short bookcases crammed with romance novels and we sit on wicker furniture and Frida pours from a real pot.

'You think I should check out Holmqvist? Do you have any new information the police should know about?'

She shrugs and shakes her head.

I stir my tea with a silver spoon and I take a sip and fuck me it tastes good. Smooth and mild, made in bone china with love. Not love, obviously, Frida doesn't love me, but with care.

'I don't have information,' she says. 'I just get a vibe, quite honestly. Don't you?'

I don't think anyone could not get a vibe from David Holmqvist.

'He says he doesn't own a gun.'

'Oh, well in that case . . .'

I finish my cup and Frida refills it.

'You know, where we're sitting right now, it's at least twenty kilometres in any direction until we get out of Utgard forest,' she says. 'And twenty may as well be two hundred, with the woods so thick. The pine harvest is long overdue. And I have to live right next to that creepy ghostwriter. I feel fine, honestly, when Hannes is here. When Hannes is with me I always feel safe, I've never met a man that would worry Hannes. But when I'm on my own up here, I don't know, I just wish he'd left Mossen village after the arrest back in the '90s, instead of changing his name and staying put.'

I excuse myself to use the toilet. It smells of rose water and there's a trio of hand creams in the lace basket as well as the miniature soaps I saw last time. I stare at the romance novels on the shelf, and squirt lily-of-the-valley nail cream into the creases of my palm and work it into my cuticles. It smells like Mum a long time ago, that early version of Mum, the real Mum, the original Mum who I miss so much it makes my bones ache.

Frida drives me back to my truck. I get out of her car and she passes me a round tin from her back seat.

'What is it?'

'I did a big bake last night for the elderly I tend to. Made a few too many. Take it home, it's a sponge and it's sunk a little in the middle but the flavour should be okay.'

I take it and promise to return the polka-dot tin. I climb into my truck and turn the key in the ignition and the headlights come on and I love them. It's two degrees. Light drizzle. The wipers squeak as they get going and I reverse out of Holmqvist's driveway and head down the track towards the top of the hill. As I turn to start the descent, I feel something bang in the back of the truck, in the open bay. I frown, trying to remember if I left anything in there. I look back through my rear-view mirror but it is dark and the rear windscreen's dotted with raindrops. I click on the rear wiper and that's when I see him.

13

He's trying to crouch down under the window, but I guess he's also trying to hold on to something, on to the metal bar above the rear windscreen. I can't see much. He's about an arm's length away from me, just a piece of glass and a row of seats in between us. I start to breathe too fast. The wiper blades. I can't see who it is but it's not a kid. Too big to be a kid. I drive faster. It's a full-grown man. Must be.

But then my breathing slows a little as I realise that I'm the one in control. He can't get me. As long as I don't stop then he cannot get to me. I'll call the police and then I'll lock the doors and then I'll park up right outside the station. I'm in here and he's staying out there.

I'm at the base of the hill when he starts thumping the rear windscreen. I can feel it and I can hear it, fists smashing against the glass. He's trying to break through to the back seats.

I accelerate hard and swerve around the track. The knocking stops and I hear him falling about, rolling around in the back of the truck. I feel it too, the subtle change in handling as the weight swings from side to side. My heart's racing. I pass Taxi's house doing seventy and finding every single pothole I possibly can. The truck lurches up and down and feels completely solid, like it wants me to push it harder, like it's taunting me for driving around on asphalt all this time. I pass Hoarder's caravan and see the dim light and carry on. Still can't make out who's in the back, he must be flat out back there.

The road widens and I push up towards one hundred. Then I slow down and indicate and bounce up onto the main road and out of Utgard forest. I hear a bang and look in my mirror and see someone jump from the back of my truck. The figure lands on the track and rolls over and then he gets up and dashes into the trees. It's twilight, the time the locals call 'elk o'clock'. I don't get a good look at him. Could have been anyone.

I pick up my phone and accelerate to a hundred and ten. My tongue's dry. I look at my phone screen and then up at the road, then back to it. It's shaking. I'm shaking. I drive towards the police station and under the E16 and my pulse is starting to slow. I see Tammy's van in the distance. I call.

'Thai green, hot to trot, double rice, crackers, ten mins. Got it.'

'No,' I yelp. 'Not that, don't put down the phone.'

'What's wrong?'

'You still have that gun in your truck?'

'The starter pistol? Yeah, 'course. Why?'

'Can I borrow it? I'll be at your van in five minutes. You'll need to shutter up for a while.'

'Okay.'

She is the one person I can rely upon to say 'okay' and not ask questions. I approach the town and head past ICA and park close to her takeout van and breathe. I'm sweaty. I check the rear-view mirror and there's nobody there. I'm fine. But then I check it again.

Tam's standing with her hand in her jacket like a Chicago gangster in a movie. I unlock my door and fall out to her.

'What happened?' she asks.

I pull my head up from her shoulder and breathe deeply and peek into the back of my truck and tell her.

'What piece of ratshit would do that?' asks Tammy.

My right hearing aid crackles. It's getting wet in the rain. I cup both hands and raise them over my ears as guards.

'Did he leave anything in the pickup? Any evidence?'

Tammy stands up on the wheel arch of my truck and shines the torch of her phone into the open rear. Nothing there. No evidence. And then she reaches in and picks something up and shows it to me.

It's a gold-coloured paperclip.

'You going to the cop shop?' she says. 'I can close up for the night and come with you if you want.'

'I'll go tomorrow,' I say, my hands still over my ears. 'Can I borrow your pistol just for tonight, though?'

'You know it just goes bang, right?'

'It would make me feel a whole lot better,' I say.

She passes me her starter pistol and the paperclip, and my fingers are still trembling as I take them from her. I look at the gun. I'm getting close, I can feel it. Why else would someone hide in my damn truck? I'm getting close and somebody out there just gave me a warning.

14

I wake from a shallow, fitful sleep. Tammy wanted me to stay at her place but I couldn't, I had to get my hearing aids into desiccant immediately, had to dry them out.

I didn't open my one, sealed, pristine bottle of rum last night. I came close but I did not open it. There are whole weekends I don't remember from my London days and I will not allow myself to go back to that.

My phone says 7:13am and I switch off the 7:15 alarm and get up and walk through the flat to my front door. I push the chest of drawers away from the door and look through the fish-eye security lens. Nobody there.

Back in the bedroom, I take out my aids and pick up the starter pistol I left on the bedside table last night. I take it into the bathroom and set it down on the toilet seat lid. I shower and the hot water feels good. I let it pummel the back of my neck, my head leaning forward, the heat accumulating under my skin. Water dribbles down my chin, around my shoulders, off the tip of my nose, not a tip really, more of a nub, a rounded part-Saami nose inherited from Mum.

I've missed laundry day. The slot allocated to my flat, to Flat 4, is Thursdays, and I missed it. I won't be able to do laundry till next week now. Someone climbed into my truck last night and scared the crap out of me, and today I'm worrying about laundry.

I sniff the armpits of a grey sweater on the sofa and slip it on along with other cleaner items. The microwave pings and I add a spoonful of lingonberry jam to the porridge and eat it pacing from the living room to the bedroom and back again and back again. I'm tired from last night's encounter with David Ghostwriter Holmqvist, or whoever it was. Gavrik's a small town nestled between a river to the south and a range of hills to the east and Utgard forest to the west and another forest to the north. It doesn't need a hunter hunting people. Doesn't fucking need it.

I head to work and the town feels livelier than usual but it's not TV crews or tabloid reporters, it's hunters. It's men, some women, but mostly men, off from work for a few days, stocking up on ammunition and gear. Buying and talking and gossiping. You might think that Swedes are tight-lipped and stoic and you'd be about right but we also gossip like hell.

The office is as it always is except that the stack of newspapers on the front counter is twice as tall as usual. I go in and make coffee. Nils is on the phone to a potential client, trying to sell him a half-page near the obituaries and birthdays, prime real estate in the paper, lots of eyeballs on those pages, lots of 'community investment' in that section.

Lars coughs to get my attention.

'Bet you'll be happy not to visit Mossen village again after this has all blown over,' he says, his spectacles resting on his bald patch.

'True,' I say. 'Each time I get back from that place I just want to stand on top of a mountain and look out. I want a long-distance view where I can see whatever's coming.'

Lars smiles and makes a little noise, then slips his bifocals back down onto his nose.

'Do you know what a *tête de veau* is, Lars? I know you cook. Have you ever heard of it?'

'Can't say that I have,' he says. '*Veau* is veal, maybe one of the cheaper cuts like shoulder or shin?'

I google it and the results are in French so I click on Google Images and oh my God.

'Lars,' I say.

He pushes his glasses up onto his head again.

'It's a calf's head, brain and all.'

'*Vive la France*,' he says, going back to his work.

I stare at the grid of images, all pale-pink glutinous fibres and jellified ears and eyes. I click on videos and play the first YouTube clip because I can't not.

Oh God, David Holmqvist actually did this and he was doing it the moment I arrived at his house.

I stop the video and call the police station. Thord picks up.

'You busy?' I ask.

'Medium,' he says. 'It's the Coroner who's busy now. Post-mortem results should come in later this afternoon. That why you're calling?'

'I want to see you,' I say. 'Right now.'

No reply.

'Thord?'

'What? Listen, I'm tied up for a bit. It'll have to be later.'

'Lunch?' I suggest, pleadingly. 'Hotel's open today. I need to talk. Meet you there at noon?'

'You really want to eat there? What about a burger?'

'No, I need some veg,' I say, almost throwing up. 'I'm gonna get scurvy or rickets if I don't get some food that's been grown in the ground. I'll pay.'

'Noon,' he says. 'See you then.'

Murder's not how I imagined it would be. I thought the whole town would swing into action somehow, that there'd be midnight searches and TV crews and 'do not cross' tape everywhere. But it's not like that. There has been no floodlit manhunt. People talk a little more but the town's almost as quiet as it ever was. There's a killer out there, maybe two killers, and people are still getting their hair cut and their fishing rods mended and their recycling done.

I need some structure to the story so I switch both aids off and focus on my screen and on my notes. I download my digital Dictaphone recordings and my phone voice memos and order them. I split what I have into stories and then rearrange them to try to get the local perspective, the think-piece, the effect on the community. Lars is right, my job is to reflect how this event affects our readers. I'll need to talk to someone at the school, maybe the headmaster, maybe some parents, and I'd like a statement from the local hunting association and maybe one from someone who investigated, or was close to, the '90s Medusa cases.

My notes are a mess so I tidy them up and print them out. I need to visit the strip club on the E16. And the taxi driver in Mossen. I search the internet for his phone number.

'Hi, this is Tuva Moodyson from the *Posten*.'

No answer. But then I realise my aids are off, so switch them both on.

'You there?' I hear him say.

'Yes, I'm here, sorry, bad connection.'

'You need a taxi?'

'No, Mr Svensson. I'd like to have a chat with you please about the murder in Utgard forest, I'm writing a piece for the paper.'

'I know. You've been talking to the whole village. I heard.'

'Can we meet, maybe in town? Can I buy you a coffee this afternoon? Say, McDonald's at three?'

'No can do,' he says. 'That's my busiest time, so to say. I'm ferrying kids all over the Kommun from different schools, and taking them all home.'

'What about after that? What time do you normally finish?'

'After that I've got my own son to deal with. I'm sorry, I'm too busy for this.'

He wants to put down the phone.

'Well, listen, I'm great with kids, in fact I used to work in a kindergarten when I was younger. Maybe I could pop by for half an hour when your son gets home and help you out a little and we could chat then?'

He coughs and then I don't hear anything.

'Mr Svensson?'

'You like kids?' he says.

'What time should I come by?'

'Come at six,' he says. 'Not sure what I can tell you that the others haven't, but I want this scum caught so whatever I can do to help. See you at six sharp.'

I trawl old reports of the Medusa murders and print out a map of the locations where the bodies were found. Then I add Freddy Malmström to the map. The bodies are well spread out, they weren't found close to any particular house or feature. I catch a faint whiff of sweat from my jumper and reach down into my drawer and take out my perfume and spray, as discreetly as I can, onto the bobbly wool under my armpits.

'No sprays in the office,' Lars says without looking up. 'You know the rules by now. This is a newspaper not a beauty parlour. No nail varnish, no nail clipping, no scent.'

I stick up my hand in a gesture of apology and then he smiles and turns away and I rotate my hand and extend my middle finger.

I save my stories as separate files and think up some headline ideas. Then I print off the company details of the strip club, and photos of Hannes Carlsson's hunting club I found on Facebook.

My stomach rumbles. I grab my coat and my handbag and slip on my outdoor boots and open the door. The bell rings and I feel the air on my face and it's starting to turn. The air is changing.

I zip everything up and take the long route to the hotel because the short route is about three minutes and I'm too early. I walk past strangers and acquaintances, nodding and saying '*Hej*', and avoiding the puddles on the pavement. I pass the stationery store which closed down a while back and turn left and see the queue. *Systembolaget* is the state-owned alcohol shop. It opens at noon in Gavrik because the

town is so goddam small. It's a part-time liquor store and the usual
Toytown dignitaries are lined up outside and I'm about three bad
decisions away from joining them. I recognise a few from arrests and
business liquidations over the years. Some were caught drunk and
disorderly and some were caught drink-driving, back when they had
jobs and families. Most of them are suited and booted, which is bizarre
because I wear jeans to work and so do most people in the town if
they're not in uniform. But these are not good suits, they're not
cared-for suits, they're not pressed or dry-cleaned suits. They're loose
and patchy, shiny elbows like mackerel skin, frayed trouser bottoms
where they drag on the paving stones. I walk past and turn left and
up towards the hotel and the factory. The wind's not blowing in the
right direction or I'd smell it, sugar in the air, a liquorice breeze that
I loved when I first moved here and that I still love now.

The sign, slightly left of centre, says *Hotel Gavrik*. There are two
outdoor candles flanking the entrance and these are lit only on days
when the place is open for lunch: Mondays, Wednesdays and Fridays.
They tried opening five days a week but they lost money. Three
days works, there are enough customers for three.

I walk inside and it's warm but it smells faintly of damp. The
pine-clad reception has a Halloween pumpkin with an electric candle
flickering inside. Premature. I turn right and see Thord sitting down
eating a lump of bread, so I join him.

'Hi,' I say.

'I've got thirty minutes then the Chief wants me back.'

'No problem.'

I look around the pale green room and recognise pretty much
everyone. People nod to me and one woman waves and then pulls
back her hand like she's just made a mistake.

'Salad, meatballs, pie,' he says, holding up the laminated no-choice
menu. 'You want water?'

I nod, tasting something bitter in my mouth, and he walks off to
a trestle table covered with a paper tablecloth. He pours two small

tumblers of water from a jug and takes a handful of paper napkins. He's got a wiry frame and a decent face and I fancied him for my first month in Toytown. I kissed him one time after too many rum and Cokes at Ronnie's bar and let me tell you, those teeth didn't get in the way at all. From time to time I still dream about those seconds, that's all it was, a few snatched seconds in the alley beside the bar, right before everyone came out and Thord and I separated and laughed and then never spoke of it again.

The owner-receptionist-waitress comes in from the kitchen and gives us each a mean bowl of salad. I can eat this at least, I can stomach this, it's not meat. The edges of the leaves are brown and there's too much vinegar in the dressing. But I get it down.

'Talk to me about David Holmqvist,' I say. 'He was arrested for the '90s killings?'

Thord places his index finger to his lips and leans towards me. He nods and I notice tiny flakes of dandruff at his temples and some in his parting and even a few in his eyebrows.

'And never charged,' he says. 'It wasn't him. We had fax records to and from his publisher in London. He's a funny old stick, always has been for as long as I've known him, but it wasn't him. Dave isn't a nature person, he doesn't know the woods. Experts from Stockholm reckon the murderer back then was a woodsman or at least someone who spends a good deal of time in Utgard forest. That's the profile. Medusa is a villager, or else someone who visits them woods regular. Dave's an indoors kinda guy. Chief don't like him much though. Something about Dave frightening his daughter years ago, some kinda misunderstanding at school.'

I finish the salad and the bowls are taken away and my lips are still tingling from the acid. Almost as soon as they're gone, the main course arrives. I've had it before. It's not bad. On any other day I would happily eat it.

Thord tucks in. I notice a white flake fall from his hair and land in the brown sauce next to his mash.

'Do you have a suspect?'

He looks up and I can see the shape of a meatball inside his right cheek and it's almost too much.

'Not yet but we're working on it.' He chews and swallows. 'A sighting of a man riding away from the area on a motorbike, carrying what might be a rifle case, foreign plates, but that could have been anything. No make or model or registration number.'

'Any other leads? Anything off the record?'

He swallows.

'You'll get the post-mortem details later on just like everyone else.'

I lean in. 'Come on,' I whisper. 'If I dig up something I'll return the favour, I promise.'

He takes a sip of water, looking into my eyes the whole time. He leans closer.

'Shot from a range of between fifty and one hundred metres.' He sniffs and looks around the room. 'Mid-torso, heart and lung, died straight away.'

The owner-waitress-receptionist asks us if everything is okay and we both nod.

Thord watches her walk away.

'The eyes,' he lowers his voice to where I can only lip-read him, 'were cut out very cleanly, some kind of short, curved blade.' He eats another meatball. 'The ballistics boys are still working on the weapon profile. But anyone with half a brain knows it was a rifle that killed old Freddy Malmström. They'll be able to tell us more soon enough. And one of the Mossen villagers has a CCTV system and he's released the tapes to us, well I say tapes, they're actually DVDs, but we're checking to see what cars came through on the day of the shooting.'

'Which villager has cameras pointing out to the track?'

He shakes his head. 'Can't say and it don't matter who, it just matters that we have them. We're checking the alibis of anyone on our watch list, and anyone that lives local or knows the woods real well. So far, all the villagers have alibis except one.'

'Your ghostwriter pal doesn't have an alibi, does he?' I ask, searching his eyes for a clue.

'Well, if that's the case, it's probably because he spends all day writing books, at home, alone. I tell you, I know Dave pretty well and he is not our man.'

'Last night I visited Frida and Hannes Carlsson in Mossen village,' I say. 'Someone climbed into the back of my truck while I was eating dinner with them, and stayed hidden in there till I got to the main road. I don't know, didn't get a good look, but it could have been David Holmqvist.'

'What?' His mouth is open and I can see potato on his tongue. 'Why didn't you come to me with this?'

'I'm coming now,' I say, searching his eyes. 'God knows what he was doing and what he had planned. He hopped out into the trees otherwise I would have brought him straight to you. And another thing . . .'

Thord looks at me.

'He cooks calf heads,' I say. 'Did you know that? He cooks their heads, whole.'

Thord places his knife and fork together on the plate, remnants of instant mash and reheated meatballs tucked under the cutlery.

'He have a weapon with him in the truck? You think it was him, but did you actually see him?'

I shake my head and scoop some mash onto a piece of stale bread. I haven't touched the meatballs or the sauce and Thord doesn't seem to have noticed.

'Listen. Still don't sound like Dave, but I'll talk to him,' he says. 'The weird food thing ain't nothing, it's just the way he is. I'll make sure he don't bother you again.'

The plates are removed and replaced with thin slices of dry apple pie with squirty cream on the side.

'Don't like that village much,' Thord says, licking cream from his fork and looking up at me. 'Woods are too big and the trees are too tall and too thick. It's time to harvest, I'd say. Time to do some thinning.'

15

After lunch I drive to Tammy's takeout van. I hand back the starter pistol because guns scare the shit out of me, even pretend ones, and she lends me the can of Canadian bear-spray she bought on the internet. Looks like a small fire extinguisher. She reckons it's better than the starting pistol because it's a deterrent *and* a weapon.

Police have released a statement following the post-mortem. It's brief and it says less than what Thord told me at lunch. The cause of death was a gunshot wound, and the eyes were removed. They don't mention the 1990s Medusa murders.

I slip under the motorway and head through the waterlogged fields outside of Utgard forest towards the Mossen village turn-off. I sync my hearing aid with my phone's Bluetooth. I dial and wait.

'Hello?'

'Hi Mum, it's me.'

'Hello Tuva.'

'How are you feeling today, Mum? Good day or bad day?'

'Oh, you know.'

She sounds weary. Maybe it's the medication or maybe she's tired. Probably it's both.

'You remember I'm coming down tomorrow to see you. I'm sorry I haven't been for a while, work's been hectic. I'll try to get there by early afternoon, about one o'clock suit you?'

'Oh, that'll be fine.'

I can see the turn-off for Mossen and the gap through the solid wall of trees.

'Can't talk for long, Mum, I'm working on a story.'

She says something but I can't hear the words.

'Mum,' I say, louder and clearer. 'You're breaking up. I'll see you tomorrow at one-ish. I'm looking forward to it.'

There's a crackle on the line. 'What did you say, Tuva?' She sounds irritated. 'Try to speak slower. Now, what was the last thing you . . .' And then it's all static and hiss.

'Bye, Mum,' I say loud and final.

'Tuva? What . . .'

I end the call and my stomach feels wrong, the way it always does when I talk to her on the phone, except twice as wrong because the conversation didn't finish with niceties, the niceties she and I know so well, the ritualistic nothing phrases of 'mind how you go' and 'okay then' and 'hope you have a good night,' that cushion each ice-cold goodbye. None of that. Just static. And now I'm in this goddam village again, the trees either side of me, my hand flicking off the indicator. It gets dark and I slow down to forty.

According to the dash display it's five degrees above zero and my tank's three-quarters full and the service is overdue. I drive past Hoarder's place. I see him outside, my headlights mowing him down. I realise that I'm driving at him as he's coming out of an outdoor toilet, the little hut with the heart on the door, and I imagine how awful this must be for him, how un-private. He lives in a remote forest to get away from people and here I am shining two halogen headlights in his face just seconds after he's taken care of business. Does he even have a sink in there? How does he wash his hands?

I drive on and it's not long before I get to the taxi driver, Viggo Svensson's house. For some reason I'm expecting Viggo Mortensen, the actor from *Lord of The Rings*. Well, I'm expecting Viggo Mortensen wearing a taxi driver's jumper and slacks and a name badge. I know this is ridiculous but that's the image I have because he's the only Viggo I know.

I swing into his drive and push the bear-spray down into my handbag and check my face in the rear-view mirror. It's not *that* Viggo so I don't know why I even bother. I leave the car and see the CCTV camera on the corner of the house pointing at the track. I look the little red building over, and find two or three more cameras and a security light on each wall, the type with a motion sensor.

'You must be Tuva,' says a man opening the front door.

He's no Viggo Mortensen, that's for sure. He's grey. That's what I see. Black hair, grey skin, narrow shoulders, a dull white shirt, a grey tie, black jumper with company logo, grey trousers, no shoes, dark grey socks.

'Yes, thanks for agreeing to talk with me. I really appreciate it.'

'Not at all,' he says. 'And this is Mikey.' He stands aside to reveal a miniature version of himself. Father and son both have grey, sullen skin and bags under their eyes. Except the boy, this Mikey, he has something else. An expression of absolute terror.

'Hi, Mikey,' I say, crouching down to shake his hand. He's not clinging to his dad's leg, he's just standing there, skinny and still, chewing his lower lip in his mouth.

'Mikey's a bit shy,' says Viggo. 'He'll come out of his shell soon enough.'

We walk inside and Viggo looks stiff when he moves. The house is small but well-kept with coasters on tables and magazines stacked neatly away on shelves. There's a high whining noise in my ears and it's uncomfortable so I try to adjust my hearing aids. I end up switching the volume down a little which helps but it's still there, an intense squeak right at the top of the audible scale.

Viggo's cooking something for Mikey so I try to engage with the boy by helping him to park model trucks and tractors near the kitchen table leg. There are two high chairs pushed against the table, two identical high chairs.

'Does Mikey have a brother or sister?' I ask and then immediately regret the question in case someone died.

'No,' says Viggo. 'But he does have lots of friends. He's a popular little man at school so if they pop over, we're all prepared, nice and ship-shape, so to say.'

I note he says 'if' and not 'when' and wonder whether anyone's ever come over for a playdate with this haunted little boy.

Viggo puts Mikey in the chair. The boy looks big enough to sit on a real chair but he seems comfortable, skinny as he is. Viggo places the macaroni and beef stew in a bowl and gives it to Mikey. The boy eats it like he hasn't eaten for days.

'You can ask me questions if you like. I expect you wanted to come here because I know everybody in the area, with the profession I have and so on.'

The squeaking noise in my ears is still there. I smile at Viggo and at his dyed-black hair and silver-grey temples.

'I imagine you've driven everyone in Gavrik Kommun at least once.'

'I'm the local transport, so to say. Keep up to date on all the gossip from the schoolkids I ferry around. They know it all, they do.'

I look around and notice for the first time that the cottage is full of houseplants. There are potted plants of all shapes and sizes on every window sill, every worktop, every inch of available shelf space.

'Hannes Carlsson is my best client. Most of my work is driving kids and the elderly, all paid for by the Kommun, but I drive Hannes quite a lot. Drive him from work or a game.' He pauses. 'Or from wherever he's been.'

I nod, but I'm looking at the plants. Spider plants, money plants, miniature ferns, they're everywhere. I recognise the ceramic pots from ICA Maxi. And that background noise is still there. I turn back to Viggo.

'Do you have any ideas who shot Freddy Malmström?'

'Well, that's a direct approach,' he says. 'Just came straight out with that, didn't you, like you're Hercule Poirot or something.'

'I'm sorry.'

'No, no, a direct approach is the best approach.' He pours three glasses of water.

'I do have a few ideas, yes. I'd rather not talk in specifics right now because . . .' He gestures towards his son with his head, the long black hairs of his fringe moving as if to point to Mikey. 'I think it could be PETA, or one of these anti-hunting, pro-animal rights people, could be them.'

I nod.

'Could also be accidental, maybe a hunting incident gone wrong. I thought about this last night. What if a hunter shot Freddy mistaking him for an elk, then realised his mistake and whipped out Freddy's you-know-whats.' He points to his eyes, a clue the boy clearly has no trouble interpreting. 'So he can frame the '90s killer, the so-called Medusa Murderer – but it's just a theory.'

I nod again, less enthusiastically than the first time.

'Anyway, Medusa's a stupid name.'

'It is,' I say.

'It's ridiculous,' he says.

I nod.

'Oh, and have you met our two resident eccentrics yet?'

I almost spit out my mineral water. Just two?

'Sorry, you mean . . .?'

'The wood-carving sisters,' he says, eyes wide, hand sweeping back through his hair.

'Yes, just briefly.'

'You know what they do? I can't talk about specifics in front of the . . .' He mouths the letters to spell *boy*. 'But you know what those two make up there at the top of the hill?'

'Yes.'

'I've never picked them up in the taxi so I haven't chatted with them, thank the Lord, but I know all about them. People talk, you know. Those sisters make special, you know, special ones, custom-made ones, did you know about that?'

I nod.

'Well, it's just not Christian, if you ask me.'

I hadn't noticed them before, but there are crosses on the walls and a leather-bound bible on the coffee-table in the living room. The high-pitched noise is still there, fingernails over blackboard, steel fork against porcelain, mosquito in a dark bedroom.

'They make little devils, let's be quite clear about that. I heard rumours they use their own.' He makes a coughing noise. 'Body hair, even their own nail clippings.'

I nod. It's amazing how a few days can lessen the impact of these facts. I'm not at all shocked hearing this now, and yet I know it's weird as fuck and he's right to be worried.

'They use animal . . .' he looks down at Mikey, who's finishing the last mouthfuls of his macaroni, 'bits and pieces, did you know that? They get some big cheese from Karlstad or Gothenburg request something twisted and immoral, they'll make it for them if the price is right. Oh, yeah. Rumour is they got money troubles and they'll take any job they can get hold of. I heard they made a . . .' he mouths the word *troll*, 'with a . . .' he mouths the word *penis*, 'made from stuffed, preserved deer meat.' He pauses. 'A deer organ, so to say. Well, I ask you, that must be criminal, mustn't it? I also heard, although this was a few years ago, I have to admit, that they made one of these satanic little creatures with real eyes. I heard, from a reliable source so to say, that they made the thing with actual badger's eyes. I ask you, what kind of people would do that? I heard they got that order, probably for thousands of kronor, y'know, they have a bad economy that pair, and they caught and killed a badger, they're both real good shots, you know. Always out there in the deep woods, shooting this thing and that, and then they took out its eyes, and preserved them.'

Mikey is looking up at his father now with even more terror than before.

I point to the boy and Viggo stops talking.

'Well done, son, you ate it all up. That'll put hairs on your chest, that will. Let's get you down from the table so you can play a bit with the nice lady and I'll fix you some fruit.'

Viggo stands by the sink and uses a metal baller to scoop out marble-sized balls of honeydew melon while I park toy cars with Mikey. I'm trying to play but it's not easy, the kid won't even look at me. He shuffles from room to room, so I follow him and that background noise is still there. I find more houseplants and even more crosses. There's a door with a heavy mahogany sideboard pushed up against it.

'Can we play in that room?' I ask Mikey.

He stares at me like I just threatened him.

'What's in that room, Mikey?'

He's holding an Action Man and he clings to it so tight that his nails are digging into the brown plastic.

'Games,' he whispers.

'Your games?'

He shakes his head.

'Shall we play in the kitchen?'

He runs away and I follow. I get a strange vibe from Viggo, and my gut says something bad has happened here. I arrive at the kitchen table and then the halogen spotlights in the ceiling flicker, but they stay on. Viggo looks at me with a bowl of perfectly round melon balls in his hand and a tea towel tucked into his grey slacks.

'We get more than our fair share of power outages here, Tuva. The electricity's a bit iffy.' The lights flicker again and Viggo places the bowl down on the kitchen table. The noise is still there. 'It's because we're at the end of the line just here, so to say. We're right at the very end of the line.'

16

I tune my truck's radio to a Saturday breakfast show and pull onto the motorway, little Mikey's haunted face still vivid in my head from last night. My hand taps the key fob hanging from the truck's ignition and it rattles and my shoulders loosen a little. I'm driving south towards Karlstad in the slow lane at one hundred and twenty and it feels pretty good to be honest. No traffic, and a loop of chart music on the stereo, and a bag of wine gums open on the passenger seat.

I'm still driving through forest much of the time, still green on my left and green on my right, but it's more open. I can see far ahead and behind with no risk I'll need to reverse. A taxi drives past me in the northbound lane and I think it's Viggo but I'm not sure. I cross rivers and overtake lumber lorries full of logs and see signposts to small towns and cross-country ski trails.

I'm avoiding the news for the first hour. On the passenger seat sits a new merino wool shawl I bought for Mum and a tube of the hand cream she likes and a small princess torta cake she'll probably not be able to eat more than a teaspoon of. I'm looking forward to spending a few hours in Karlstad before I drive back north past Gavrik to the strip club. It opens at 3pm.

Sushi. I'm daydreaming of good sushi. Not London good or even Stockholm good, but still. With extra wasabi and a plate of pickled ginger on the side, thank you very much. I'm going to sit at a bar in Karlstad and eat little strips of melt-on-the-tongue sashimi and look out of the window at streams of Saturday shoppers. It's a taste of civilisation and the only downside will be Mum's reaction when she sees me. Her lack of reaction. I can just about remember her hugs and her baking from before the crash. Proper hugs, no rushing to disengage. And her stories. She read bedtime sagas with gusto; special voices for characters, different facial expressions, the lot. Now her stories are more like dreams than memories.

A TV4 van passes me on its way to Gavrik. The satellite dish on its roof is clearly visible over the motorway's central reservation. And then Lena calls so I switch off the radio.

'You heard?'

'What?'

'Tuva, it's that ghostwriter in Mossen village, the one you interviewed. It's looking more and more like he's the man who shot Freddy, at least that's what the town thinks. Checkout girl at ICA, you know the one, the pretty one, she sold her story to *Expressen* and it got printed today. He comes across like a complete sociopath.'

'But is there any new evidence?'

'Where are you?'

'I'm on the E16. Halfway to Karlstad to see my mother.'

'I'm really sorry. Can you postpone?'

I look over at the princess torta, the bright green icing starting to sweat in its plastic container. Shit. I'll have to make it up to her.

'I can turn around at the next exit.'

'Okay, fine, I'll see you at the office unless you hear from me in the meantime.'

I take the exit and drive under the E16 and then loop back around to join the northbound lane. My stomach aches. Mum could be gone this year, this actual year, and what am I doing about it? If Dad was around, he'd ... I don't know ... He's not around, it's just me and I'm not doing half of what I should be doing. Maybe if I drop in midweek to surprise her, the hospice will let me in for an hour.

I accelerate to one forty and switch on the news and it's all David Holmqvist. It's all 'pigs' hearts' and 'books ordered specially'. 'Books on how to butcher big game' and 'he never had any friends, nobody ever visits his house'. I roll my eyes and overtake a two-section lorry with slices of house roof strapped to its back. Statements from locals are fed to me: 'Never felt safe around him' and 'I heard he had an accomplice' and 'he creeped me out' and 'I heard he's got no alibi'.

Then the story shifts to a statement from a Lund-based criminal psychologist. She doesn't talk about David specifically, not even about the Mossen bodies. Her voice is all textbooks and sensible shoes. 'Statistically speaking, most serial murderers are white middle-aged, middle-class males. They tend to have little social awareness and there's often a history of abuse of some kind.'

Just before the Gavrik exit, I spot a sign for the strip club:

Enigma Gentlemen's Club. Exit 84. High-class Entertainment. Stop By and Say Hi.

The mass of Utgard forest looms on my left as I approach the exit. I turn and join the road to Gavrik. Everything looks like it did yesterday. I pull up outside my office and Lena's waiting in reception wearing sneakers and a tracksuit.

'They're in ICA right now, the TV crews. He's doing his weekly shop like he always does on a Saturday, at least that's what this article says.' She shoves a rolled-up copy of *Expressen* at me. 'Cashier reckons her dad, now long dead, once saw Holmqvist deep in Utgard forest wearing plastic shoe covers over his boots. Get over there, take lots of photos, don't let them steal the story from you.'

I nod and take the paper and turn back to my truck.

'Call me if you need me or Lars to back you up.'

My back to her, I stick the rolled-up *Expressen* in the air in acknowledgement and skid off towards the supermarket. I park in a lorry unloading bay and grab my camera from the back seat and head inside.

I run past the bottle recycling machines – the ones that suck in plastic and spit out money – and I overhear two teenage boys chatting.

'Eighty grand they paid her. Eighty fucking grand.'

'I heard it was a hundred and eighty.'

I run past and through the entrance barriers, scanning around, trying to find a commotion, jogging to the tills.

'You're too late, Tuva.'

I turn and see the guy I usually go to when I pay and he's restocking discount chocolate bars and salt liquorice.

'Sorry, they left five minutes ago, about ten of them plus Holmqvist. They just left.'

'Thanks,' I say, tapping his shoulder and then barging past paying customers to get back to the exit. I jump in my truck and speed back towards the motorway, and then turn and drive under it. The day's sunny but there's a grey cloud over Utgard forest now, one of those clouds with a distinct dark edge and I can see rain falling from it in sheets.

I get to the Mossen entrance and pass Hoarder's place and then Taxi's place. I accelerate hard up the hill and a piece of gravel hits my windscreen and chips it, an acne scar on an otherwise flawless surface.

I approach the wood-carving sisters' workshop and I see lights ahead of me and my heart races a little. Is it the TV crews driving towards David Holmqvist's house?

No. It's a 4x4 heading my way and I can't remember where the damn passing places are. They're not marked. I slam my foot on the brake pedal and my seatbelt digs in between my breasts.

The truck keeps heading at me like it's me that should reverse but I don't see why. I look in my mirrors and I can't find any passing place, just this narrow dirt track with a drop either side of it. I start to reverse slowly and the 4x4 comes at me a little too fast. It's closing on me, so I put my foot down. I start sweating. It's like the elk all over again. I press the button to open my window and it's not raining but it smells like it will. The 4x4, one of those tall Volvo SUVs, is in my face and it speeds up and I'm gripping my steering wheel hard but I can't do it. The reversing's too difficult. The Volvo accelerates and I see his face now through my chipped windscreen. It's

Hannes. He looks mad, or maybe just impatient, like it's ridiculous that I'm reversing this slowly and I'm holding him up. I check my mirrors and there's a bend behind me and still no passing place. Sweating, nowhere to go, I turn the wheel and veer down into the ditch. My wheels skid, and my wine gums scatter across the floor of the truck. I come to a shaky stop resting at an angle on the slope. I look over to my left and see Hannes Carlsson speed off. No thanks, no wave, no flash of headlights. Ignorant fuckpig.

I exhale and turn the wheel and accelerate slowly. My tyres slide a little and then they bite into the walls of the ditch and drive straight up and out and then I'm back on the level. Thank you, Hilux. I close the window and drive past the sisters' smoky workshop. As I approach David Holmqvist's house, I see the trucks and vans parked in his driveway. There's no place left for me, so I leave my truck in the road with my hazards on and grab my camera.

Outside Holmqvist's front door there are two cameras on shoulders and one on a tripod. I see three other photographers and a couple of reporters with made-up hair and painted faces. No sign of David.

'Tuva,' a guy yells to me from the centre of the pack. It's the guy from before, the bearded Stockholm slick-back from the cop show.

I nod to him and retreat back a little so I can see the first floor windows and the veranda. All they show is pine trees reflecting back at me. I pull out my phone and check my contacts and dial David Holmqvist's number. No reception. I pace back towards my truck. Patchy reception, but something. No pick-up. I call again. No pick-up. I call again.

He accepts the call but says nothing.

'It's Tuva Moodyson. I'm outside your house.'

'Are you behind all this?' Holmqvist asks me. 'Whatever it is that you think I have done, I have not done.'

'Wasn't me,' I say. 'The girl from ICA sold her story, pal. And now you've got a gang of reporters at your front door.'

'You think I don't know that? Well I can tell you, I've got impor-
tant work to do up here and I have enough food and supplies for
weeks, if not months, so that's what I think of you and your gang.'

'They're not my gang, David.'

I hear a screech from the direction of the sisters' workshop. The
walls of spruce each side of me flash blue.

'The police are here, David. I don't know what you've done, if
anything.' I watch Thord and Björn walk purposefully up to David's
veranda-covered front door, flashbulbs strobing their faces and dark-
blue uniforms.

'Police!' Thord shouts, knocking on the door. 'David Holmqvist,
open up.'

Holmqvist's still on the phone to me, but he's not talking. Then
I start to hear him sob. I can hear his mouth burbling and spitting
through tears.

'Is there anything you want to tell me, David? This may be the
last chance you get, is there anything you want to let me know?'

'Call my lawyer for me, his name's Oscar Krevik. And . . .'

'Go on. I'll call him for you. Oscar Krevik. What else?'

'I can't live like this. I keep myself to myself and still I get harassed.
You think Hannes and Frida are the perfect couple, don't you? I
heard she's been giving you home-cooked food, her famous house-
wife stews. They're not perfect, Tuva.'

The police are banging on the front door again. I can hear it from
out here and I can hear it through the phone like an echo. The
reporters are trying to question Chief Björn. I hear Thord bark at
them to get back and give them some space.

'Hannes is a beast,' David says.

There's a commotion at the doorway. I see it open and I see the
other journalists inch forward, shouting over each other. David
Holmqvist walks out, his phone pressed against his ear.

'Hannes is a goddam beast, Tuva.'

17

They walk David Holmqvist to the police Volvo. They don't say 'David Holmqvist, I'm arresting you . . .' like they do in the movies. Maybe they're not arresting him. They get into the car, could this be for his protection or something? Thord sits in the back seat next to Holmqvist, and Björn reverses at speed away from the flashbulbs. I take a flurry of shots with my camera and then jump back into my truck.

I'm parked the wrong way so I do a quick three-point turn with the other hacks beeping and complaining as I turn, and then I drive after the police car. I feel like Hannes earlier, because I'm driving forwards and in front of me somewhere is Björn still reversing. I drive fast but don't want to get too much in his face. I see flashes of light in my wing mirrors as the TV crews start catching up, and at the bottom of the hill I reach the police Volvo and they've managed to turn around someplace because they're driving forward and I'm pleased about this. It's a relief. The clouds darken even further and then they burst open like water from a broad showerhead in a fancy hotel. I turn my wipers on full speed but still I'm squinting through the windscreen as the droplets bang and bounce off the chipped glass. The sound from the roof of the Hilux is there but it's okay. I'm fine. We pass Taxi's house and then Hoarder's house and as we turn onto the main road the light levels bounce back up and the shower ends just as fast as it started. I can't see a rainbow but a rainbow's due.

I google Holmqvist's lawyer and call his mobile, but he cuts me off and tells me he's already at the station. It takes twenty minutes to reach Gavrik, and I guess the TV vans are a little way behind me. I pull up in time to see the lawyer – fine blond hair, golf jumper – lead his client into the station. Thord closes the door and locks it behind him.

Looking around at the shiny wet town centre, I see a few people milling around. There's only one person I don't recognise: an older lady who looks a bit like Tammy, wearing a bright red coat, and riding a bike. I see my office and then realise what I have to do. I've got one chance at this. So I drive up the back street and past the hotel and wait there out of sight. I see the TV vans arrive. I sit and wait until the last one passes me and then I drive off out of town the same way I just came. I'll get the police statement from Thord later. When the police confronted Holmqvist, I'm pretty sure he left his front door open. Or at least unlocked.

I drive west out of town and call Mum.

'Mrs Moodyson's phone.'

What? My throat closes up. Is this it? Already? After my missed visit? My vision blurs at the edges. I need to say things. Hear things.

'Is Mum okay?'

'Who is this, please?'

'This is Tuva, her daughter.'

'Mrs Moodyson is out today. Can I take a message for you?'

Out?

'Where is she? Who is with her? I was due to visit today.'

'I'm not sure, my shift just started. Can I get her to phone you back when she returns?'

'Please tell her Tuva called.'

How can she be out? How? I feel dizzy not knowing where she is. I always know where she is. What if something happens now and I can't find her? I clear my throat and wipe my forehead on the back of my hand and pull a wine gum from my pocket and let it sit on my tongue. It's a green one and it's dusty.

I park up at Holmqvist's house and it looks like nothing's happened here. The only marks of change are the carved-up gravel and the muddy tyre grooves from the vans. I step out of my truck and get hit by sporadic drops of rain, fat drops tumbling from the sharp points of pine needles far above my head.

The front door's ajar. I look around and then head back to my truck and get my camera and Tammy's bear-spray. I place the camera strap around my shoulder like a handbag and walk inside.

'Hello?' I call out. 'Anybody home?'

No answer. The place is immaculate like a holiday rental on day one. The stainless steel countertops are gleaming and the floor's polished and buffed and the cushions are plumped. I slip my boots off and walk further inside. My nerves are prickling. Not supposed to do this. Only chance I'll get. There's no basement, thank God, I don't think I could handle going underground right now. Lena's explained to me that most houses in the area have no basement because the land is so boggy. The water table's about as high as it can be without us living in a goddam lake. I walk around in my socks and have to be careful not to slip, and I feel more vulnerable without my shoes on, less able to defend myself. The ground floor doesn't feel quite real, except for the kitchen area. It's like nobody ever comes here but it's here just in case they do. Like when I came. I see the espresso machine with its drawers and grinders and steam wands and dials. Above it there are three sharp scoops, also stainless steel, of different sizes, like you see baristas use in cafes to measure out the ground coffee. Under the window there's a sous-vide machine, at least I think that's what it is, like a vacuum-pack thing for slow-cooking. There's a door near the kitchen sink. I pull on my wool gloves, not ideal but they'll do, and open the door and step inside, and now I really am intruding. I'm being rude but I need this story – a full report of the Medusa murders compared to Freddy Malmström's death, no holding back. If the police won't make the connection, then I will. I'll have the local perspective, from the inside; quotes and diagrams and a detailed analysis of what we know and what we don't. I'll be as comprehensive as I can be and I'll focus on the community and on the victim's families, the things national papers gloss over.

I see racks bolted to the wall with lined-up boxer shorts hung on them, three to a rack. All white. I see a washing machine, and an ironing board with a can of spray starch on it. There are three vertical drying cabinets set against the wall for wet coats and hats. I open the first door and see shelves and shelves of dehydrating mushrooms. They're Karl-Johans, I think, Porcini, the expensive Disney type. Each shelf is packed with wafer-thin slices and they smell strongly of the wild. I check the other two drying cabinets and they're full of other mushrooms. I walk out and head to the foot of the staircase. It's the kind with no back risers, the see-through kind. I look around and step up and that's when I trip the alarm.

The noise is a squealing pulse. I switch off my aids without pulling them out because I can't be without them in a place like this. I run up the stairs expecting the police to arrive any second and then I realise that they're all tied up and they won't be coming and there's no panic. Make the most of this opportunity, Tuva.

The master bedroom. The walls are covered in mirrors and I mean every fucking wall. The bed's unmade. I turn left and find a clean bathroom with a grey towelling robe hanging on the back of the door. There are two other rooms up here and both the doors are closed. I head to the first and push down the handle.

The bedroom's carpeted. There's no guest bed or any furniture at all. The walls are covered with simple white shelves and each one's laden with identical white box files. Six shelves high, across three and a half walls; there must be close to a thousand files. I step closer and the distant hum of the alarm is just detectable in my unaided ears.

I find 'P'. Two files on Pearls marked 'Pearls I' and 'Pearls II'. One on Prairie dogs and one on Peru and one on Playing cards and then three files on Pantomime. In the other direction, I crouch down and find Oysters and Opera and Ocular surgery and Ospreys and Oslo. I open Oslo. The paper is graph paper, the kind with tiny square boxes. Holmqvist writes with a very fine hand and he must use some kind of draughtsman's pen. Page upon page of research and snippets of dialogue heard on travels, and small maps of street intersections. I put Oslo back and walk over to the window. It's not mirrored at all from the inside. Looks normal. I see my truck and then turn and stroke my fingers across the edges of the files. Black holes and Berettas and Batteries and Bat Mitzvahs. He has a lifetime of information up here. Damascus and Disguises and Dragonflies and Diphtheria and Dior and Dionysus. It's like Wikipedia in paper form. I'm impressed and bemused by the sheer amount of work. I do research all the time for my articles, but this?

I turn out of the room and onto the landing. My gloved hand's on the door handle of the second guest room when I feel something at my back. Coffee breath. Warm. Damp. I spin around on my axis and lift the canister of bear-spray but he's got his hand on my arm so I can't use it. He's shouting at me. I shake my head. I CANNOT HEAR YOU. I struggle to loosen his grip on my arm and then I focus on his lips.

'What the hell are you doing here?'

I point to my ears and then I switch my aids back on and the siren bursts into my head.

'The door was open, I was checking to see if Holmqvist was here.'

Viggo frowns at me. His breath reeks of Nescafé and sleep.

'This alarm is hurting my ears and he's clearly not home. I'm leaving.'

'He went to the police station,' Viggo says. 'You should know, Tuva. You followed him out there.'

I sigh and keep my finger on the top of the bear-spray.

'Okay. I wanted to see if there were any clues here before the cops came. Guilty.'

Viggo nods and walks downstairs and I follow with my hands clasped over my ears.

'You think you could give me a lift back home down the hill? I came up here for a stroll, doctor's orders, so to say, but now it's getting late and I need to cook the boy his dinner.'

I look at him. It's the last thing in the world I want to do right now but with the alarm pulsing in my ears I feel I have no choice. I nod to him.

We drive back down the hill and I pull up to his red house. I see little Mikey in the garden playing with a hosepipe and he waves to me.

'I told you to stay indoors until I got home,' Viggo says to Mikey in a flat tone.

Mikey stops waving.

'See, he likes you a lot, Tuva. He's got excellent taste, that one. Hasn't stopped yabbering about you.'

I smile to the boy and he runs up to my truck and comes over to my door and knocks on the window.

'Hi Mikey, you remember me?'

He doesn't smile, but he nods. I've never seen him smile. I open the truck door and he tries to pull me out of it by my hand.

'Sorry, little man, I've got work to do.'

'Could you watch him for ten minutes while I make his dinner?'

I look at Mikey's grey eyes and pull my truck into the driveway. Ten minutes in the garden won't hurt. I hear a distant gunshot. Then another. The grass is waterlogged from the downpour, puddles gleaming on the grass. Another gunshot. Two more. Mikey grabs my arm and tugs at it to follow him indoors. I pass the threshold and see houseplants and a box of ammunition on top of the bookcase and that whining noise is still here.

'Is it safe to have them out?' I point up to the box of bullets lodged between two miniature ferns.

Viggo smiles. 'Mikey can't reach up there. Plus, it's empty, so . . .'

I'm going to tell Thord all this and I'm going to make him listen to me.

'Viggo, can I ask you,' I'm scanning the room for clues, anything that looks out-of-place. 'What's that high-pitched squeak? It's probably my hearing aids, but I get a lot of feedback in your house. Can you hear it?'

'Oh, it's not you,' he says, smiling and pointing to the plug socket on the kitchen counter. 'It's the mouse-repellers. Have them all over the house. They're ultrasonic, so to say. Only kids and rodents can hear them. And you, I suppose.' He looks down at his son with his gaunt little cheeks and his dark circles under his eyes. 'I don't think it bothers Mikey any more, he's got used to it. Before Mikey was born I used to poison the vermin, but that's not safe now. Tried acid buckets but these ultrasound things work pretty good, they use the building's electrical wires as conductors. They turn the little mouses and rats half-crazy they do. Now, Mikey, get to the table please, dinner's ready.'

I look over at the little boy and I know he can still hear the piercing squeals. I pass the two identical high chairs and wave goodbye to Mikey and leave.

18

I wake up early for a weekend. My neighbour's swapped me his Sunday laundry slot with my Thursday slot for the next two weeks. I need his slot, my clothes stink. The room in the basement's a good place for me. It smells of synthetic meadows and artificial forests and man-made ocean breezes and that's just the way I like them.

I walk upstairs with a basket of tangled sheets and bras and jeans and pillow cases. They're warm and soft from the dryer, and they remind me of Mum before she lost him. Before I lost both of them. The light bulb in the stairway has blown. I get inside my apartment and put all the clothes and bedding away and then I go to the office, feeling clean and a little more organised like I can face what lies ahead even though I have to work all day and I still haven't seen Mum. I'll get down there soon. She's my constant niggle, my tiny itch of guilt just behind my ear.

My heart says drive-thru so I follow my heart. When I arrive at work, it's already open and there's someone lingering on the other side of the street. The guy runs off as soon as I get to the office door. I don't see his face. Inside, the lights are on and the computers are off.

'Hi Lena,' I say, placing a McDonald's coffee down on her desk. The coffee's pretty good actually. It's the best in town but that doesn't say much.

'Hi yourself,' she says.

'What's the plan?' I ask, sitting down in front of her desk.

She drinks and then reclines, the red underside of her baseball cap casting a warm glow over her elegant face. She breathes deeply and then she straightens up and looks at me.

'I'm increasing circulation for the next issue, an extra thousand copies. I want the murder and your analysis to be front and centre, but I want the usual stuff, too. Just because someone got shot doesn't mean that Håkan from the hardware store forgot about his triathlon personal best, or that Margit from the bank doesn't want to read all about her charity jumble sale. That stuff stays, but it's at the back and it's lean. You write about Freddy from a Gavrik point of view, try not to sound like the police or like you have theories or you're investigating. Local people want facts and they want it clear and they want to know how, if it all, this is going to affect them in the coming days. Does that make sense?'

I nod. 'Do you know David Holmqvist, Lena?'

She shakes her head. 'Know of him, but don't think I've ever met the man. 'Course, when I see his photo on the news I think maybe I've seen him on *Storgatan* or at the movies, but he looks pretty normal, don't you think?'

'I have no idea if he shot Freddy Malmström.'

'Not your job, Tuva. Now, listen up because I reckon what I'm about to say is important because someone smart once said it to me.'

She takes a slurp of coffee.

'You get a story like this maybe once a decade in a town like Gavrik and you gotta make the most of it. Now, I see you're working long hours and covering all the bases and that's great. But you need to think about the printed word. What you write in the next issue will remain. Those words will stick around. For ever. You need to write well and with purpose and with courage. Your articles will follow you around whether you like it or not. So stay focussed on the story and on the local perspective, don't get too fancy or too speculative. I want it direct, I want it relevant, and I want it so you're still proud of it when you're my age, yes?'

I nod and walk to my desk and check that it's not too early and then I pick up the phone and call Thord.

'Gavrik police.'

'Hey, just wanted to check in about David Holmqvist. What's his status, please?'

'Holmqvist is a person of interest, Tuva, you know that already.' He sounds tired. 'No arrests have been made but he's still here at the station, if that's what you're asking.'

'What about his house, are you searching it?'

'You know I can't talk about that.'

'I have two neighbours saying they've seen official cars round there, that's all.'

He sighs.

'Off the record, nowhere near the record, I can tell you that forensic teams are working with Holmqvist's permission.'

I pause for thought, staring at the pen pot on my desk. Thord has stopped calling him Dave.

'There anything else or can I get back to work?'

'Ballistics results?'

'White coats at the National Forensic Centre are quick, but they're not that quick. Detailed report may take another week.'

'Have they told you anything?'

I hear him sigh down the phone. 'Eight millimetre. Most likely an older rifle, that's all I know. No more details.'

'Thanks, Thord. Talk soon.'

I make a note of the gun details and then put on my coat and my boots and say bye to Lena and get into my truck. It's four degrees. My clothes smell fresh and I put a weekly reminder on my phone so that I never forget another damn laundry slot. I join the motorway and head north, towards Dalarna. The view's static. It's rolling by, I don't mean that, but it's unchanging, the same trees, the same colours, the same milky sky. I drive and drive and it's like a retro console game with shitty graphics. Grey road, white sky, green pines. I call Mum but she doesn't pick up.

Exit 84. I see a shipping container in a field with a sign across it saying *Enigma Gentlemen's Club*. The container's placed at an angle and there's a line of black crows or ravens perched on one end of it. Must be twenty of them. I drive off the motorway and pull into the parking area of the strip club. It's big. They were optimistic in the business plan when they designed this place. I drive towards a puddle the size of a duck pond, engine oil slicking its surface with desperate, twisted rainbows. It shimmers and I drive through it to the back of the club. I see four cars and I recognise one of them. My eyes strain as I focus on the Volvo's number plate, and then I drive around and head back out to the motorway.

Hannes is here.

I drive north. The woodland thins a little with farmers' fields on my side of the road, and granite boulders with glacial battle-scars on the other side. I take it easy in the slow lane. Three on a Sunday afternoon and Hannes is in a strip club. I kind of feel sorry for him, but then I think about Frida and what lies he must have told her. A lorry comes up behind me laden with brand new Volvos without number plates, like newborn babies that haven't been named yet. I swing over to the fast lane and accelerate up to one forty. Who goes to a strip club on a Sunday?

There's a pair of hawks or falcons or something, circling at the horizon. They look untouchable up there, utterly safe and confident, like they can see the whole forest and beyond from up there, far beyond.

I take the next exit and join the southbound lane.

It's five degrees and I think about how I'm going to write the articles for the next issue. I've got four days. Mum's fine, don't think about that, not now, she's okay. I'll call her and explain. I want something I can show to *The Guardian* or *The Washington Post* in a year's time. I need to write something and hit the sweet spot, where I get the right words down in the right order and they actually move people. And it has to be accurate. No sloppy bullshit that might add to the distress of the families, it needs to be one hundred per cent correct.

The sky's featureless on the way back to Gavrik: no birds, no planes, no nothing. The clouds look like they start at head height and there's not quite enough air underneath them for us all to breathe comfortably. I jangle my key fob and hear the batteries clink together. I need to order more but I have enough for now.

I take Exit 84 and pass under the E16 and approach the strip club again. Hannes is gone. It's half past four and there are two other cars in the customer parking area and about five in the employee area. Locals don't like to talk about Hannes, but maybe the employees here will. Hannes is a hunter who knows the woods and I don't like how close he is to Chief Björn; it doesn't sit right with me. I lock my truck. The building's made from corrugated steel, like an aircraft hangar or a warehouse on an industrial estate. I put on some lip balm and smooth down my hair and then I walk over to the entrance.

19

The door's so heavy I struggle to get it open. Then the music hits me. An R&B song from the '90s with a baseline that beats through my bones. I feel it. The woman at the counter looks up at me and speaks. She's had lip implants or fillers or something. I can't hear her and I can't read her swollen lips so I cup my hand to my ear and step closer.

'Two hundred,' she says. 'Two hundred to come in. Open till eleven.'

I pay in cash and adjust the volume of my hearing aids, and she pushes something onto the back of my hand. It's a stamp, a little red heart symbol close to a vein. In the corner of the entrance, on the plastic wipe-down flooring, there are two mousetraps baited and waiting.

The woman with the lips turns back to her magazine.

I walk in. It's dark but I expected that. There's a black stage with three vertical poles and there's one woman up there on the central one. She's topless and I stare at her. This is weird. Five minutes ago I was driving on a road and now I'm staring at a half-naked woman. Just like that. She's blonde but she's dyed her hair dark brown and she's kind of awkward beautiful.

I walk further in and stand with my back to the bar. The room's big, maybe thirty tables. I see three punters. There's one table of two guys drinking beers and watching the stage, and one table against the wall with a guy having a private dance.

'What are you drinking?' the barman asks behind my shoulder. I turn and he looks familiar somehow. He's got a solarium tan and there's a scar running from his lip to his ear and the faint, white line glows like a smile in the club lighting.

'Give me a sparkling water with ice and lime, thanks.'

'Lemon?'

I nod and he mixes me the drink.

'One hundred.'

Back in London, one hundred kronor would equal about nine pounds and even for London prices, nine pounds for a glass of water would be fucking outrageous. I pay him and take a seat. I'm frowning because I don't want people to think I'm here to watch strippers but I know they don't give a shit why I'm here. The two guys look bored as they watch the equally bored-looking woman on stage rub herself against a steel pole. The music changes and it's 'Roxette' and I'm relieved.

The girl from the stage steps off and a stunning black girl replaces her. She looks like a model but she can't dance too well and she seems uncomfortable near the pole. The earlier girl from the stage walks over to me and leans in close to my face. She's got a thin, Lycra dress on now; the kind of dress that I wouldn't even wear as a swimming costume.

'Hi,' she says.

I smell fake tan and it's quite overwhelming. Fake tan and perfume.

'Hi,' I say.

'I'm Savanah.'

'Tuva.'

'Would you like me to dance for you, Tuva?'

'Can we just have a chat?' I say, 'I'm happy to pay for your time.'

She says something but I can't hear it clearly. I cup my ear and she takes my hand in hers and leads me towards an arched doorway next to the stage. Her hand's smooth and warm and slight.

'Lucky bitches,' I hear one of the two beer guys say as we walk past their table.

We go through to the back and the music's quieter here.

'Private booths,' she says.

There's a bouncer guy leaning against a wall. Savanah winks at him and he goes back to playing some game on his phone. Savanah leads me into a booth with a black, leather chair and a table and an ice bucket. She closes the curtain.

'It's a thousand for fifteen minutes,' she says.

I laugh a little conceited laugh that I instantly regret. 'To talk?' I say. 'No, I just want to talk with you. How much for that?'

She smiles. Her teeth are so white they look weird. They're white but they have even whiter patches, unnaturally white patches, in the centre of each tooth.

'It's still a thousand.'

I look at her and sigh through a smile.

'Okay.'

'Go ahead and talk,' she says, turning away from me. 'I'm a great listener.'

I see her start to pull down the shoulder straps of her white Lycra dress so I laugh again and stand up. I touch her shoulder, slick with moisturiser or something, and she turns. In one swift move, she removes my hand and guides me back down in the black leather seat. I can see her ribs through her dress.

'I'm sorry,' I say. 'Please keep your clothes on, Savanah. I just want to talk with you, to have a chat. Is that okay?'

She looks a little disappointed or maybe annoyed. Then she smiles and sits down on the other armchair in the booth and crosses her legs.

'You wanna buy me a drink, Tuva?'

'You want what I'm having?' I say, pointing to my glass.

'Sure,' she says, pressing a button on the table between us.

The bouncer pops his head in and Savanah starts to say something but I cut her off.

'Glass of water, please. Thank you.'

He looks at her and she nods and he leaves.

'You a cop?' she asks.

'I'm a reporter, I work for the *Posten*.'

She shrugs, her bottom lip extended.

'*The Gavrik Posten*, the local newspaper.'

She lifts her head. 'I'm not local, I live in Karlstad.'

'Long commute,' I say.

'Four-hour round trip. But it's only three days a week and the mill guys tip real well. I like it up here, we get good regulars. It's not the mill guys that mess around trying to grab us y'know. It's the boys, the stag parties and the college pricks. And they tip lousy, too.'

'You get the mill managers up here, I heard,' I say.

She shrugs.

'Carlsson's up here quite a bit, I heard.'

'What do you want, Tuva?'

'Freddy Malmström, the man who was shot. Did he come in here?'

'The guy who was killed by that ghostwriter? Yeah, I seen him in here quite a lot but I'm not his girl and I never danced for him. He likes Candy, he's got a big thing for Candy. Well, he did, before.'

'Is Candy here today? Can I speak to her?'

'She hasn't worked since it happened and nobody's seen or heard from her. She spoke to the cops and all, and then she just upped and left.'

'You have any idea why Freddy Malmström was killed, Savanah?'

'Yeah, I do,' she says as the glass of water arrives through the curtain. 'Cos that ghostwriter shot him in the head and everyone's saying he stole his eyeballs, that's why.'

'He was shot in the torso,' I say. 'In the chest.'

'Okay.'

'Are you Hannes Carlsson's girl, Savanah?'

She snorts and crunches an ice cube between her teeth.

'I wish.'

I frown and shake my head.

'Daisy's his girl. He's the best tipper in Värmland, that's what they say. He's a gentleman too, Daisy always tells us so. He comes back here with her few times a week and never lays a hand on her. Not inside the club, anyway. He's got a good economy, he's clean and nice, and he smells good.'

When the fifteen minutes are up, Savanah walks out through the curtain and beckons me to follow. I look down at my phone. Seven missed calls. Five from Lena, one from Thord and one from Mum. The bouncer's watching TV now, an unbranded flat-screen model bolted to the wall. The sound's off but he's reading subtitles.

I look at the screen.

They're reporting from Utgard forest.

They've found another body.

20

'Them redneck hunters,' the bouncer says, opening a can of Diet Coke as he looks up at the TV.

The bouncer doesn't understand. The hunters are the ones getting killed. Or maybe he does understand. This town feels altogether more dangerous now. Two bodies. I give Savanah my business card and she shows me to a back exit.

I step outside and the wind catches around my neck and I shiver. As I walk to my truck through piles of sticky leaves, I get glimpses of an image in my head. It's Dad and he's lying in David Holmqvist's spare room, the one I didn't have time to look in. He's the new body. In that unseen room. I shake the image away and spit on the ground.

I drive out of the strip club car park and a beat-up Volkswagen with blacked-out windows passes me on its way in. Two guys, early twenties, heavy metal screaming out of their speakers.

The southbound lane of the motorway's quiet. I call Lena.

'You heard?' she asks.

'Just now. What do we know?'

'Not much. A body was found and Björn tells me Karlstad are all over this now, they've taken control of the crime scene. Body was found deep inside Utgard forest, somewhere called 'Badger Hollow'. You heard of it? Can you get there? I want you there.'

Fuck. *Inside* Utgard forest. *Deep* inside.

'I'll find it,' I say. I swallow even though there's nothing in my mouth. I swallow a big, hard, dry nothing. 'I'll use the GPS on my phone.'

I accelerate and my truck shakes slightly in the crosswind. There's no traffic, just me and a straight road. I look to my right and see Utgard. The northernmost edge looks like a fortified wall of dark spruce. I jangle my key fob and plug my mobile into the charger.

Radio on. I scan through the stations and find a newsflash from Radio Värmland mentioning the new body. No gender or identity. They pull up a two-day old soundbite, a chat with the retired librarian from the local school, a snippet where she talks about Holmqvist's eyes, his guilty lifeless eyes. I turn it off.

Closer to Gavrik, I see a police car and slow the truck down to a hundred and ten. I get off the E16 and drive under the motorway and head towards Utgard. I pass a large gravel area I haven't noticed before. It has a few dozen diggers parked up or maybe it's a scrap-yard. Then I turn right, where Mossen's grey gravel spills out onto the main road.

As I pass between the pines, the dash shows the temperature drop from plus three to minus three. I tap it with my finger which is an utterly pointless thing to do with a digital reading, and nothing changes. I open my window a little and feel the cold around my neck like before at the strip club. The track crunches inside my hearing aids. I switch the heated seat to max and drive past Hoarder's house. His caravan lights are on. I go past Taxi's house. He's home, too. It's Sunday and it's too late for church so where the hell else would they all be. I drive up the hill and through the swamp and past the wood-carving sisters' place. They're sanding and polishing. I get to Ghostwriter's house and the parking lot's full of police cars, marked and unmarked; one ambulance and one mountain rescue fire truck. The house itself is dark, and striped crime-scene tape joins each supporting column of the veranda.

I park half in a ditch because it's the only place left. They're all in the woods somewhere so how am I going to find them? In Stockholm or Chicago, reporters locate the crime scene and report and then go back to the office and write it up. Here, I have to find

the damn scene in a thousand of acres of dark repetition. I grab my
phone and my ski jacket complete with bright colours to show that
I'm not a bloody elk, and I take my woolly hat and a bar of Marabou
milk chocolate and a torch. I pick up my handbag. Is a handbag the
right thing? I feel it should be a backpack with pockets and straps.
In my handbag I've got a can of bear-spray and a flattened sandwich
and my camera.

I walk over to the other side of the track and peer through the
trees, my boots still firmly planted on gravel. I squint into the murk.
It smells like old compost, like rotting earth. I can't see anything. I
go back to the other side of the road and stand in front of my truck.
It looks exactly the same, a million upright sticks above uneven
earth. Some pines have fallen in a storm and lodged against the
others, their angles ruining the verticality of the whole. I hear foot-
steps. No, it's just the wind. I look around and it's getting dark even
though it's only five. From the direction of the sisters' house, I see
a figure walking towards me. It's Frida and she's lifting one walking
pole in the air as if raising a hand to wave.

'Frida,' I say, some relief in my voice.

'You heard?' she asks. 'They found another one.'

'Where are all the police? Have you seen the body?'

'No,' she says, licking away a bead of sweat from her upper lip
and stopping in front of me. 'The hunting team found him when I
was down in Karlstad. I haven't seen this one. He's up at Badger
Hollow.'

'Where is that?' I ask. 'Can you show me on the map on my phone
so I can go check it out?'

Frida looks at me like I'm insane. She doesn't laugh, she frowns.

'You think you'd find them? You wouldn't have a chance. Do you
really need to get that deep into the woods just to photograph it?
Isn't there someone else at the paper who can do it, someone local?'

I shake my head.

'Well,' she breathes in hard and puts her hands on her hips with the loops of her Nordic walking poles dangling from her wrists. 'I guess I could take you but I need to be back home by seven-thirty for Hannes's dinner. You got proper boots on?'

I look down at the two-thousand-kronor boots I bought in Karlstad two winters ago.

'Yeah.'

'Well I don't, not for this. Let's swing by my house on the way out, it's kind of on the way to Badger Hollow anyway.'

We walk to her place. It's the exact same walk we did the last time a body was discovered in Utgard forest. It feels much shorter this time because now I know how long it is. It's still too foresty for me, but alongside Frida, I'm okay. She emits a confidence that no wild thing would ever question. I walk pretty close to her side, her walking poles clattering against my boots once or twice along the way. She goes into her house and I stay outside. I look at the grey timber outbuilding with the moss roof. The light's on inside. I can see the hut's built on a stone foundation, with spaces and gaps for ventilation.

Frida comes out with boots and a long stick with a ball on the end of it.

'What's that?'

'My elk stick. Carved Norrland oak with a knot at the end, it was my grandfather's. Never been used on an elk but I reckon it'd make one think twice.'

She slaps an orange neon band around my arm and puts one on herself. She presses mine at a certain point and it starts to flash.

'Have we got torches?'

'Better just to use your eyes,' she says, not looking at me. 'They'll soon adjust and then you'll see fine. You got a torch, you got a thousand mosquito bites, that's what I say.'

She walks fast and I have to slow-jog to keep up. We traipse through her waterlogged back garden and over a rocky slope and out onto a patchy gravel track. I have to concentrate when she speaks because it's difficult to lip-read or see her facial expressions out here in this murk. She tells me all about her day. Church, then delivering frozen meals to the local elderly, then a few hours in Karlstad to shop at the department store. Same routine every Sunday. She tells me Saturdays are for cleaning up and cooking.

'Do both your parents live in Karlstad?' she asks.

'Mum lives there, Dad's dead.'

'I'm sorry,' says Frida.

I wave it away with my hand. 'Long time ago.'

'At least your mum's not too far away, does she pop up to see you often?'

My throat feels tight and I can't swallow.

'Mum's not well, so it's me that visits her. I go whenever I can.'

I look around. We've been walking for a few minutes, that's all, maybe five minutes, and I'm completely lost. I can't see a single sign of humanity, except for Frida. No lights, no cars, no houses. It's dark but not completely dark and the strip of sky above our heads is pale grey and starless.

'Wait one second,' I say.

'What is it, Tuva?'

I look around me, staring into the black pines, turning on my heels, trying to see things. The beasts are out there and I'm trying to spot them behind the trunks and the rocks.

'I'm not good with nature, Frida. I mean, I really hate it. I mean, I really, really don't like this right now.'

'I know . . .'

'I'm not kidding,' I say, placing my hand on her forearm. 'See, I'm actually shaking, I'm not faking that.'

'I see that,' says Frida. 'Tuva, listen to me.' She stares into my eyes and I see blue, and it's comfort right there, something that's not dark green or earthy. Her eyes are blue and clean and sharp. 'I grew up in Norrland,' she says. 'And compared to Norrland, this is a walk in the park. Up there we have wolves, bears, lots of bears, and we have big country, not like this, I mean vast wilderness. And I was always fine. As a kid, with no stick and no knowledge and no police that, by the way, are only about two kilometres away, I was always fine. This all looks scary but the animals are so spread out and so petrified of us, we have nothing to worry about. Listen, sweetie. Follow me, stay close behind and focus on my armband or my jacket. Keep up and we'll get you there real quick and then we'll get you back out to your truck.'

'Okay,' I say. 'I'm okay now. Thank you.'

She says nothing, just walks off. I concentrate on her armband and block out everything else. I'm deaf but I hear everything, every twig snap, every owl hoot, every branch creak. I thought it was eerily silent in these places but I was wrong. It is eerily fucking noisy.

I speed up and walk so close behind Frida I'm almost touching her.

'Tell me some more about Norrland,' I say. 'Why did you move here?'

'Because of Hannes. He got a good job at the mill, straight out of school, so we moved down here. He's from up north as well.'

'Don't tell me you two were high-school sweethearts?'

'Oh, but I will tell you,' she says, pride in her voice. 'I used to work in the Sibylla hot dog stall on the main street of our little town. Was a nice job for a teenager, they paid pretty good. Hannes was popular with all the girls in school and he messed around a lot. Anyway, one day his parents told him he had to take responsibility and grow up. So when he approached eighteen, he started dating me. It was all dances and flowers and moonlit walks on the rocky hills outside of town. He was so romantic, I was swooning about with a massive smile on my face.'

I feel slightly queasy at this story and all its eighteenth-century faux-romantic chauvinist bullshit but I don't say anything. I'm at work.

'Then he got the job and bought a car and drove it over to my hot dog stall. He told me, I'll never forget it, he told me, 'Frida, you're too beautiful to serve people hot dogs. It breaks my heart to see you working here in a uniform and a hat. You're too good for this. I want you to be my wife.' He thought I was too pretty to hand out ketchup. He'd got the job at the mill that very morning. So we got married and moved down here and this is where we've been ever since. It's like something out of a movie, really.'

There's a noise to the right of us. Frida stops walking and that freaks the hell out of me so I stop and kind of hide behind her like a kid.

'It's a bird,' she says. 'It's just a bird.'

She strokes my shoulder and I'm placated like a kitten. My breathing slows and her hand on my shoulder makes all the difference in the world.

We walk on.

'Is it much further to Badger Creek?' I ask.

'Badger Hollow,' she corrects me. 'We're over halfway there.'

The gravel's gone now. I'm walking over rocks and through boggy grass and over knotted tree roots designed specifically to hold on to my boots and trip me up. I'm warm except for my cheeks and my nose. My pulse is beating loud in my ears.

'Let's cut through here,' Frida says, turning left towards a rocky outcrop covered in brown ferns.

'Is that the only way?' I ask. 'We can't stay on this track to get there?'

'We could,' she says. 'But it'd add a good couple of hours, and I need to get back to fix Hannes his dinner before his poker game. Come on, this is a shortcut, it's fine, I've done it a million times.'

But it's not fine, it's darker. The strip of light grey above is muddied by a criss-cross of spruce branches. Can't Hannes fix his own fucking dinner? I see things that aren't there, eyes and antlers and snakes hanging in trees. We get to a boulder field and scramble over the slippery rocks, Frida helping me, my boots losing purchase on damp moss and wet granite.

Then I see lights. They're not clear, just sporadic splinters of white light, broken by branches and trunks, and I want to walk faster. I'm happy to see something ahead so I speed up. I hold on to Frida's hand and walk towards the lights and I hear voices now, men's voices, and the depth and calm of their tone is reassuring. I'm smiling even though I know I'm heading towards an eyeless corpse.

We wade through brambles. They scratch my legs and tear my trousers before I get through to the clearing on the other side. I have to fight to free myself. We skirt around marshy land, reeds and tall grasses swooshing about our faces, and then we reach the men. They've placed torches and lanterns in the trees to try to light up the space. There's no tape and Thord isn't turning people away. It's just five men standing around a dead body in a hollow. I can see the victim's hair sticking out from under a tarp sheet. Damp. Grey. Medium-length.

'Who's there?' A voice booms out.

'Frida Carlsson. I've got Tuva Moodyson with me.'

I hear grunts of reluctant acceptance and see Thord walking towards us.

'You shouldn't be all the way out here,' he says, looking cold and tired in the harsh white light of the lanterns.

'I don't want to be,' I say. 'Let me ask you a couple of questions and take a few photos then I'll be out of your hair.'

'No questions,' a man from behind Thord says. He has the beginning of a beard, and I can see a Bluetooth earpiece hooked onto his ear even though there's no reception out here. It's flashing. 'Karlstad homicide are in charge of this crime scene.'

'I'm from the local newspaper,' I say.

'Good for you,' he says, turning and walking back to the body.

'Is it a man or a woman?' I ask.

The Karlstad cop with the Bluetooth thing in his ear walks back over and stands next to Thord. The air is all leaf mould and spores.

'Didn't you hear me? Get back to wherever you came from and let us do our job.'

'Is it a man?' I ask.

I see Thord nod ever so slightly as the Karlstad Bluetooth guy tells me that's my last warning.

'Have the victim's eyes been removed?'

Karlstad Bluetooth guy crosses his arms. 'You got one minute to leave the crime scene before I arrest you for obstructing police business.'

But Thord nods.

I shiver.

'Last question, then I go home, officer.' I need to know if Holmqvist was locked up when this murder took place. 'Was the victim killed in the last twenty-four hours?'

Karlstad Bluetooth guy unclips the handcuffs from his belt and Thord shakes his head.

'Okay, I'm leaving,' I say, turning and grabbing Frida's hand as I go.

We retreat a few steps and I take out the camera from my backpack. Then I turn and point it and take a flurry of photos. The flash reflects off the damp trees around me like sheet lightning. I see the police, at least three of them, turn and walk fast in my direction.

I grab Frida again and we run back to the boulders.

My heart's racing.

'You shouldn't mess with the police force like that,' Frida says. 'They're only doing they're job.'

'I know,' I say. 'So am I.'

21

My pillow alarm vibrates. I get up and stretch and climb into the shower and notice the scratches and cuts on my legs from last night's hike through Utgard. I pull out a barb from my thigh and a spot of red appears in its place. So, brambles can draw blood through thick denim jeans, who knew? Think about that next time you eat a blackberry.

I rub moisturiser into my face. Soon I'll need to move to my heavy winter cream because my nose and my eyelids are getting dry.

David Holmqvist is inside the cop shop two minutes from my apartment. Locals are gossiping, whispering in ICA that he's killed two men. Others discuss the case at the bus stop and reckon he's killed all five. There are only three cells in Toytown and it's likely Thord is preparing one right now.

But the town hasn't changed one bit. I drive and I see people cycling down *Storgatan* with their lunchboxes in their baskets, and I see old ladies scurrying along thawed pavements with spikes strapped to their sturdy leather shoes. Everybody has something to do, just not very fast.

When I get to work there are no copies of last week's issue left on the counter and everyone's waiting inside Lena's office. I hang up my coat and kick off my boots and join them.

'We haven't started yet, Tuva, I'm just explaining what you told me last night.'

I nod.

'So I had a chat with Holmqvist's lawyer this morning and he reminded me of our legal obligations, not that I needed any reminding. We report whatever the hell I decide we report, don't worry I told him that in pretty basic language, but we can't risk jeopardising any prosecutor's case against Holmqvist if he ends up getting charged with the murders.'

'What does that actually mean?' asks Nils, an elastic band stretching between his fingers.

'Not much for you, but Tuva, Lars, just be extra vigilant when it comes to fact-checking and sources.'

I look at Lars and he's staring up at the ceiling, his bald patch shining at me. He's probably rolling his eyes from behind his over-size glasses.

We split to our separate territories: Lars to the printer and Nils to the kitchen/office and me to the desk closest to the counter.

'You see the body last night? Any idea who it is?' Lars asks.

'Didn't see it,' I say. 'Well, I saw it but it was already covered with a sheet.'

'This is a lot for a town like Gavrik to cope with,' Lars says, like it might tip the place over a cliff. 'This is the last thing we all need after that business in the '90s. I wish it would all just go away. We just want a quiet life, not all this.'

I call the police station and Thord picks up. He sounds more officious than usual and I guess he's being watched by someone regional, someone of rank.

'Thord, it's me. Press conference today or tomorrow?'

'Noon,' he says, and puts down the phone. I look at the receiver like it's his face and he just made an obscene joke.

The first part of the morning's spent collating photos and prior-itising what writing I need to do. I have three full days and I almost hope nothing else happens because I can barely hold on to the stories as they are, never mind accommodate developments. Lena will give me as much space as I need for this, to explain the pattern in the victims, to lay out the facts as fairly and as impartially as I can. I need to visit the paper mill up north, as that's where some of the '90s victims worked. I write all morning with one eye on the clock and my aids switched low, but still on.

At 11:45 I take my camera and leather jacket and pull on my boots and walk over to the police station. I invited Lars to come with me but he said he wasn't in the mood.

It's like before, but worse. There are maybe twenty journalists, no BBC or CNN, it's just Swedish press so far, but we've got representatives from Gothenburg and Malmö joining us now. I'm told there will be a third cop starting work here after Christmas and I reckon they need her now. It's still Björn giving the statement but he has two good-looking guys behind him, one on each side, both wearing suits. I take my seat on the front row and check my Dictaphone and my camera and then I notice one of the suits staring at me. He's the guy from last night with the beginner beard and the Bluetooth on his ear. He's had a shave. Looks good. I nod to him but I don't smile and he just ignores me.

Björn starts. Same preamble as before. He speaks into a nest of brightly coloured microphones as flashbulbs light up his face.

'Welcome all, thanks for coming. Yesterday, at 13:22, a call was placed to the Gavrik district police station by a member of the Utgard forest hunting group. Said member informed us that a body had been discovered close to the area commonly known as Badger Hollow. When officers arrived at the scene, they discovered a deceased male in his fifties or early sixties. His identity is unknown at this present time. I would like to appeal for information and request anyone with a missing friend or relative matching that description to come forward. This man was not an official member of the Utgard hunting team. He was found with a rifle and a leash, but no dog.'

I raise my hand and the Chief points to me.

'Was the victim found with his eyes intact, sir?'

'I can't comment on that yet.'

'Do you know the cause of death?' asks someone behind me with a thick *Skåne* accent.

'A gunshot wound to the chest area.'

'Is it the same weapon used in the murder of Fredrik Malmström?' asks a woman with a clear radio voice.

Björn sniffs. 'I can't say but it appears to be of a similar calibre.'

Radio woman perks up again. 'Was the same weapon used in the '90s murders used for these new murders?'

'We can't say yet,' says the Chief, 'but the National Forensic Centre in Linköping are running ballistic tests.'

A woman with a video camera on her shoulder, I think she works for a small outfit in Dalarna, asks, 'Will hunting rights be cancelled for the rest of the season?'

'No decision has been made at this time.'

A man on my right with trousers too short for his legs asks, 'Has David Holmqvist been charged with any crime?'

'Nobody has been charged in connection with this incident.'

A tabloid woman at the back with thick blonde hair I'd kill for, wrong choice of word, asks, 'Was there was any sexual element to the crimes?'

The Chief looks uncomfortable. 'Not that we're aware of.'

More flashbulbs.

'What will the police do to make sure nobody else dies in Utgard forest?' I ask.

'We've brought in specialists from the National Homicide Unit, and we will decide what to do about hunting rights at the earliest opportunity.'

A woman with a chestnut-brown spaniel bursts through the doors to the conference room and everybody turns.

'Ma'am, this is official press only.'

'It's my husband,' she says. No tears, no sorrow, no emotion at all.

She strokes her dog and rubs his long, soft ears. 'We had an argument yesterday and then he took off with Jumbo.' She looks down at the dog and then up at Björn. I recognise her face from somewhere but can't place her. 'He hasn't come home and I know it's him out there in the woods. He goes there sometimes.' She looks down at the dog again. Her skin's loose like she's a smoker who's been on too many holidays. She quietens her voice. 'I can feel it. It's Rikard.'

Cameras pivot on their tripods and flashbulbs explode in her direction. The dog growls and she pulls it tight under her chin and backs out into the entrance foyer of the station. Thord follows her as Björn tells the press conference that questions are over can we leave in an orderly fashion, as if we're Boy Scouts. When I get through to the counter, Thord and the woman have already slipped through the heavy door with the push-button code lock. The other reporters are right behind me and we exit in one lump.

The sun's out. Photographers are checking their cameras, hands shielding digital screens from the light. Two TV types walk over to their outside broadcast van and several others start making recordings, stiff smiles and microphones, good-looking people with their backs to the police station. The liquorice factory chimneys cast long shadows down *Storgatan*. I can see one guy preparing for live broadcast and the other newspaper reporters are chatting and sending tweets.

I'm hungry for grease and I need some air so I walk towards McDonald's and see a figure seated on a fold-up stool outside the pharmacy, with placards and leaflets and a small table with a clipboard. The wind picks up. There's a biro attached to the clipboard with string. It's Bengt Gustavsson, the Mossen hoarder.

'Bengt, how are you?'

'Oh, keeping out of trouble. Have you walked over here to sign my petition like a good Christian?'

'Depends what it's for,' I say, smiling, the low sun warming my cheeks.

His face drops. He stands up from his fold-up stool and I notice his cold sores again, and then his eyes narrow.

'Are you okay?' I ask.

He talks through breaths, straining to get the words out. 'You're ...' he says, his nostrils flaring. 'You're all the same.'

'I'm sorry,' I say, backing off slightly, checking behind him in case anyone else is around.

He grabs the lapel of my leather jacket.

'What do you think this is actually made out of? You call this fashion? It's barbarity is what it is.' I pull back and he lets go of my lapel. Nobody's coming to my rescue, nobody's noticed.

'Come on, Bengt.'

'Don't,' he says, still pointing at my jacket, stepping back. 'Biggest mass-murder in the history of our planet. Do not be one of them. I'm dead serious.' He raises his voice. 'Meat, leather, hunting, sport, murder.' He thrusts a leaflet at my face. 'Meat, leather, hunting, sport, murder.' I can see a froth of white spit at the corner of his mouth. 'Why don't you educate yourself, Tuva Moodyson. Before it's too late.'

22

I spend the rest of the afternoon at my desk sorting my stories, drafting headlines and cleaning up quotes and making a string of appointments. I schedule meetings at the paper mill and the strip club, and one with the local hunting association chairman. There's a scrolling newsfeed at the base of my computer screen in case anything new comes in. Three separate journos pop in to say hi and ask for local restaurant and hotel tips and they all have the same look on their face as they open the office door. The bell rings above their head and they see our bobble wallpaper and our beat-up pine desks and our PC monitors the size of microwaves. They look amused and nostalgic and then I answer their questions and they look disappointed. One asks for the route to the crime scene. He asks if he can drive all the way in or will he need to rent a quad bike to get there and I just laugh at him.

I look up at the muted TV on the wall, subtitles blinking underneath faces, and I recognise the woman on screen.

'Isn't that the owner of the stationery store?' I ask. 'The dreary place that closed down?'

Lars looks up and nods and goes back to his typing.

I leave the office. I see Bengt in the distance with his placards and his bright white socks and his anger management issues, and then I turn the other way to my truck. I drive for about five minutes to *Eriksgatan*, the street I recognised on the TV, and park up next to the stationery store woman's house. There's a film crew outside and she's talking from her front doorstep wearing a bright purple fleece and black leggings.

I walk up to the journos and plant myself in between them, thrusting my Dictaphone under her chin.

'Oh, say now, you're a local girl, ain't ya?'

I nod and the other journalists scowl. At least one of them is broadcasting live and absolutely hating me right now.

'I was just telling your friends here, I knew Davey from way back when. He was one of the best customers I had before that damn supermarket expanded down the road and began selling cheap pencils and bad quality paper and such. I'll never shop in there, y'know, I drive all the way to the ICA in Munkfors these days on principle.'

'Do you think David Holmqvist is capable of such a crime?' asks a man wearing a woolly hat.

She purses her lips and the skin around them wrinkles and puckers into deep ravines. Her lipstick has bled.

'He was always a strange child,' she says. 'Used to come into my store, sometimes alone, sometimes with his little friend, and spend an age pottering around, I didn't really mind much because he was a good customer, just like I told you. Even back then. He'd be specific, very specific about what paper and pens and notebooks and journals he wanted. I had to get it in special from the depot and if I got it just a little bit wrong, a one-hundred-and-twenty-page refill pad instead of an eighty-page, say, he'd not go near it. Like it was poison. He'd not even touch it, just leave the store without saying nothing, or reordering or nothing. I reckon he thought he was the boss of me somehow because he bought so many supplies, box files and printer cartridges and such. Davey bought almost as much as the liquorice factory bought, or as much as the *Posten* bought before they all started going to the damn supermarket, or ordering everything on the internet store.'

The woman licks her index finger and pushes it through her eyebrow. She opens her eyes wide and adjusts her posture for the cameras.

'Did you think he was dangerous back then?' I ask.

'Well now, let me see. It was a few years ago now, but yes, I do remember thinking, well that boy won't be babysitting my grand-kiddies anytime soon, and that's a fact. He had cold eyes, you know what I mean, like them ones you see on the news. There wasn't any 'good morning Irene' or 'how's business Irene' about him. He'd walk in wearing them pull-on shoe covers. I told him he didn't need to, and he'd pass me a great list of bits and bobs for me to get hold of, all in this tiny, girly handwriting he had, I needed a magnifier glass in the end just to read it. He never did me any harm, but yes, I'd say he most likely had it in him to slaughter young Freddy Malmström, no doubt about it.'

'If he did do this, why do you think he did it? What was his motive, do you think?'

'See, I'm not so sure about this one. I've seen films about it and such, documentaries, real good ones that you can learn things from, you know the kind. I'd say, and I'm no expert, but I'd say he was envious of Freddy and this other fella they just found. Always got the feeling Davey had no friends or family, so I suppose he slaughtered those boys out of envy. It's as green as poison ivy, that's what I always say, but twice as deadly.'

'Why do you think the victims are all male?' I ask. 'Why do you think the perpetrator attacked middle-aged men?'

'You mean Davey Holmqvist?'

The guy to my right nods, something his camera won't pick up.

'I can't say, to be honest, maybe he was jealous of these good family men, you know, like I said. Freddy had a wife and a boy and a proper job. He went to work every day up at the school, not just staying at home all day writing ghost stories in his bedroom. Freddy was a Christian man and I'll bet you the other man they found was, too. Ghost stories, I ask you.'

The interview winds up and I drive back to the office with my recording. When I get inside I see Lena and Lars watching TV with the sound turned up. I slip my boots off and angle my neck up to see the picture. It's the ICA Maxi checkout girl again, the pretty one. I reckon without her looks she'd be forgotten about by now, but here she is taking her second fifteen minutes of fame. She's being interviewed with the supermarket sign in the background, must be standing facing Tammy's takeout van. She's next to an older woman with short white hair and a butterfly brooch on her uniform.

'Like I told the paper,' the pretty girl says. 'He'd come in and buy just the weirdest stuff. I seen him buy pigs' snouts he specially ordered, like their actual noses. I seen him buy tails and trotters and one time he even ordered in ...' she stops for a moment, either for effect or to rethink, 'testicles. Don't know if they were bull or pig or what, but they sure were big and I had to pick 'em up in their little Styrofoam packet and bleep them through my till. Eurgh, I still shiver just thinking about them bull balls.'

The other woman with the brooch starts talking as soon as the younger one finishes, keen to get her voice on TV.

'There's a rumour in this town,' she says, looking at the younger girl for a split second before turning back to camera, 'I don't know if it's true so don't quote me, but I heard David Holmqvist came on real strong to a girl at the school when he was studying there back in the day. Now, I'm not one to spread gossip, Lord no, but I heard on pretty good authority that he was trying to romance a girl in the year above him who was a little bit slow, poor lamb,' she points to her own head. 'Not retarded or nothing, she was in the normal school and now she's moved away with her parents to Spain or someplace hot, but I heard from an authority figure, that's all I can say about him, that Holmqvist tried to court her and she'd wanted none of it. Poor lamb, the school had to intervene or so I heard, they had to bring his parents in and all sorts.'

'Was any crime committed to your knowledge?'

'Well, let's see, you'd better ask a judge or lawyer or somesuch about all the technicalities, but in the eyes of the Lord, I'd say yes, a hundred per cent, yes a crime was committed I'd say.'

The younger girl sniffs.

'All I got is facts, what I seen with my own two eyes. He'd come in every Saturday like clockwork, sometime around two in the afternoon. He'd visit the meat counter but rarely the fish counter. He'd come to me even if I had the longest queue, and he'd have a pretty full trolley and most of it was meats. And a lot of teabags, all sorts of like fancy herbal types. He'd have a coupon most weeks, one cut out of the *Posten,* or one from a letter. He'd be very particular about the way he'd put items on the conveyer belt, I never seen anyone do it quite like him. He'd have to have them all fit together, the boxes and packs, like a game of Tetris or something, all one layer thick, no single item on top of another one. Always took him a while. Lots of heavy-duty cleaning products. And he never bought our bags, always brought his own ones made from some kind of brown sackcloth or something. He'd pack pretty slow so we offered him help a couple of times, but he'd shake his head and mumble something. Then he'd pay at my till and to tell you the truth I'd always get the shivers when he came up that close. He'd like pay and he'd always have this little pocket knife attached to his wallet and he'd get out his card and he was one of them who clamps his hands around the machine so nobody else could see his code, you know the type. And he'd be sweating by then and I reckon he was looking at me, I don't know what he was thinking but he usually had one hand in his trouser pocket and I don't know but I didn't like it, I didn't feel comfortable one bit. Then he'd like go and come back the next Saturday, same time.'

Every resident of Toytown has a story about this guy.

About ten minutes before I decide to leave for the day, I see a newsflash on the base of my screen. David Holmqvist has been arrested for the murder of Freddy Malmström. No mention of the other murder.

I call Thord and the line's engaged so I redial and redial and redial.

'It's me.'

'Hi, Tuva.'

'Well?'

I hear him sigh on the other end of the line.

'Press conference tomorrow. I'll reserve your seat for you. Gotta go.'

My hearing aid beeps, battery low, final warning. I pop it out from behind my ear and pull off a piece of fluff from the earpiece. I pop open the tiny compartment and the battery springs out. I push it off the desk into the recycling box and open my key fob container and peel off the sticker from a new one and wait for a minute and then I push it into place.

I head over to Tammy. I need dinner but really I need to talk to a person, an actual person. I need her. She's serving a couple in matching coats as I arrive so I wait in line.

'Hej!' she says when I get to the front of the queue, a dimpled smile all over her face. She leans forward and gives me an awkward half-hug out of the serving window. 'You look tired.'

I nod and breathe in the spicy lemongrass steam. Smells good. My belly rumbles.

'Let me feed you, I got something good over here, pad thai, the genuine real deal legit one hundred per cent authentic.'

I smile and nod enthusiastically.

She's really something. I watch her work in her cramped van, the van her mum converted years ago, and it's impressive how she keeps it so clean and organised, small containers of chilli and coriander and shallots and finely-chopped spring onion all ready to garnish. She takes a long pair of chef's tweezers and picks up a steaming clump of shrimp noodles, glossy with oil and sparkling with tiny gems of chilli and garlic. She pushes it into a shallow plastic box and sprinkles herbs and peanuts on top, then sticks a wooden fork in.

'You know you could open a restaurant in Karlstad one day and you'd make an absolute killing, millions. Your food is that good.'

'I'm an engineer,' she says, leaning from her serving window, her weight on her elbows. 'Or at least I will be in two more years. You think I want to serve food to ungrateful white people for the rest of my life? I'm gonna move south and design bridges.'

Another customer, someone who's phoned in an order, arrives, says hi, takes his plastic bag full of boxes of rice and Thai red curry, extra mild, and pays Tammy. I stand back while this takes place and finish my box of noodles.

'Asshole,' she says as the customer walks out of earshot.

'What did that guy do wrong?'

'He's a skinny ratshit,' she says.

I gesture for her to elaborate.

'Typical Swedish crap, no offence. Dude orders from me twice a week, sometimes more, always the mild, creamy stuff. It's about as Thai as you are but they want it so I cook it. He comes down here one time last year and we start chatting and he's seems okay. But then he starts talking about cooking and asks if I eat proper food when I'm at home.' Tammy does quotation mark fingers when she says 'proper food'. 'He asks if, when I'm not working, do I cook, y'know, meat and potatoes and sauce, that's what he called proper food.'

'My parents used to say the same about pasta.'

'Well your parents are different; this guy's an acorn-dick if I ever saw one. So I confronted him and told him that this and food similar to this was proper food for millions more people, tens of millions more people than his version of proper food. Gets pretty hot behind here in summer, and I was fuming that time. He told me it's junk food, but don't get him wrong, it tastes good, he buys it doesn't he. All this veiled racist bullshit. Skinny ratshit. He looks at me with his watery eyes and talks down to me. So I tell him if he thinks it's junk he should stay home and cook his cod and boiled-egg sauce. He didn't come back for a few months after that. Then one night he turns up all snooty-faced and thin-lipped and orders a fucking green curry easy on the chilli. Ratshit asshole.'

23

The police press conference starts at ten and it's the same people as before. Some are staying in the town hotel and they look restless and tired, like they're ready to quit Toytown and head back to reality somewhere south of here. The police have identified the latest body, the one found in Badger Hollow, as a mill worker called Rikard Spritzik. Björn confirms that Spritzik's injuries are similar to those of Freddy Malmström. Someone removed his eyes. The victim was found with a large amount of cash on his person, around five thousand kronor.

The Chief takes his glasses off and lets them dangle around his neck.

'Any questions?'

Everyone in the room seems to lunge forward, arms raised. Me included.

He looks at me and says nothing. Time slows down. Everyone's waiting for him to say something and I'm getting hot in my boots and this feels like some kind of unspoken warning. He blinks.

'Tuva.'

'Chief Andersson, are you connecting the murders of Fredrik Malmström and Rikard Spritzik with the three Utgard murders of the 1990s?'

Björn doesn't look at Thord, he just swallows and widens his stance like he's been expecting this question and rehearsing for it.

'We are keeping an open mind at this time and would urge

members of the public to come forward with any information no matter how insignificant it may seem.'

A guy with a centre parting asks, 'Has anyone been charged yet for the murder of Fredrik Malmström?'

'Not at this time.'

'Is David Holmqvist still being questioned?' asks a woman behind me with a Danish accent.

'Mr Homlqvist is assisting us with our enquiries.'

Centre parting perks up again. 'Is it safe to go into the woods?'

The Chief scratches his chin. 'Residents and visitors should be vigilant at all times. I would urge—'

A voice cuts off Chief Björn's answer. It's a guy with a bow tie and patent leather shoes, I don't recognise his face, but he has a nasal Stockholm dialect.

'Is there a serial killer in this town and if so how long before he kills again?'

Flashbulbs light up the Chief. He pulls the two halves of his glasses apart and holds them by his neck. He glares at Bow-tie man and then he nods and smiles. 'Thank you, that's all I have to say at this time,' he says.

I leave and get into my truck and drive up the E16 to the strip club. If there's one place local guys might let their guard slip and reveal something, it's here. I've got an appointment at noon before the place opens for business.

The day's as cold as wet socks in January and the rain's falling in squalls. It's falling against my driver's side window like someone's spraying a hose at me, and as I walk from my truck to the strip club entrance I have to cover my aids with my hands.

The door's locked. There's no bell or knocker so I thump on it. It opens and I find a woman older than my mum, maybe seventy or so, in a floral dress with bright white collar, and patent leather shoes.

'Are you Tuva?'

I nod and smile with my hands still cupped by my temples.

'Come in, dear, come in, you'll catch your death out there.'

I walk in and the place looks completely different. Ceiling spot-lights are buzzing and lighting the main room in a bright, forensic glare. The pipe of a vacuum cleaner coils on the floor, but the business end stands erect like a cobra's head. We sit at one of the tables by the stage, nearest the gleaming poles, me and a woman who looks like the goddam Queen of England.

It's the same scarred barman as before, the one with the tan. He's shuffling a deck of cards and he doesn't seem to recognise me.

'What are you drinking, dear? It's all on the house,' says the old lady.

'Just a water please, I'm driving.'

'Two negronis if you don't mind, Lucas.' She turns to me. 'Water's for rodents, that's what my grandmother used to say.'

I smile and tell myself to take a sip, a micro-sip, and that's all.

The room's faded and worn. The seats and the carpet are frayed, the stage pock-marked with dried chewing-gum patches like lichen on tree bark. But the punters won't ever notice, they don't come here for the furnishings.

'Can I ask you about your clientele, please?'

'You can ask me anything you like, dear.'

'Is Hannes Carlsson a regular client, and if so, who's his favourite girl?'

'Oh, not specifics, dear. I'm afraid. I'm in the business of discretion, have been for over forty years.'

'Has this place been open for forty years?'

'Goodness me, no. Before this, I used to manage a rather exclusive pampering house for local gentlemen. The paper mill employed three times as many men as it does now, did you know that? And they paid very well, too. Many of those gentlemen engineers and technicians came from far afield, from the south, the north, the west, from all over. They needed some attention after a long day working pulp at the mill and so I managed a very professional, dedicated team to do just that.'

'What happened? The mill downsized so you shut up shop and turned it into this?'

'Well, it's a little more complicated than all that, dear. You remember the dreadful business in the early 1990s? The three unfortunate incidents?'

'The Medusa murders?'

She takes a long slurp of her negroni and straightens the hem of her dress.

'It just so happens that those three were mill workers, well two of them at least, I think it was two, anyhow, they were members of my establishment.'

'Did it have a name? Was it a members-only club?'

'No and yes, to those two questions, my dear. No and yes. I moved to Spain once the pampering house closed down, lots of Swedes down there, lots of ex-pats, some real characters.' She looks at the barman. 'That's where I found Lucas. But now I'm happy to be back in Sweden.'

She jiggles in her black leather armchair and puts down her drink. She takes her manicured hand with its blood-red nails, and probes the side of her seat. I have visions of her pulling out a pink thong, but no. She brings her hand up to her eyes.

'Five hundred,' she says, holding up the banknote and admiring it. Then she opens her stiff, leather handbag and takes out a matching stiff leather purse and slides the note inside.

'Was Rikard Spritzik, the most recent victim, a regular here?'

'Couldn't possibly comment, dear.'

'He's dead,' I say. 'He's no longer a client.'

I see her gesture to the barman, then down the remainder of her negroni.

Savanah walks in from the back room in jeans and a thick wool jumper. She's not wearing any make-up and her hair's swept up in a ponytail and she looks magazine-beautiful.

'Savanah, darling, do you know a Richard Spritchdick?'

'Spritzik,' I correct, and offer a little wave to Savanah to say hi. 'Why you asking?'

'The body they found in Utgard forest two days ago has been identified as him,' I say. 'The police confirmed it this morning.'

I look at her face change. Savanah knew him.

'Was he a regular gentleman client, darling?' asks the old lady.

Savanah straightens her back and drags her palms over her scalp as if pulling off a wig.

'He was pretty regular, yeah. Nice guy. What,' she steps closer to me and lowers her voice to little over a whisper. 'What the hell is going on around here? First Freddy, now Rik? Why is this happening?'

I shake my head and look at the old lady. Neither of us has an answer.

'It's guys getting shot,' Savanah says. 'I know it's just guys dying, not us, but I don't feel safe no more.'

'You're safe while you're inside my four walls, my dear, I can guarantee you of that. You know we're safe here, we've got protection, there's nothing bad happening to any of my girls, that's for certain.'

'Poor Rik,' Savanah says, still standing over us. 'I think he's got kids. This ain't supposed to happen to people like him.' She looks at the old lady. 'I think I'm gonna skip my shift today, I feel kinda sick after all this. That okay with you?'

'Of course it is, dear,' says the old lady. 'Still gotta pay your appearance fee though, them's the rules.'

Savanah looks at the old lady and the old lady looks back at Savanah.

'Fine, I'll work.'

This place feels like the spider at the centre of the web. Maybe the killer's a jealous ex of one of the dancers, or maybe I'm joining up the wrong dots and it's just that most Shitsville guys drop in here from time to time.

I give the old lady my card and thank her for the drink I hardly touched. I leave and it's a relief to get back out into the rain. I sprint back to the truck with my hands over my ears and get in and turn the heating up high. It's damp, but not cold. I unhook my hearing aids and place them near the fan so they can dry out a little, I can't afford for them to malfunction.

Next appointment is with Benny Björnmossen, the local hunting association chairman. I drive at a steady one twenty with my wipers on full. I park outside my office in the usual spot. The town's quiet. I reach back into the truck and pull on my ski jacket and hook my aids back on and pull my hood over my head.

Benny's office is located above Björnmossen's gun store on *Storgatan*. There's a sign outside with a wild boar on it and the motto: *A Shot Not Fired Can Never Be Regretted.* He buzzes me in and I walk through a separate entrance next to the shop door and up a narrow set of stairs that creak with every step. At the top, I see a door slightly ajar. The ceilings are low up here and the place stinks of old cigarette smoke. I knock and walk in.

'You Tuva Moodyson?'

I nod.

'Come in and sit down, Tuva. I'm Benny Björnmossen.'

I take a seat. The room's long with windows front and rear. In the centre is a big old desk covered with papers but no computer. Behind the desk is Benny and behind him there's a circular card table with a green baize top, and behind that is a row of grey metal gun cabinets all bolted to the wall.

'Suppose you heard what they're trying to do to us, you mind if I . . .?' he holds up a box of Marlboros.

I shake my head. 'Trying to do?'

'Hunting rights,' he says, taking a deep drag on his cigarette. He looks like he's smoked all his life. 'The government's trying to rescind our legal rights, our God-given ancient rights to manage our woodland and preserve our way of life and protect the balance of nature, you gonna write about that in your paper, you gonna write what I just told ye?'

'I'll record our conversation, Mr Björnmossen,' I say, bringing out my digital Dictaphone from my jacket pocket and placing it next to a pile of papers on the desk. 'It's all on the record so you have nothing to worry about.'

'Two men dead and that's a damn shame. In fact, it's a crime. But they caught the fruitcake that done it, that ghost-story boy from Mossen village. So now do you think we can get back to doing what we do around here? Oh, no,' he says in an exaggerated Stockholm accent, 'we must assess the situation and ascertain the best way forward for the 2016/17 hunting season in Gavrik Kommun. Did you ever hear such a heap of steaming horseshit in your entire goddam life?'

I smile and shake my head.

'I guess they're worried about more fatalities,' I say.

He blows smoke out from his mouth and sucks it up through his nose. 'Why are they worried now this fruitcake ghost story boy's locked up over there in the police station, and gonna be in Karlstad court for trial soon? What this town needs more than anything – you should put this down in your newspaper – is to get back to normal. We're hunting people and we need to hunt. We need to come together and cull the old bulls and the excess calves and we need to manage our land so our grandchildren can live here long after we're all gone.'

'So who decides if the hunting licences are revoked?'

'The bureaucrats, of course, the men in suits, and most of them have never picked up a goddam shotgun in their lives, never mind a rifle. Why the hell should pen-pushing beer-bellies tell us what to do in our own woodland?'

'Could you offer a compromise? Hunt in the other forests but not in Utgard?'

'You're missing the point entirely.' He stands up and adopts a schoolteacher pose, like I'm a thirteen-year-old pupil. He's wearing a belt with a steel buckle in the shape of a diamond. 'Utgard's the biggest forest around and it's the best one, too. It has the biggest quotas and it needs the most managing. Carlsson does a good job leading the team and, after me and that taxi driver in Mossen village, I'd say he was just about the best shot around here.'

My hackles rise.

'The taxi driver? You mean Viggo Svensson?'

'If that's his name. Fine shot, I've seen him out at the gun club, but no hunting group will have him, none around here anyway. Oddball.'

Could Viggo and David Holmqvist be working together? They're not welcome in Hannes's hunt team so maybe they've set up one of their own?

'What do you mean by oddball?'

Benny looks down at my Dictaphone. 'Listen, what's important here is that it's a crime not to continue with the Utgard elk hunt till the quotas have been filled. That would be the real crime.'

'The quotas are that important?'

'Sweden has the highest density of elk in any country in the world,' he says, puffing out his chest like it's some sort of achievement. 'That's a proven scientific fact, watertight and cast iron guaranteed. Elk or moose or Bullwinkle or whatever the hell people call them, they're everywhere and they munch the pine saplings and they need controlling.'

'I suppose the police and the Kommun are putting people's safety before anything else.'

'Now you get it,' he says, nodding, his eyes a shade warmer than before. 'You write that in your newspaper. It's time we got our priorities straight around here and keep on hunting just like always and that's a fact.'

I leave, slightly bewildered, with a list of hunting teams and their leaders and their territories, and a chart showing the relevant seasons and the start and end dates, from elk to beaver to wolf to bear to wolverine to wild boar.

Back in the office, Lars and Lena are finalising all the non-murder stories and Nils has a client with him in his office-slash-kitchen. I write for a few hours and try to make sense of the strip club information and why David Holmqvist killed these two men, and if he did it alone. Whatever evidence the police have, they're keeping it close to their chests. I'll push for more ballistics detail from Thord when the experts in Linköping have finished their work.

I head home and park up. I walk into my building and pick up my post and walk up the stairs towards my apartment. The light bulb's still out and the foyer's shadowy. I climb the final steps and there's something half-lit in my doorway.

There's a troll sitting on my mat.

24

The thing's right here on my mat, it's right here. I calm myself and hold on to the stair rail and breathe. There's nobody around. It's basically just a carved doll. But it's not. It's loaded with a thousand bedtime stories and with ancient folklore running rich through my bone marrow. I stare at it. I'm in a building with thirteen other apartments. I'm about twenty seconds from a public street with traffic lights and delivery vans. I approach the troll and it's as tall as my shin. I look down at its eyes. They're half closed like it's drunk or sleepy or high or ill. Its hair is thick and matted. It's a she. I get to my door and stretch my arm to unlock it, leaning over the troll so as not to touch her. I step over her and into my apartment and turn on the lights and half close the door. Then I reopen it.

I'm looking at her back from inside my apartment, at her stumpy legs and at the sprout of ginger tail coming from her trousers. Not so scary from behind. I'm okay. I can close the door on her any time I want. Except that she'll still be there. I check my phone in my pocket and approach her from behind, my hands outstretched as if about to lift a baby with a leaky nappy.

It's cold. *She's* cold and hard. I hold her by the waist and slowly turn her around. Her eyes have me, they're some sort of dolly eyes, the kind where an eyelid moves up and down over a dead eyeball, and she's got me.

'That's enough,' I whisper. 'Enough of this town.'

I thrust her down onto my laminate worktop and let the front door close and walk away from her into my living room. What is this? I rub my eyes and scratch an itch just inside my nostril and I turn around and walk back to her. She's almost my height now.

I inspect her at a safe distance. She has real hair eyebrows, but doll's eyelashes. Her face is pine, sanded smooth, with red cheeks and freckles painted here and there. She has a wart on her chin, perhaps the nub of a twig once upon a time. I look at her ears. They're oversized and they have wooden blocks lodged behind them. Hearing aids? I see hair sprouting forth, like hair from the ears of an old man. The same ginger hair makes up her tail. Her mouth is sad. She's dressed in dull grey clothes and she's barefoot. I touch her feet, then recoil. I'm panting. She has toenails, human. They must be human; curls of yellow nail glued to each wooden toe. Do I confront the sisters? I can't take this to the police, it's hardly a crime, it's a gift, a fucked-up gift, but a gift and probably a valuable one at that.

My throat's dry. I pour a glass of water from the tap and drink it in uncomfortable gulps. Who orders these? And where the hell do they put them? In a living room on display like a fine piece of porcelain? Or in a private room, to look at and fondle? I step back over to her and tug at her clothes. They're made of little pieces of old sack but they're carefully sewed together and hemmed. It's good work. Neat. Her top has a red stain at its centre. It's been glued to her pine body but the trousers have a drawstring made of twine, so I undo it. For a moment I'm a five-year-old girl again, and I want to see what's underneath. I tug down her rough little trousers and see a glimpse of curly dark hair between her pine legs and then there's vomit in the back of my mouth. I grab my handbag and open the front door and slam it behind me. I run down the steps two at a time with sour images of those sisters in my mind, images that don't belong there, not now, not ever.

I should have thrown it out of the window. I run onto the street and it's silent like a movie scene. There's no wind, just a damp chill in the air, and a faint hint of liquorice every now and then.

I jump in my truck. Feels safe here. My truck with its torque to get me out of trouble and its Toyota toolkit in the back and the canister of Canadian bear-spray beside me on the passenger seat in my handbag. I switch on the engine and jangle the key fob and it rattles, so that's fine. I get flashbacks of the pubic hair. It's the real deal, human hair, and the taste of vomit returns to the back of my throat like a burning reflux. I drive off in a skid. *Storgatan*'s empty, a few cars but the shops are all shut and nobody's around, probably some reality TV show drawing them all home like moths to a light bulb. Lars told me once that his TV is his best friend and his broadband connection is his family, especially in the winter months. He said they keep him going. TV and coffee and alcohol: the holy trinity of cold countries.

I don't know where I'm going. In London, I'd head to a friend's or a pub or a cinema or someplace with crowds, but there's nobody here. The office is locked and the lights are off. The cinema's closed tonight because it's only open on Mondays, Wednesdays and Saturdays. I drive out towards McDonald's and there are no cars in the drive-thru lane. I pull a left towards Tammy but she's taken a break and shuttered her van. I call her mobile, no pickup. Now I get a little panicky, like where the fuck is the whole town? Most of the flats and houses I can see from the car park are dark. The acid's still there in my throat. I floor the accelerator and squeal round a roundabout, hitting about as much grass as tarmac. I head out to the motorway because I need some speed to wind down, but then I change my mind and turn off and drive underneath it. I get to the digger graveyard, or rental yard, or whatever it is, a huge car park for earth-movers in the middle of nowhere, and carry on.

I'm heading for Frida, I realise that now. I've tried everybody else I know in Toytown, and if I drove down to Karlstad I wouldn't get there until midnight. I need ten minutes and a cup of tea with an actual human being. And yeah, I know I'll have to drive past the wood-carving sisters, but big deal, they're older than my mum.

Pines. Hoarder's house, a dim light in the caravan. His solar lights are twinkling like quartz crystals amongst his cabbages and parsnips. Taxi's house, I see his Volvo with a pop-up kids sign still on its roof. Up the hill, past the marshes and then the sisters. The smell of smoke. I can hear folk music faintly from their workshop. They're carving and don't look up as I speed right past them. Ghostwriter's house is dark, striped blue tape reflecting in my headlights. The tape's wrapped around his veranda like a gift-wrap ribbon. As I'm looking at it, I sense something ahead of me and slam on the brakes. In my head, it's an elk as big as a house, the elk that wrecked dad's car, but no, it's a tree, a pine laid across the track at an angle. I stop about three metres from its branch tips, my heart pounding, regretting coming here at all, what the hell was I thinking.

I call Frida with my hazards on even though I'm not sure they're strictly necessary out here. She picks up after one ring.

'Hej, I was just thinking about you,' she says.

I can hear music in the background, perhaps she has the radio on. 'Oh, really?'

'About your mother. I was wondering if you wanted me to add her to my food roster. I could deliver some meals to her, maybe a bulk delivery of frozen meals once a fortnight or even once a week? I like to get down to Karlstad on Sundays to go shopping so it wouldn't be a bother.'

'I . . . the hospital take care of all that.' It's hard to say all this out loud. My voice is catching slightly at the back of my mouth. 'Thanks for thinking of her, though.' I pause. 'Frida, I'm here. I'm near your house and there's a big tree down across the road.'

'You're here? Gosh, I wished you'd called first. Hannes is going to slice that tree up in the morning, but there's not much I can do about it this late. Let me drive and pick you up, I'll be there in two minutes. Is everything okay?'

'No, no. I don't want to put you out. I'll head back home now. I'm sorry I came straight out here, I should have checked.'

'Nonsense, it's always nice to see you. I'll be there in just a jiffy, hold on.'

I keep the lights on even though my beams get lost in the prickly needles of the spruce. It's another corpse in a way, a fresh one. Still looks alive to me. I pull my bear-spray close to my thigh and feel safe out in front, in the light, but vulnerable, very vulnerable, from the darkness that is every other direction. I can see the blue police tape at David's house in my wing mirror, the loose ends fluttering in the breeze around the veranda posts. And I think about that troll and her ears and her . . . hair. My breathing's almost normal now, but I can see sweat all over the steering wheel, a glistening slug-trail of my own palm sweat.

Headlights are coming towards me from the other side of the tree. I get out of the truck and lock up.

'Tuva,' Frida shouts. 'Best thing is if you climb kind of through the branches and over the trunk, that way you'll stay in my head-lights.'

The route she's suggesting, straight through the bushy centre of the tree, looks impenetrable. But Frida has a point. The tip of the pine and its upturned roots are not on the track, they're in the woods on either side, in the darkness. I climb through a tangle of stiff branches. They're scratchy but not like brambles, they don't hurt or make me bleed. Then one whips me in the face and I get a cheekful of wet needles. They smell fresh after the grossness of that troll. I climb over the trunk, my jeans rubbing against the rough bark, and fall to the other side.

As I pass the branch tips and see Frida, I almost collapse with relief. She's holding her arms out wide for a hug and somehow Mossen village, past the marker that is this fallen tree, feels like a different place. It's okay. The dead spruce divides heaven and hell. I hug her and she smells of lily-of-the-valley.

'Come on,' she says. 'I've got some soup on, let's get you inside.'

25

Frida's car is warm and clean and it smells like it's been valeted.

'You look like you've seen a ghost, Tuva. What happened to you?'

'I'm okay,' I say. 'It's stupid, really.'

We drive up the track to her clearing and I see the sloping mansard roof of the house. There are lights on in every window, lights near the entrance on wrought-iron posts, and lights beaming out into the woods. They've got so many lights that this almost feels like a normal place in the centre of Utgard forest.

'Someone played a trick on me, that's all,' I say, an apologetic tone in my voice. Frida looks over at me as she parks in front of the grey outbuilding. 'Somebody left a troll on my doorstep and I think it was probably made by one of your neighbours.'

'Eurgh,' Frida says, and I laugh although I don't know why and that sets her off laughing too. I laugh harder and I have to stop myself. I'm angry as hell and I'm laughing.

We get out and the front porch is neat with ornamental heathers planted in painted wooden containers. The light inside the grey hut is on. We go into the house. Smoke. I see the fire in the living room log-burner and I see Hannes next to it reading a newspaper. My newspaper.

'You all right?' Hannes asks. 'Driving out here like this, Frida was worried you were in some kind of trouble.'

'I'm fine, just had a fright, that's all.'

He folds up his copy of the *Posten* and shakes my hand. He's

156

wearing an expensive-looking navy jumper and it's clinging to his solid torso. It has a little zip open near his neck. He has weathered skin and tiny hairs on his cheeks just above his beard line.

I slide off my shoes and my coat. We head to the kitchen and it smells like a commercial for something wholesome and warm. I see a vat of liquid bubbling on the hob and head over to it, the smell drawing me closer.

'Chicken soup?' I ask.

'Needs a few final touches,' Frida says. 'I'll just be a sec.'

I watch her walk out into the garden and the grey hut's outer security light switches on. I breathe in the soup, the steam moistening my face, and then Frida comes back into the kitchen and brings Hannes with her.

'Pheasant plops, I call them,' she says. I frown and she walks towards me with a blue rubber ice-cube tray. 'Little blocks of frozen pheasant stock, from birds Hannes brings home. I make concentrated stock and freeze it like this and then when I make a soup I just . . .' She pushes out three brown ice cubes into the soup. 'Plop, plop, plop,' she says. 'That's instant depth of flavour right there.'

She stirs the melting ice cubes into the soup and my stomach grumbles. I think it's inaudible to them. I hope so.

'Sit down, let me get you a drink, you look like you could do with one.'

'Just water, thanks.'

'You can have a small glass, surely?' says Hannes as he takes a bottle of white wine from the fridge and opens it. I watch as a bead of cool water rolls down one side of the bottle. 'You get pulled over by Björn or Thord, you just tell them you drank Hannes Carlsson's Chablis and then they'll let you be on your way.'

The cork pops out and he pours me a large glass and I decide to do what I did in the strip club and sip the top ten per cent.

Frida pours three deep bowls of steaming soup and brings over a loaf of brown bread on a board.

'Can you get the butter?' she says to Hannes. 'The whisked one, please.'

It all looks wonderful. I'm getting nourished and I haven't even tasted a mouthful yet. I'm sitting at a clean table with a napkin and a glass of cold white wine and a bowl of hot soup. I ease down into my chair, my posture slipping as I start to feel relaxed and a little tired. We drink and we eat. The warm bread with whisked, salted butter is delicious and the soup is rich and earthy and I eat two deep bowlfuls.

'I was wondering,' I say, the wine loosening my voice. 'Have you read any of David Holmqvist's books? Do you know what he's written?'

'I don't read fiction,' Hannes says, like the question was only directed to him. 'I'm too busy for made-up stories, got no time for all that. Now, you give me a good history book or an encyclopaedia and I'm right as rain but I stopped reading fairy tales when I started shaving.'

'And like I told you before,' says Frida. 'We're not even sure what he's written.'

'Hannes, what do you do for relaxation? You have any clubs or places locally you like to hang out?'

He sits up straight and leans towards me. 'I hunt.' He refills my glass and I realise I've drunk the whole thing. It tasted so good with that soup.

'Oh, no more, thank you. I've already had far too much.'

'Nonsense,' Frida says. 'You can either stay here in the spare room, or else Hannes will drop you back home, won't you Hannes?'

'Well,' he says. 'I'm on my third glass, so best not risk it.'

'I know,' says Frida. 'We'll call Viggo, how about that. It's his job after all and we get very good rates with Viggo, only two hundred and ten into Gavrik.'

They both look at me.

I smile and let go and nod and Hannes fills up my wine glass.

'Is Mikey's mother around?' I ask. 'How long has Viggo been a single dad?'

'She left after the boy was born,' Hannes says. 'Reckon she'd slept with half the Kommun by then and at least half of my hunt team.' Hannes and Frida look at each other. 'Karlstad girl, not from around here, she was a weirdo, that one.'

'So,' says Frida, changing the subject. 'I need to do the weekly shop tomorrow so how about I drive your truck to your office in the morning and then Hannes can bring me home later on. I promise I won't crash into anything. Is that okay with you two?'

I nod and smile. Hannes nods.

'Now, cloudberry pie. Let me take those bowls.'

I stand up and feel slightly light-headed from the wine. I'm so out of practice since London, where wine was for sale in every corner shop and supermarket. I take the bread plates and walk them over to the sink.

'Not for me, thanks Frida. I'm full, it's all been so delicious.'

'Just a smidge,' Frida says, pinching her fingertips together. 'Half a smidge.'

'Okay, you persuaded me.'

She slices the pie and brings out a big bowlful of Chantilly cream with black vanilla specks. She takes a spoon and quenelles balls of cream onto the three plates as expertly as a chef on TV.

The pie tastes incredible. Not too sweet. 'Sorry if this sounds rude,' I say, finishing the last of the cream. 'That was so lovely but can we call Viggo now? I need to work early tomorrow morning to get the next issue of the *Posten* out, it's an important one for me.'

'No problem,' says Frida, clearing away the plates.

Hannes calls him.

'Viggo'll be here in ten minutes,' he says.

Frida drives me to the fallen spruce and we hug goodbye. She gives me a dog-eared novel as I disappear into the needly branches. It's called *Cowboys and Wedding Bells* and it looks like vintage paperback bullshit. I thank her and see Viggo on the other side seated in his Volvo. I check my truck's locked up and then I jump in the back seat of his car.

He doesn't say much, just confirms the price and destination. The car's warm and smells a little musky. He drives fast and smooth through the twists of the road, and my eyelids start to feel heavy. I'm warm and I feel my chin hit my neck a few times as I drop off.

I wake up in the digger yard close to the E16.

26

I'm sober in a second. The Volvo's cold, the engine's been off for a while. My seatbelt's tight and my mouth is dry.

I have to think, have to be smart right now, no missteps.

'Engine trouble?' I ask, and then I spot the tea-light candle on the dash in the centre of the windscreen.

'No trouble,' Viggo says, facing forward like he's still driving, the collar of his fleece jacket giving him a straight jawline in the darkness of the car.

I'm trying to think fast but the wine's still there in the background, sluicing around and messing with me.

'Why did we stop?'

He presses a button on the central console of the Volvo, under the pathetic little candle, and a song starts to play. I look to my right and see the door's locked, the little plastic nub flush against the window sill. I slide my hand to the door handle as the first bars of 'Unchained Melody' drift out of the speakers at low volume. The door won't open.

'Child locks,' Viggo says softly from the front seat, his face still in shadow, his head still pointed forward. 'For protection.'

I'm sweating now. My feet are hot in my boots but the air is chilled and I can see my breath cloud in front of my eyes.

'Viggo, what are you doing?'

No answer. The song continues. The candle's flickering and I can see small souvenirs dangling in front of it. They're in silhouette like

Viggo; small mementos hanging from string under the rear-view mirror. It's a cross, some kind of crucifix. And a Swiss army knife. And a little figure. It's a tiny troll the size of a kiwi fruit.

'I thought you didn't approve of trolls, Viggo.'

I see his shoulders shake as he laughs an inaudible laugh.

'The sisters didn't make this one. This one's a good troll, it's a *hustomte*, a gnome to take care of things, no menace here, Tuva, not in here.'

I pull my handbag up from between my knees. No phone reception.

'What do you want?' I say. 'I don't like this.'

He seems to deflate a little and his shoulders slump down. I notice he's wearing cologne, a scent I last smelt back in the '90s: a unisex perfume that used to be sold in a black bottle.

'Well that's not what I wanted at all, now is it?' he says. 'I can never get these things right.' I see him shake his head. 'I thought we could just, chat, you know? Like adults, no children around. I liked our time the other night, with Mikey, you were really great with him.'

He pauses and I stop searching in my bag with my hand.

'He's a good kid,' I say.

'He's not an easy child,' Viggo says. 'You were really something.'

'Listen Viggo, it was nice to meet you and Mikey. But don't do this. Just let me out now and I'll get a friend to pick me up. Let's just say this never happened, okay?'

He turns to face me and the candle lights up one side of his face.

'But it did happen,' he says softly with what looks like a caring expression. 'It is happening.'

I rattle in my bag and find the canister with my hand.

'Okay, now shut up. I've got a weapon here that will put you in the hospital. Let me out.'

'So do it,' he says, turning back to face the windscreen. 'Unchained Melody' peters out and we're left in silence once more. 'Do what you like to me, I don't really care. I thought we could have a, not a date really . . . just a grown-up chat, so to say. I thought I'd make a little effort, as you've been so nice to me and Mikey.'

I take a deep breath and unclip my seatbelt.

'Let me out, Viggo. This is over.'

'Is it because I'm not a hunter?' He pauses. 'Because I'm not like Hannes and the others, all bravado and muscles and hunting stories, is that what this is about?'

I shake my head and start to answer but he holds up something between the two front seats.

'Well, you might want to take a look at this, Tuva.'

I have my fingertip on the white tip of the bear-spray canister. I take the square piece of paper from him.

'Turn the light on so I can see this.'

'If you focus, you'll see it.'

I bring it closer to my eyes and then realise I'm obscuring my view of this freak's head so I hold it up to the window and try to keep one eye on that fleece collar.

'It's a target sheet.'

Viggo sits up in the driver's seat and raises his chin a fraction.

'All nines,' he says, cocky again. 'Bet you Hannes and his so-called poker buddies couldn't get three nines. Nope. You think I'm not man enough, well I can shoot as good as an army sniper.' He looks back at me. 'Better than a sniper, Tuva. Now you've seen the proof.'

'Here's the deal,' I say. The windows are steaming up and I know that the longer this goes on, the more likely it is I'll end up face down in a ditch with my throat slit. 'This was nice, I got to know you a little better. Thanks for the effort. I have a boyfriend in Stockholm, but otherwise I think you're a real nice guy. Like I said before, I have a weapon in my hand but if you unlock the car right now and let me out then we're quits. All right? Unlock my door and we'll forget all about this and we'll move on.'

I watch him. His breathing's faster, his silhouette rising and falling like he's sobbing but he's not. I see his arm extend towards the tea light. He pinches it with his fingertips and now everything is dark. It's pitch black and as cold as a freezer. I'm watching him.

He turns on the engine and the headlights fly forward and pick out a sleeping hoard of diggers and dumper trucks.

'Let me out,' I say quietly. 'It's time.'

He releases the handbrake.

'You don't need to drive me anywhere.'

'It's what I do.'

'Think of Mikey,' I say. 'He needs his dad. He doesn't need you to put this taxi into drive or pull away or do anything else. Think of little Mikey and unlock my door.'

Nothing. I look at the bear-spray and then out at the caterpillar tracks of the diggers.

'Let me out now!' I scream as loud as I can. 'Now!'

He presses a button and there's a clunk sound and the little plastic nub on my door pops up. I fall out of the car onto the muddy gravel and scramble away towards a dumper truck.

He drives off slowly and carefully, the *Beware, Children on Board* sign still erect on his taxi's rooftop.

I use my phone to find Tammy's number but my hands are shaking so bad I keep getting the wrong person; first Tina, my hairdresser, then Savanah, the girl from the strip club. I stand on a pallet and get one bar of reception. Still trembling, I tap the screen and get Tammy and call her.

'Kitchen's closed.'

'It's me.'

Her tone changes instantly, like she understands exactly what I've just been through from those two useless words.

'Where are you? You okay?'

'I'm at that weird digger lot near the underpass to Mossen village. I'm okay, but—'

'I'll be there in five minutes. Are you safe?'

'Yes.'

'Hold tight, Tuva, I'm coming.'

I rest against the wheel of some kind of excavator and the hard rubber tyre is as tall as I am. Somehow I'm not as cold as I was in the car. It's dark but what little light there is bounces off the machines so it's not like being in a forest. I'm not expecting elk or wolves or snakes in this place because it's all reassuringly metallic and mechanical.

It's been two minutes. My eyes are starting to acclimatise and my head's calmer now, though my heart's still stressed, it doesn't move on so fast. The sky's amazing. There are so many stars that I want to open my eyes as wide as possible to try to see them all in one go. My hearing aid beeps a battery warning and I search my jacket pocket for my key fob and it's not there. I remember I gave the bunch, minus my apartment key, to Frida back at the house. That's fine. I'll have them tomorrow and anyway the battery will last twenty-four hours or so and I have more at home and the one in my other aid's practically new out the box. But nothing for my hand to jangle. My hearing now has a life expectancy.

Above me, a large cloud moves over from somewhere else and the sky falls dark. I hear something and then I spot a headlight.

In seconds she's on me, hugging me, kissing me, asking me if I'm all right. I'm tired. I'm happy I have Tammy here in this digger graveyard, but I'm so, so tired. I jump on the back of her bike and she passes me a helmet. My tongue tastes bitter. She starts the engine and turns onto the road and the throb of the bike feels good. I'm tight against her back like a shipwrecked child clinging to a lifeboat. I'm hugging her waist so tight, my chest warming up, nestling my nose into the smooth leather of her jacket. I'm safe.

She takes me home and we walk up to the flat together and go inside.

I'm about to explain everything when she points to the kitchen worktop.

'And what the fuck is that?'

27

Tammy picks up the troll and inspects it fearlessly, like it's just any old Cabbage Patch doll.

'Found it earlier,' I say. 'That's why I left the flat, I wasn't planning to leave. Found it here and just freaked out, Tams, just look at it.'

'Looks like a local girl, born and bred.'

'Can you dump it for me? Can you just get it out of here?'

'Who gave this to you?'

'Likely it was made by a couple of sisters in Mossen village, they carve this crap for handicraft fairs and Christmas markets. Don't know if it's a message or a gift, but this place is starting to get inside my head.'

'Do you have to keep going back to that shitty village? Can't you do some desk time and send Lars out there? Those people are even worse than my customers. You're dealing with the crème de la fucking crème of Gavrik's rednecks and perverts.'

We share half a bottle of rum and wash it down with Diet Coke. I feel normal again. Tammy's my lifeline, my umbilical cord to the outside world. She tells me her mum's gone travelling, no Skype contact for the last few weeks, and I realise just how different our mothers are.

I tell her more about what happened with Viggo.

'If I ever see him, I'll . . .'

'I know,' I say. I've stopped shaking now thanks to the rum but my heart's still pounding. Part of me keeps imagining what could have happened tonight if he'd driven off with me and part of me shuts that down because it's too awful.

'You gonna talk to the cops?' Tammy asks.

'Tomorrow. I have no idea what he was trying to do.'

'I have an idea,' she says.

I take a deep breath. 'In a way, it was just a candle. He didn't try to get in the back seat with me, he hardly even looked at me.'

'You let the cops decide what to do,' she says. 'You need a lift in future, you call me.'

We hug and I persuade her I'm okay and that she can go home and leave her bike here until morning. She takes the troll and agrees to throw it down my building's garbage chute on her way out. I almost pity it. I pull out my aids and strip and pull on a nightie I've had since I was a teenager. Then I climb into bed and curl up into a ball to sleep.

I wake up hot, my pillow alarm shaking my head from a vaguely enjoyable dream. I have a hangover on top of a hangover, rum on top of wine, and all mixed together with stale adrenaline. No more drinking. It's too much of a relief, a blissful escape, a warm blanket. What happened in London can't happen here. I'm done.

I shower and pour brightening eye drops into my eyes. As a retired optician, Mum hates these drops. For me they're a godsend. I scrub my face with an exfoliating cream to try to rid myself of October paleness, of that dull skin look. It works. I have colour now, albeit mild-sunburn colour.

As I brush my teeth I think about Viggo. He didn't even touch me, didn't even say one inappropriate thing. I've had worse in bars and house parties. But it was him. In a taxi. That's what was scary. It should be a place of safety and it always has been for me, drunk or sober, awake or asleep.

I'll tell Thord and I will never again fall asleep in a taxi.

I pull out a frozen loaf of white bread and toast two slices. I have no butter but I have chocolate spread which I heap on the toast with a spoon. Water. Two paracetamol. More water. I walk to work and it's sub-zero, or exactly zero, the worst temperature for me, raw and cutting. I turn to look at the Grimberg liquorice factory and get hit in the face by microscopic ice crystals and they burn my already beat-up cheeks. My hair freezes, each wet strand hardening and pulling chill down into my scalp. But the cold helps me to think. I remember the old cathouse by the E16 and the articles I need to email Lena today and the stories I haven't even started to draft yet.

Frida's waiting outside my office. She jumps out of my truck as I walk past with my collar turned up and my hands deep inside my pockets.

'Morning,' she says.

'Thanks for driving this in, and thanks for last night.'

'Hannes drove actually, asked me to pass the keys to you and tell you he's very impressed with your truck. You get home okay?'

I almost tell her everything but I'm too hungover to face it all again. I just nod and then she smiles and reaches into my truck and passes me a tray of four coffees.

'Wow,' I say, staring at the McDonald's coffees in their little McDonald's takeout cups. 'You didn't need to do this.'

'I felt bad,' she says. 'We should never have given you all that wine. And then you had the cost of the taxi. Hope this makes amends.'

She passes me a paper bag.

'Muffins,' she says. 'Not home-made I'm afraid, just McDonald's. I got two different flavours for you and your co-workers in there.'

'Thanks, they'll love you for ever.'

She waves that off.

'I'd better go, Hannes is picking me up from ICA in an hour and I've got lots of food to buy.'

She hands me my truck keys, plastic fob jangling nicely, and walks away. I go inside and the bell rings above my head. Lars and Nils look suspicious when I hand them each a coffee and muffin.

'What I do?' asks Nils, an XXL ice-hockey jersey pulled over his shirt in honour of tonight's big game.

'How much do I owe you?' asks Lars, his glasses on the end of his nose.

But Lena takes hers like she's been given coffee and muffins by reporters her entire life and I realise that she probably has, just not by us. Nils is called in by her as I step back out to my desk.

I load up the stories I organised yesterday. Six distinct articles with one gaping hole. I need to talk to Rikard Spritzik's family. I pop two more paracetamols as my head starts to thicken and then I switch off my aids and get to work.

Three hours. I write some good copy, pasting in quotes and information snippets and focussing on local issues and the town's police. I've completed four of my six pieces by lunch. The first five pages will be the murders – the timeline, the similarities between the two, the similarities between these and Medusa, the local perspective with quotes from various townspeople, and a shaded column headed 'What We Know'. The things I can't write about yet: the niggling thoughts I have about Viggo and Hannes, about the strip club being central to the crimes, about people being scared or just unwilling to talk, throb in my head like a parallel hangover. At least the writing's cathartic, it's pulling me back to centre, to who I was before I arrived here in Toytown, and also to who I'll be when there's nothing left keeping me here and I get to move away to the biggest goddam city that'll have me.

Lena opens her door and says something I can't hear and gestures for me to come into her office.

My fingers find the little buttons behind my ears and then the audible world returns. First, a jingle specific to the hearing-aid manufacturer, then whirs and whistles and the sound of Lars photocopying in the corner. Hurts my head a little. I walk through and sit in front of Lena's desk.

'How much have you written?'

'Almost there.'

'I've had a few calls, Tuva. Last night and then again this morning. Local people, local businesspeople and councillors who have asked me for a favour.'

I frown and lick my lips. They're dry and my lip balm's still in my truck.

'Now, I've had this before, not exactly this, but similar. We have a responsibility to tell the truth and to report the news so that our readership can follow what's happening. These locals, they would like us to do so in as positive a light as possible. They don't want Gavrik to come out looking like a den of violence or a place which is dangerous to visit. Does that make sense?'

'Well, it is pretty dangerous right now, wouldn't you say?'

'We have three major advertisers threatening to pull their contracts if we don't run the stories sensitively. I've given this a lot of thought. It makes me sick to the stomach, but I think we can walk a line where we're professional and accurate but still, well, still patriotic to the community.'

'I'm not paid to be patriotic to the community,' I say. My headache is coming back, tightening my forehead. I rub the bridge of my nose and push the skin between my eyebrows. There's no fucking way I'm writing anything other than the truth. I've seen the damage caused by inaccuracies and bias: collapsed court cases and broken families. 'What about freedom of the press, what about journalistic integrity?'

'Yeah, I think I've heard about those things too, but this isn't a Wikileaks exclusive, it's crimes affecting local people. And you are, in a way, paid to be mindful of the community, they're the ones who pay our salaries, the readers and the advertisers. We don't have some rich benefactor or multinational parent company, Tuva. It's just us four.'

'Who's complaining?'

'It's not important *who's* complaining. I want you—'

'I'll be sensitive if you tell me who complained. Otherwise you can write your own damn stories.'

She closes her eyes and inhales and scrunches up her face for a minute like a child.

'Benny Björnmossen, he's head of the local hunting association.'

I nod.

'The woman who owns the caravan park down by the reservoir, the one with the water-ski contests each summer. Can't remember her name, Petra something, cousin of Chief Björn? Anyway, she's worried sick about next year's season, about cancelled bookings. Talked about hiring herself a lawyer.'

'Okay.'

'And Hannes Carlsson.'

Shit.

'He called yesterday. He was pretty reasonable, understands our responsibilities, blah, blah, blah. But he talked a lot of high and mighty about the common man's right to hunt his own land, and how we don't need outsiders from big cities poking their noses in. Talked about his people taking care of the problem themselves.'

I rub my eyebrows the wrong way, each one towards the centre of my forehead to ease the tension in my sinuses.

'I've written four and I've got two left,' I say. 'I'll get them to you ASAP, then you can see what you think.'

'Smart,' Lena says. 'Smart of you to think long-term. Lars is calling for you.'

I turn and find Lars standing at his desk with a phone in his hand, his moist palm cupping the receiver like the damn thing doesn't have a mute function.

'Got a Savanah for you, she didn't give a last name. I'll put her through to your desk.'

28

'I need to talk to you.'

Savanah's whispering down the line but I can just about hear her, she has good diction.

'Sure,' I say. 'Of course, I'm listening.'

'Can we meet somewhere? I want to . . .' I hear a muffling sound like she's covering her phone with her sleeve or something. I wait. I can't hear music exactly but I think I can make out a beat, a baseline.

'You still there?' she asks.

'I'm here. You say where and when and I'll be there. I'm working on a story up at the mill later so I'll need to be in your area anyway.'

'The gas station,' she says. 'The Q8 gas station, north of the club, it's on the way to the mill. Meet you there at twelve-thirty.'

My dash reads ten degrees as I drive up the E16, sun reflecting in my rear-view mirror. Värmland looks good on days like this, bright skies with clouds drifting by like swans on a lake. The sky's a shade of blue unlike I've seen anyplace else in the world.

Clear road, so I push up to one forty and turn on the radio. Chart music and traffic updates. No breaking news, though, nothing major. Court date for David Holmqvist's preliminary hearing. He's held under 'reasonable suspicion' rather than 'probable cause' so they need to move fast. The gossip and rumours have moved away from broadcast news to social media. Some of the stories make me laugh they're so ridiculous. Someone tweeted that David Holmqvist used to kill cats as a child, and that he used to shoot them with an air rifle and then cook them and eat them. But I checked with Thord and there have never been any records of feline torture in Gavrik or in any of the surrounding towns. A cat was stolen once in the '80s, part of a divorce case gone sour, but no harm was done. Nils mentioned there was gossip back in the day that Holmqvist and Bengt Gustavsson, and one of the victims, were all lovers. He reckons our friendly neighbourhood hoarder and writer are both locked in the closet and don't want anyone knowing it. And then there was a rumour that Holmqvist was a world authority on the occult, that he wrote on the subject using pseudonyms and the book sales had earned him a fortune. Well, I've been inside his house and his research is eclectic to say the least, but I saw nothing on black magic or the dark arts. But then I didn't have time to look in that second guest bedroom, did I? I've checked Holmqvist's tax records and he's earned pretty well over the years, well above the national average, ten times more than the wood-carving sisters, but nothing extraordinary, nothing like Hannes Carlsson.

I drive past the strip club and see its heavy front door propped open with a bucket and mop. I call Thord and sync the phone to my hearing aid and I tell him what happened last night in that taxi. Not easy to explain how unnerving it was. I can hear the words as they leave my mouth and it sounds like Viggo pulled over and switched off the engine and then he hesitated to let me out and then he let me out. Thord tells me he takes this very seriously and he'll contact Viggo immediately and I say thanks.

Thirty kilometres further north, I turn off the E16 and into the petrol station. These places are mini-worlds of their own this far north. They are vital. With just one gas station, I can survive. I can fill my thirsty pickup and I can buy headache pills and I can pick up firewood and I can buy tampons and I can get basic foodstuffs – and I can meet a source for a chat and a cup of coffee.

There are no other cars around. I pull up to the pumps and fill up and move my truck away from the forecourt, and go in to pay.

Savanah's ten minutes late. She pulls up next to the truck in her old Saab and there's a stalemate for a moment as we both look at each other, both eager for the other person to make the transition into unknown territory. I open my door and get out and then I climb into the passenger side of her Saab. It smells like fake tan and those cardboard air fresheners in the shape of spruce trees. Pines. Can't get away from them.

'Thanks for this,' she says.

'No problem. Thanks for talking with me. You want to go inside and get a coffee?'

'Let's chat here.'

I nod and look around her car. There's a rip in the back-seat upholstery and a heavy book's lodged in the tear. Beside the book is a laptop and a heap of exercise books.

'You studying?'

'Part-time. At the university in Karlstad. Law and Psychology. I just started my second year.'

'Wow.'

'What do you mean, wow? Because I'm a dancer?'

'No, just that your course sounds kind of heavy. I did media studies and that was hard enough.'

'Oh.'

'What do you want to talk about? Mind if I record?'

She doesn't seem to hear me. She's looking forward now, her eyes glazed.

'It's Daisy,' she says. 'Well, it's everything, really. I'm starting to get scared. There's something happening, and somehow we're all involved in it.'

'How do you mean?'

'Daisy's getting paid more now, she told us. Well, she told Candy and me. Daisy's getting paid by Hannes not to dance for any other clients, not even to talk to any. It's like she's his personal property now, like he's in charge of her because he pays her more.'

'So she's not at the club any more?'

'No, she is. That's what he wants. He wants her at the club at her usual times, for when he drops in, but he doesn't want her flirting or dancing or even on stage when he's not there. He told her he has eyes on the inside and she reckons he means the guy working the bar. So she's earning double what we earn now – and she earned the most even before – and for less work.'

'What does your boss say?'

'She doesn't care two hoots. As long as we pay her our nightly fee to work, she's happy. She's a Madam of the old school and she likes things the way they used to be.'

'Like in the cathouse?'

'She was a genius Madam, so they say. She ran the place like it was Microsoft or something, and she was connected to all the important local people. She'd send out girls to private events, all sorts of weird stuff, big money, S&M games, dares, erotic asphyxiation. Sex with guns, crazy, nasty stuff. That was back when the mill had guys crawling all over it, before the big machines and computers came in. She was getting fully booked most nights, girls came from all over to work there. And then . . .'

She pauses and looks at me. Her eyes are shiny and her lips are almost blue without their lipgloss.

'And then business dried up because men started getting killed off by that ghostwriter and he was only eighteen years old at the time. They say he came into the cathouse one night looking to lose his virginity, and the mill men stared at him and then laughed at him, jeering and rubbing his hair and asking if he was there for a job and how much did he cost and would he do this thing to them and would he do that thing. So he ran out. Then the bodies started showing up in those woods; bodies with no eyes. They lost some of their best clients. They were either dead or else they stopped coming because it was too dangerous.'

'So she knocked it down and built the Enigma.'

'Well, she moved to Spain, you know that, right? She moved to Spain for years but still owned the land where the cathouse used to be. Came back a few years ago and built the club when she realised her money was gonna run out sooner than expected. There was three killings back when the cathouse was open. Then it shut and there was no more killings. Then the club opens up and we get two new killings. So, what I'm trying to tell you is the place is still cursed. The ground it's built on, not the building, it's bad ground.'

'Did David Holmqvist ever try to get into the club?'

'Thank God, no. Not that I've seen anyway. I would have heard about it if he had. But me and the girls have seen something. Well, I say *seen*, really we've felt something, someone sniffing around behind the club fence, past the end of the car park, you know. It's the edge of the woods there really. We reckon, well, we've all felt it, someone's out there watching the club, someone's spying on us.'

'How does Hannes Carlsson treat Daisy?'

Savanah snorts and clicks off her seatbelt.

'Real nice. He pays her double, you heard me say that, right? Double money, and he's not been rough, not done nothing she didn't want to do. He tried it a few times – some weird nasty shit with his poker buddies, she said. Some fucked-up game in one of them hunting towers, but she said no. I reckon he goes to someone else for all that, but I don't know for sure. He's one of them controlling types, like my ex. He's jealous as hell and he can't stand seeing her with anyone, not even for a chat. One night I saw Hannes come into the club and Daisy was talking to this lad at the bar. He was just a kid, some stag party from Hicksville-by-the-Bog. But the kid was cute, one of those tanned guys that works out and uses all the creams, he was a real cutie. Hannes went nuts. He grabbed the guy and threw him out the club, straight out the front door and into the snow. Daisy went after him, tears spraying out of her eyeballs like fire sprinklers, and Hannes was trying to drag him over to the motorway, probably to kill him or something. Daisy pulled him back and nothing else happened, but I saw he could be a nasty piece of work if he feels outranked or outmanned. Maybe he's got a needle dick but I wouldn't know because Daisy won't tell me.'

29

I drive north through open farmland dotted with clumps of leafless birch trees and piles of boulders. Birds circle overhead. The fields are waterlogged and the farms are small and marginal. I know because I've interviewed some of the local farmers and most of them this far north make their real money from winter snowploughing and gritting and salting, all paid for by the Kommun.

I turn off onto the mill access road. I want to see Hannes in his professional habitat, ask him some carefully worded questions about Daisy in front of his colleagues, just to see how he reacts. The barriers are down where the train tracks cross the road. I'm the only vehicle on either side of the railway. Thankfully there's no piercing sound, just flashing lights and a horizontal bar. A train comes from my left. Each carriage is loaded with hundreds of pine trunks. The trees have been stripped of their outer shells and stacked like pencils in a tin. Steel prongs hold the timber in place as it rattles north to the mill to be turned into toilet rolls and newspapers and banknotes. The train is long. Carriages of recently cut spruce, a dead forest moving from left to right as if on a showreel.

The barrier lifts. I drive over the uneven surface of the tracks and my phone rings. Private number.

'Tuva Moodyson.'

'Hello Tuva, it's Kent here from SPT Mills.'

'Hi, I'm on my way to you now. I'm about ten minutes away.'

'Well, I'm sorry to hear that, Tuva, because I have some disappointing news. You see, management have called a last-minute meeting that I will need to attend. It'll be in progress all afternoon so we'll have to rain-check your tour of the new bleach processers I'm afraid.'

'That's okay, I just need five minutes.'

'Why don't I email you later and we can talk dates then. My diary's pretty full.'

'Five minutes,' I say. 'Can we walk and talk?'

'No can do. But happy to reschedule. Now, I've got to go.'

The mill's chimney smoke is visible in the distance as I make a U-turn. There are piles of lumber stacked near the plant, and they're longer and taller than cruise ships. Kent's been badgering me for weeks to get exposure in the paper for his new machines and the local jobs they'll create. Is Hannes avoiding me? Is this cancellation his idea?

Back in the office I check in with Lena and Lars. Lena wants me to start writing my old stories as well as covering Holmqvist, now that the court hearing's been announced. She wants me to split it fifty-fifty with Lars so he can get back to working part-time. I agree but I have so much more I need to write about Medusa, so I'll just have to work nights. I've been in Toytown for three years and I'm going to get one prize-winning story out of it, or at least one piece that will get me noticed. The big city dailies might have better paper quality, their hacks might be household names, but nobody writes the victims' angle better than I do.

Lars barely looks at me. I draft a couple of quick slice-of-life articles about a new cycle path and the refurbishment of Ronnie's bar, and I feel nothing as I write the words. I used to take pride in these stories. The locals need to know so I need to write them, but now they seem pointless. I write them brainlessly and then I look up Rikard Spritzik's wife's contact details. Her name's Stina Johansson; she's kept her family name. And I know her, or of her, she's a doctor in the local *vårdcentral* surgery. She's never treated me when I've had an ear infection or complications with my aids, but I recognise her name. I find her home address and leave the office and get in my truck.

She lives in a smart neighbourhood, behind the liquorice factory, overlooking a wooded valley. It's close to Lena's place. Well-maintained little gardens and apple trees. I park on the street and knock on her front door. No reply. The lights are on so I knock again, and then I hear a dog barking and a girl with plaits in her hair comes to the door.

'Hi, your mamma home?'

'She's at work.'

At work? Same week as her husband's murder and she goes to work?

'Thanks, honey. Bye.'

I walk away from her and I'm frowning. Why did I call her honey? I never call anyone honey. I hate that kind of baby talk. And she was no baby, she was a teen, maybe fourteen.

But she is the exact same age as I was when Dad died. Her mum's left her to fend for herself just like mine did. Nobody to comfort her, nobody to explain. She's dealing with losing her dad and she's all on her own like I was. Like I am.

I drive to the *vårdcentral* surgery. I walk inside and take a pair of plastic blue shoe covers – there are hundreds of them stuffed inside a basket by the front door – and I slip them over my boots. I take a numbered ticket and sit down. I'm registered here so this should be the easiest way to meet Stina Johansson.

My number's called and I walk up to the reception and give my personal ID number and get told by a guy about my age to go to Dr Khan's room. I shake my head. I've prepared for this. I point to my ears and tell him I have an infection related to my aids and I want to see Dr Johansson. He fumbles and coughs and rattles though his notes like a newsreader with a broken autocue. He tells me to take a seat and he'll call me when Dr Johansson is free.

I wait for ten minutes before I'm called. I recognise her from the police press conference. Dr Johansson is kind-looking but her face is gaunt and her eyes are tired. I walk in and sit down.

'What can I do for you, Tuva?'

I sit down.

'I'm so sorry about your husband, Dr Johansson.'

She nods at me like she's heard this twenty times already today. 'Thanks. What can I help you with today?'

'I'm here to check that you're okay, actually.'

She frowns and looks uncomfortable. She's prettier than I remember from the cop show, weathered and wrinkled, but attractive.

'Me? Oh, I'm okay, considering. Now, I just have a ten-minute slot until my next patient. Please, what can I do for you?'

'I'm investigating whether David Holmqvist was working alone. Will you let me ask you a few quick questions?'

Johansson stiffens.

'Absolutely not.' She crosses her arms and her legs. 'How dare you come in here under false pretences? If there's nothing wrong with you, Tuva, then I must ask you to leave.'

'I'm sorry,' I say, trying to claw this back. 'I lost my dad as a teenager and I want to report this story in all its detail so that justice can be served and so that nobody else has to suffer and no more kids have to grow up without a father.'

'No.' She stands up and ushers me to the wide door of her office. 'Don't ever do this again. Leave us alone.'

I walk out towards the piles of magazines in reception. Her mobile rings. I hear her gasp and then I turn to see her lean against the frame of her wheelchair-accessible door. She's asking 'Why?' over and over again. I walk slowly back to her doorway, stepping softly and holding out my hands in a gesture of charity, of help. She looks at me, her eyes half-closed, and ends the call.

'Are you okay?' I place my hand on her arm. She's shaking. The receptionist guy and two patients peer around to look at us and I hold up my palm as if to say, 'it's okay, I've got this' and reverse into her room and close the door. She steps away and turns her back on me and takes three deep breaths. Then she turns to me, her skin pale, her face suddenly older than before.

'Just . . . Can you just leave me alone now, please.'

'Can I do anything to help?'

She looks at me like she's making a decision.

'That was my lawyer. The police just told her . . .' she takes another slow, deep breath. 'They'll probably have to let him go free.'

'Holmqvist?'

'They've got a little more time and then they'll have to let him go. My lawyer says they don't have enough evidence to charge him. I cannot believe this is happening.'

She looks around the walls of the office, at the filing cabinet and the wall-mounted defibrillator and the curtained-off bed.

'I'm sorry.'

'I've got to get home,' she says, gathering her handbag and her cycle helmet from under her desk. 'My daughter doesn't know yet, my lawyer says nobody knows yet, I have to get home to her.'

'Can I give you a lift?'

She looks at me and then looks at her cycling helmet.

'Okay. Thanks.'

We walk out to my truck, Stina whispering something to the receptionist as she passes him. We drive past ICA and I can see a white taxi parked close to Tammy's truck. It's a Volvo. My stomach tightens and I drive on. Within five minutes I'm back in the suburb I just came from.

'I want to help find the truth,' I say, looking forward at the road and choosing my words carefully. 'The bastard who did this needs to be caught, and I might be able to help. I want to write about it from every angle so maybe someone will come forward. There has to be someone around here who knows something and isn't saying.'

Stina looks at me.

'Two of my patients went missing in the '90s, both in October. One was found in Utgard forest, just like Rikard was.'

I glance over and see her touching a man's watch loosely strapped to her wrist.

'The other one was never found. They were both family men. The one they never found was recorded as missing. People think maybe he left the country.'

'Do the police know?'

'I told them all this already,' she says, running her fingers along the leather strap of the watch. 'But you know they're all related, right? That's half the bloody problem. Everybody here is related to one another. The anti-hunt guy in Mossen village, the one with the house full of junk, he's related to a judge in Karlstad. Björn, the police chief, he's the cousin of Hannes Carlsson, who runs the mill and the hunt and most other things around here. The troll carvers, they're both related to the priest at the church, and also to one of your colleagues, the old guy who used to do your job. But you probably knew that already. So, that's what you're up against here. It's like the Freemasons only worse. If you can do any better finding Rikard's killer, you do it, and I'll help in any way I can. GPs know a little bit about a lot of people.'

'I was wondering ...' I say, 'about your dog. How did it find its way back to you?'

'Police asked the exact same thing,' she says. 'Cab driver brought him to my house in the back of his Volvo. Picked him up near that digger storage yard outside town. Thank God he had his address on his collar, otherwise—'

I bite the inside of my mouth. 'What was the taxi driver's name?'

'No idea.'

I think back to that candlelit taxi. 'What did he look like?'

'Like a cab driver.'

I see the daughter with the plaits open Stina's front door with a confused expression as I pull up to her house again in my truck, this time straight into the paved driveway, this time with her mum next to me.

Stina hands me a card with her mobile number written on it.

'Find something. You can do this, you're from outside.'

30

We go to press tonight. Lena's rewriting one piece for me and I'm fixing the rest. As I work, I realise that this is the first elk hunt season where more than one murder has taken place. Or at least the first season where the police have found more than one body. It's what Lars calls 'escalation'.

I switch off my aids and bin the remainder of my lunch, and then I unscrew the cap and break the seal on a bottle of Coke. I sip and write, incorporating details from the latest police statement into my work. The police have found a boot print. This is new information. A full print close to the body of Rikard Spritzik in Badger Hollow, and also a partial print near the body of Freddy Malmström. Both with the same tread design, both a size 42. Same size as Holmqvist, but he doesn't own the matching boots. Unfortunately, half of Gavrik Kommun does. It was the bestselling outdoor boot sold in ICA Maxi last season and I'm wearing a pair right now.

I'm three-quarters through my Coke when I notice Lena walk in and point to the TV. I switch my aids back on. It's Björn, but there's no press conference, just him with his snap-together glasses, and Dr Stina Johansson, and the Karlstad homicide cop with the Bluetooth thing clipped to his ear. *Appeal for information. No detail too small. Very much an active investigation. Urge anyone to come forward.* Then Lena and Lars run past me to the front door of the office and Lena opens it and they both run out to the street. I follow them out but I can't make out what's being shouted.

It's David Holmqvist. He's being escorted from the police station to a private car, his lawyer's hand planted on his shoulder. I run to the pack of waiting journalists and cameramen but I've got no camera or Dictaphone with me. David's head hangs low and his shoulders are slumped and rounded. I watch the car drive away, snapping with my phone as the lawyer's Range Rover disappears down the street towards the liquorice factory. I look back at Thord and his face is as expressionless as a pebble and then I realise that I am being shut out.

'What's going on?' asks Lena. 'Every other journalist knew he was being released now.'

I look around at Slick-back and Fake Tan and Short Trousers, they're all there.

Lena, pointing towards the cop shop, says, 'Nobody told you, did they?'

Thord goes back into the police station and locks the door. I march back to my office and Lena goes back to work and I sit down and look at Lars.

'Why are they excluding me?' I ask.

He sits down behind his desk and pulls his glasses back down to rest on the indented bridge of his nose.

'I don't think they're excluding you, they're just not prioritising you any more. Chief Andersson's been running this town for decades. You come in, young hotshot from out of town, and you write in a way nobody in this town has ever seen before. Sure, they've seen that kind of reporting in the nationals, but not the *Posten*. I never wrote like that, not even close. Folks are worried about the town getting a bad name, some have said to me they think you're stirring up trouble as much as reporting it. Gavrik's not a wealthy town, people are just getting by and they don't want to see any more local firms going out of business.'

'Okay.'

'The articles you wrote last week, the ones linking Medusa to these deaths, asking all sorts of open-ended questions about how many more people will die, about when will the authorities bring in experts from outside, about how come the '90s murders were never solved – all that stirred up resentment. Björn's pissed.'

'I write the truth,' I say.

Lars picks up a box of Grimberg salt liquorice from his desk. It's the size of a matchbox and he opens the lid and pops a lozenge into his mouth.

'All kinds of truth out there.'

'Like the fact that you're related to the wood-carving sisters, Alice and Cornelia Sørlie? You didn't think to tell me?'

'We're not related,' he says. 'Not really. If we'd been blood relatives, you'd have known about it. Small town like this, you'd have known all about it. They're cousins of my brother's wife, that's all. I've met them at weddings, at funerals, at christenings. Seem all right to me, but if I find out one's been hunting down men in the woods I'll be sure to drop you an email.'

'You know why they left Norway? I've heard—'

'No idea,' he says, cutting me off and getting back to his typing.

That's the problem with a two-man office. When one person goes back to work in the middle of an argument, what the hell is the other one supposed to do? So I thump the keys of my computer and write gibberish for a while. I'm hot. I kick off my boots and leave them by the bin under my desk. I'm an outsider here. The police have stopped telling me what they'd usually tell me and now I have an urge to jump into my truck and drive to Stockholm and look out at the sea and at the open skies and order hot Sichuan food and listen to traffic. Just the thought of it calms me.

A journo from outside walks in and ignores the counter, just lifts the barrier and strolls towards Lena's office.

'Can I help you?' I ask.

He points to her door and then knocks on it and walks inside. I hear laughter and through the crack in the door I see them hug for a moment.

'*Svenska Dagbladet*,' Lars whispers to me.

I nod but I don't smile.

I watch the journo as he sits down in front of her desk. I can't hear what's said but I stare at the back of his head. I stare at his short grey hair and his pale blue collar and his navy jacket. He has an attractive back, groomed, a strip of tanned neck, broad shoulders tapering to a smooth waist, his tailored jacket skirting his torso. He's mid-fifties, I'd say. I can't hear the words but his voice is deep and he keeps his sentences short. Then he stands up and walks towards me and smiles and leaves the office.

Lena comes to her doorway.

'Police are looking for the barman at that strip club on the E16. Apparently he got the job with a false name. Connections to money lenders and unlicensed gambling, but they still don't have a genuine ID. Look into it.'

She closes her door. I email her everything I've written so far and step out for air. I've got a new lead, the scarred barman, and I'm happy about that. It's cloudy but dry and the air's laced with sugar. I walk a block to Mrs Björkén's haberdashery store and I go inside and the bell over the door tinkles. Nobody appears, but that's normal. I browse the buttons and the threads. This is my place, the place I come to when I need a moment to compose myself. I look at yarn of different colours and thicknesses and wool textures. I squeeze the springy balls and caress samples of felt. The needles and crochet hooks are displayed in size order, as are the pin cushions and safety pins. The shop, pine-clad, smells of my grandmother's apartment, all dust and tea and pressed petticoats.

'Can I help you, my dear?'

Jowls. Pretty smile. Long velvet skirt.

'Just browsing, Mrs Björkén, thank you. Working out what to buy for my next project.'

'Oh, do tell.'

'Just a scarf for my mother, nothing too complicated, something to keep the chill out this winter.'

'Very wise, my dear. She's a lucky one to have you.'

My innards pull tight inside my chest.

I thumb through some ribbon spools and thread bobbins. My heart rate slowing as I inhale the stale odours of the place.

'Thanks,' I say, opening the door. The bell tinkles. 'I'll be back again soon.'

I walk back to the office and sit at my desk. I type my password onto my screen and then a man walks into the reception area wearing a dark green cap and carrying a rifle.

31

I stare at the man. I can feel Lars staring at him and at the rifle pointing up at the ceiling.

'Don't worry, it's not loaded,' the man says with no hint of a smile.

'You can't bring that in here,' Lars says. 'Against the rules.'

The man cracks open the gun and places it on top of the counter and then he crosses his arms over his chest. Everything in the office suddenly feels lightweight and trivial next to that gun and its owner.

'My name is Martin Larsson. My brother was one of them that got killed twenty years ago in the woods nearby. I want to talk to whoever's in charge.'

'That'll be me,' I say. What am I doing? 'You have information for the paper?'

'You're in charge?'

He wants to talk somewhere private so I lead him out into the street to my truck. He looks at me suspiciously; doubly so once he spots my hearing aids. I tell him to leave his rifle in the office and he tells me he will not.

'You got ear problems?'

'I'm deaf. But don't worry, with these in I can hear every word you say.'

We get into my truck. It's parked facing the rear wall of the newspaper office like always. I grab the unopened bag of wine gums from the passenger seat and stuff it into the glove box. The man places his rifle down on the back seat of the Hilux like it's a sleeping toddler and he looks more relaxed now we're in the truck. I'm not worried being in here with him. Partly because it's my truck and partly because he gives off a gentle vibe and partly because Lars knows I'm here.

'Didn't mean to frighten you and your man in the office back there. I don't live nearby here. They're changing the tyres over on my truck, putting new winters on, so I don't have nowhere to leave my firearm right now.'

I shake my head dismissively. He's maybe a foot taller than me with a broad neck and large rough hands. I feel the truck leaning to his side.

'Who was your brother?'

'Fredrik Larsson, he passed in '93. Lived here and worked at the SPT pulp mill up the road. I'm based in Jönköping so don't often get up this far north, not back then neither. Saw that ghostwriter got arrested again and finally thought my family could put all this to bed. Then the ghostwriter gets released and I don't know what to damn well think, pardon my language.'

'You want a coffee? There's a McDonald's five minutes away, we could sit outside and you can keep your gun locked in the truck.'

'Sure,' he says. 'Sounds good.'

I back up and drive to McDonald's. We end up using the drive-thru for coffee and donuts and sit in the car park with the windows cracked open. I can see Tammy's takeout van in the distance, steam rising from its roof.

'Fred thought someone was spying on him back in the week before he died. We talked on the phone, joked it was the government or something. I reckon he was picked, y'know. I think the Medusa coward that done this to my big brother had him in his sights for a while before he pulled that trigger.'

'Any idea who picked him?'

He shakes his head.

'I've talked to a lot of people in the area about the shootings, Mr

Larsson. Can I run a few names by you maybe and you can tell me if you recognise anyone, or if anything rings a bell in your head.'

He takes a slurp of coffee. He's removed the lid because he can't seem to master drinking out of the little hole in the plastic.

'Fire away.'

'Well, let's start with Holmqvist. I think many people still suspect him, at least for some of the deaths.'

'Seems like a first-rate weirdo to me, but Fred never talked about him, never talked about no book writer.'

'Okay, what about Bengt Gustavsson? He's a retired soldier, lives in Mossen village.'

He shakes his head.

'Viggo Svensson? He's a taxi driver from Mossen.'

He shakes his head and bites a chunk out of a sugar-dusted donut.

'Two sisters who carve model trolls, Cornelia and Alice Sørlie?'

'Sorry, nope, never heard of none of them. Fred and me didn't talk much,' he looks down at the half-donut in his hand. 'We shoulda talked more than we did.'

'What about Hannes and Frida Carlsson? They live at the end of the road in Mossen village, at the centre of Utgard forest. He works in the pulp mill that employed your brother, Fred.'

'He the boss?'

'One of them, yes. He runs the—'

'Well, Fred did mention his boss a few times. Said he was breaking his balls over Fred's holiday time around his wedding if I remember right. Fred wanted a decent honeymoon and the boss was having none of it. Fred reckoned the boss hated him cos Fred got chatting to the boss's missus at the Christmas party the year before. Well, I asked Fred if he was flirting with her cos he was a good-looking lad was Fred and he had an eye for the ladies, but he tells me no, just being friendly. You reckon that mill boss is the killer?'

'I don't know about that, but I think you should tell the police what you just told me.'

'Well, maybe.'

'And one more thing,' I say. 'I hope you don't mind me asking this, but I've been talking to some old-timers who used to visit a place between here and the mill. It's a strip club now.'

He smiles at me and I see sugar crystals stuck to his lips. 'You mean, The Love Shack?'

'I've never heard it called that. That was the name of the brothel?'

'No, it never had no name I don't think. That's just what Fred and me used to call the place. Fred went there a fair bit I think before his wedding. He used to complain to me about the steep prices. He'd go there with a big-spender mate from the mill. Pete, I think his name was. But Fred never went back after he got married, he turned to his other vices; at least that's what he told me. He was a red-blooded young guy, y'know, into hunting and gambling and fighting. Told me he never stepped a foot inside that place after he took his vows.'

'He ever mention a man who worked there? A barman?'

'Never mentioned no men. Those places don't usually have no men working in them.'

I drop Martin Larsson off at the police station with his rifle cocked over his arm. I park and walk past my office and on up the street. The heavy glass door of Björnmossen's hunting store squeaks as I open it.

'You here to shut me down, Moodyson?'

Benny Björnmossen's sitting behind the till on a brown leather stool.

'Just browsing, I need a few things.'

He grunts and I pace around the creaky floorboards checking out racks of wet-weather gear and fishing tackle. The store smells of waxed jackets and cigarettes and rubber boots. Behind the till is a wall of small wooden boxes on shelves all behind a locked wire screen. Ammunition. Each box has a printed label with an excellent name like Hornet or Winchester or Remington or Magnum or Krag or Ruger or Beowulf.

I look at GPS tracking devices designed to be strapped to hounds. I check out scopes and high-energy dog food and telescopic tripods.

'You have any night-vision binoculars, Benny?'

He walks over to me like a cowboy in a western. His legs are bowed and I can see red bumps all over his neck and chin. At first I think they're razor burn, but as he steps closer I can see them on his wrists too. They're mosquito bites.

'Now, listen to me, if you can't see it properly then you can't shoot it properly, you understand what I'm saying?'

I nod.

'You can hunt from sunrise, or an hour before sunrise if you really know what you're doing, until sunset. That's the code. You only shoot when you can see real good so there's no need for no night-vision technology.'

'I'm not hunting,' I say. 'I want to watch bats and birds of prey, that's all.'

'Well, why didn't you say so? You like raptors, eh?'

I nod. I don't even know what a raptor is.

'Well, then, that's a different thing altogether, but still ain't got no night-vision technology in stock. Those right there should do you pretty good.' He points to the cabinet in front of me and I notice he's wearing a diamond ring, a solitaire, the kind you expect to see on a woman's hand. 'Them Leicas. Nice magnification, easy to use, anti-glare lenses. You buy them and you won't go far wrong.'

'I need some other bits and bobs, too.'

He scratches a bump on the side of his neck. 'Bits and bobs?'

'I need a big torch. I need the best bug repellent you've got. I need something I can use against animals.'

'Do you mean a gun?'

'No, something more like bear-spray or pepper spray.'

'I just got guns. Oh, and a catapult, I guess. Use them for throwing fishing bait, but you put a stone in there you could do some real injury to an animal I'd say.'

'I'll take it. And I need a backpack, a light one.' He hands me a dark green backpack. 'And a knife, please. Whatever you think is the best one.'

'I'm not being funny, miss, but you want to pay me all this money so you can go look at bats and birds?'

'I don't have anything else to spend my salary on round here, do I, Benny? I need a cap, too, one of those waxy green ones with ear flaps to keep the rain off my hearing aids.'

'You birdwatching in town or out in the country?'

'Both.'

'Well, I'd say you better take this one, then.'

He hands me a bright orange cap with reflective ear flaps.

'Don't want you being Medusa's next victim, now do we?'

'I'll take both caps,' I say. 'How much?'

He walks over to the till and adds up all the items. As my Visa card is being processed – cards take a long time to go through up here in Gavrik – Benny Björnmossen looks at me.

'I'm just gonna come straight out and say it. I reckon you'd best be careful how you write your newspaper. This here's a small town, and we got lots of jobs depending on tourism and field sports up here.'

'I write the truth,' I say, almost shouting. Then I calm myself. 'But I'm also conscious of the community. I'm careful.'

'All right. Well fine, just mind you are,' he says, pushing my knife and my boxed binoculars into brown plastic bags. 'Gavrik's a nice town, but some of your stories make out like it's some kind of hell-hole.' He scratches his neck. 'Would hate for your paper to get any problems.' He hands back my Visa card and looks at me. 'Mind you do stay conscious.'

32

I write the last of my pieces and then email them through to Lena to edit and arrange. I tell her my plan as I walk out the door.

'Well, take precautions,' she says.

I head home and find my mountain bike in the shelter by my apartment building. It's crusted with grime, and it takes me about six attempts to remember the combination to the lock.

I throw the bike in the back of my truck and drive west towards Mossen village. Past the supermarket and under the motorway and on towards the forest. It's windy and it smells like it might rain. I park up in the digger graveyard and it feels okay to be back here, considering Viggo's romantic shitshow. I hide the Toyota as best I can between an old horsebox and a rusting Honda excavator. The backpack's covered in labels and tags so I pull them all off. I stuff a packet of wine gums inside, and the knife in its stiff leather sheath, and Tammy's bear-spray and the catapult. I'm not confident about the catapult at all. I pack 'jungle strength' roll-on insect repellent, and then finally, carefully, I place the Leica binoculars on top. They'd cost about triple what I was expecting. My truck's a rental, so aside from my laptop, these binoculars are now my most valuable possession in the world.

I drag my hair back in a ponytail, and pull on the waxed green cap, the one Benny Björnmossen said was suitable for town use only. But as I have no intention whatsoever of straying more than two metres away from the Mossen gravel track, I'd say my chances of getting shot are roughly nil. I need camouflage, not protection.

I pull on the backpack and tighten the straps and then I drag out my bike. I lock my truck and gaze over towards the forest. The outer pines look like a tidal wave. I start to cycle, the seat uncomfortable between my legs, my balance a little unsteady over the saturated gravel. Still no rain, but it feels like it could come any second. I pull out onto the road and increase my speed and move up through the gears with audible clicks. The moist air freezes my cheeks and I get feedback in my hearing aids. I have about a kilometre more of smooth asphalt before it all turns to shit so I decide to enjoy it. No cars in front and none behind. I pass two magpies on the verge and they look like they're not getting on.

The turning to Mossen is marked by a small yellow signpost: *Mossen 6km.* I don't know which part of Mossen that six kilometres refers to. I'd say Frida's place is about fifteen kilometres and Bengt's caravan is about two. I guess they just picked somewhere in the middle, maybe the hill.

Now that Holmqvist has been released without charge I can feel a countdown ticking, an upturned egg timer losing sand grain by grain until the next hunter shows up dead and eyeless. The experts have said the killer is likely to be local to Utgard, with knowledge of the woods and good outdoor skills. If the villagers were normal I'd probably extend my search but one of them's hiding something, I can feel it.

Slower now, swerving to miss puddles that could be as deep as a dinner plate or as deep as a saucepan. Bikes don't come with rear-view mirrors so I can't see back to the asphalt, just forward to a mean alley through densely-packed spruce trees. The air smells musty, like a carpet that's been left out in the rain, and there are mushrooms everywhere, even some growing out of the gravel track itself. There are dozens of varieties, tall and pale, squat and dark, spongy and grey. They don't look tasty, not like a mushroom you'd get on top of a restaurant burger. Most look worm-riddled and wet. I get up to the first bend and push on, my legs getting used to the exertion, my senses attuned to the trees each side of me like some kind of primal defence. As long as I'm on the track, I'm okay. I'm going to be fine.

Bengt's place is up ahead. There are stacks of wooden pallets piled behind the house, almost up to the roofline. They're covered in ivy, an even thicker blanket than what's clinging and climbing up the rest of the walls. He lives in a house full of God-knows-what wrapped in a green cloak of poison. No wonder he moved out to the garden. I cycle past the front windows, two downstairs and two upstairs, curtains drawn across them all. Rare to see curtains in Sweden. My apartment doesn't have any. Up here in Värmland, light is at a premium.

I speed up after I pass the house, and cycle towards the caravan and the vegetable garden. The leaves and stalks are bright and they're the only colours I can see: vivid greens and dark reds and purples. His patch is immaculate. I move down to fifth gear, my thighs pumping the pedals to go faster so I can move past the caravan unnoticed. No lights are on. My heart's beating hard now and I'm breathing deep gulps. The air smells pretty good along this stretch, like rubbing pine needles between your fingertips. I keep going, eyes probing in front for the passing place I've assigned to be my parking bay for the next few hours. I think I see it, but it turns out to be a flat rock where no spruce can grow. I ride on and the air changes. It thickens and becomes more still and it smells bad, like a wet dog with indigestion. I brake sharply and miss the passing place and jump off my bike. The earth's soft. Gravel with a coating of leaves and needles and crushed pine cones. I walk my bike back to the half-moon of extra gravel placed on the left side of the track so two cars can pass each other, and peer into the tree cover. It's 4pm and the light's dropping. I'm not here for night-time surveillance and I'm sure as hell not here for a walk in the woods.

I pull my bike over knobbly roots and mossy stumps. I'd planned to drag it maybe five trees deep off the track and drop it, so it wouldn't be visible. In reality, I pull it two trees deep behind the track and lean it up against a dying birch. I want to be able to find it again quickly if I need it.

Taxi's probably still working so I'll do Hoarder first. Tonight is about downhill residents, I'll tackle uphill when I'm more experienced, when I can handle it.

I walk on the edge of the track, ready at any moment to dive into the trees if a van comes by. I pull out my bug repellent and roll it over my face and wrists. I already have something buzzing close to my ear and it's driving me crazy, like a siren inside my hearing aid. And then the sting comes. Not from a mosquito but from the repellent itself. My skin feels like it's on fire, my eyelids burning, my upper lip stinging – like someone pushed a bouquet of nettles into my face.

It settles down a little and I calm myself and tuck my jeans into my socks and my jacket into my jeans. It's not a good look.

I had planned to peer into Hoarder's caravan from the edge of his land. Now I see that the trees are too thick and it just won't work. I cross the road and jump a ditch full of pale brown water and marestail weeds lying down in the direction of flow like kelp strands in a tide. I move behind a pine but it feels too exposed so I go one tree deeper. Looking up, I see only branches, countless scratchy branches piled up towards the sky. The bottom few are dead and the rest are weighed down with wet needles. I put my sheathed knife into my jacket pocket and then pull it back out and open the sheath and touch it and then close the sheath. I place the bear-spray down at my feet. The binoculars have *Made in Germany* etched into them and they feel heavy, reassuringly heavy. It takes me a while to get the focus right and to work out how to see one image instead of a Venn diagram of two intersecting images. I rest my chest against the trunk of the tree and watch.

I can hear his wind chimes, faint and distant. I zoom in on them, the vertical bars clanging together in the light breeze. I focus up on the bedroom windows of the house itself. There are crucifixes in most of them. Hadn't noticed before. The glass is dirty but I can see little objects arranged on the window sills, organised next to each other: little figures and models, and one looks like an angel complete with a set of lace wings. The upper part of the pane has been boarded up and I can see ivy growing through the wooden cladding in several places, growing into the house and inside the wall cavities and eating it up.

There are piles of firewood stacked neatly between the house and the outdoor toilet. They're covered in tarp sheets. How does Bengt light a fire if he can't get inside his own house? Is there a back door? I notice a black cable on top of the tarps, a thick electrical cord joining the house to the caravan.

I pull back from the trunk of the spruce to adjust my position but the tree's holding me. There's a thick trickle of amber, or spruce sap, whatever it's called, dribbling down through the grooves of the rough bark and it's making my jacket sticky. I've got tree jam gumming up the front zip. As I try to pull it out of the zip it just sticks my fingers together.

I pan over to the caravan and all I can smell is gooey pine sap. Lights approach from my left, headlight beams scattered by the pine trunks. It's Viggo's white Volvo. I pull myself tight to the tree to stay hidden and then turn back to the caravan once the taxi's passed by. I don't want to pry, and I don't want to watch Bengt doing anything too private, but I have to see this. A little invasion of privacy to potentially save lives and write a really good piece. No-brainer. And anyway, Lena's sanctioned it, she told me it's okay. I'll take my time and look for anything suspicious. Anything out of place. Tracks, an outbuilding, something that doesn't fit. If the police won't do their job right I'll have to give them a push. Although I didn't fill Lena in on any specifics, and she didn't ask for any.

Gunshot.

I spin round and face the blackness of pure, unadulterated nature.

It is endless. The shot's echoing imperfectly from a thousand cylin-drical tree trunks and the boom's splitting and spreading through Utgard forest. I have no idea where the shot came from or how far away the gun is. My back felt vulnerable before, but now I feel like one of those paper targets Viggo showed me in his candlelit taxi. Like I have concentric circles painted on my back. But I'm too close to the track to be in any danger. I'm okay here, right? I'm fine.

Well, fuck me. I look through the Perspex caravan window and see Bengt and he's as bald as an egg. He's wandering back and forth and I guess he's hung his wig up for the evening. I can see his head but not his hands. He could be listening to the radio or making a bomb or loading a rifle and I have no way of telling. Instinct tells me he's probably okay. Then again, instinct told me Viggo was okay.

It's getting darker. I move out of my position having gleaned nothing useful at all. I walk up the edge of the track, my legs a little weary from the cycling. I go past the passing place, the area where I know my bike's hidden, and walk on. I kick a plastic gravel bin and then turn right before I get to Viggo's dark red cottage. There's some sort of wooden tower through the trees so I walk towards it. There's nobody up there. It's only about three metres or so off the ground, facing a swampy open area buzzing with flies and midges. I climb and the wet birch ladder feels soft and clammy in my hands. It's half-rotten. And then I'm up and it feels great to be off the ground, a layer of clear air between me and the writhing forest floor.

Towards Viggo's house and the track, there are strings of red tape. I know these indicate directions that hunters can't shoot at from the stand. Last year I wrote a short piece about local kids moving the tapes around on elk towers and the risks that posed. On the other side, towards the marsh, there's no tape. I stare at the red cottage, at the lights and the crumbling wall surrounding the garden.

My view isn't as clear as it was of Hoarder's house. There are more trees, and the branches are thicker at this height. I'm sheltered by a corrugated-steel roof topped with a layer of moss and pine needles as thick as a mattress. Viggo's security lights illuminate his garden and the track, bathing the land so that his CCTV cameras can see everything. It's a beacon of light in a dark, dark place.

I can see him at the kitchen window. Viggo's either cooking or washing up, maybe making something for Mikey. In the garden I can see a mechanical log-splitter and a set of rusting free weights, and in the middle of the lawn there's a car battery complete with jump leads. Black and red. It's just sitting there on the grass, close to a puddle, and the clips at the end of the cables are underwater. Lots of boot prints, lots of mud. He has five trees dotted around his small garden. They're fruit trees of some kind: gnarly old twisted things with sagging branches held up by timber planks and scaffolding poles. Mikey's built dens at the bases of most of them, collections of sticks and logs to make himself little hideaway places. I remember the duvet dens I used to build in my teenage bedroom. Somewhere to escape. I'm pleased these stick dens are here, safe little shelters just for him.

There's something leaning up against the loose garden wall. I adjust the zoom dial on my binoculars. It's a pile of something on my side of the stones, so not on Viggo's actual land. It's a grey pile of something. The light's getting too low now and the security lights don't reach this far. My eyes are straining to make out the details. I take a wine gum from the open pack in my jacket pocket and let it melt on my tongue. It's a white one, a lucky hit, pear flavour, my absolute all-time number one favourite. It's far better than any real pear I've ever eaten. I reckon I'm doing okay considering I'm crouched inside a fucking elk shooting tower in Utgard forest, so I decide to call it a day and go back to get my bike. I climb down the slippery ladder and my boots find the soft moss once more. The ground is never flat here. It's never flat and it's never reliable and it's never uniform. There are holes and roots in unexpected places; animal warrens and brambles where I don't need them and where I don't want them. The forest is almost black and Viggo's lights are the only real comfort save for a few stars above. I walk as quietly as I can to the wall of his garden, and then walk along it to find out what that pile is. I'm crouching to keep my face, the least camouflaged part of me, out of sight from the house.

I tread on it before I know what it is. Squinting, I look down. It crunched when my boot pressed down into it. The pile resting against the wall is almost as tall as I am. It's a pile of mice and rats. The bottom half is all bones and worms but the top part is a furry blanket of fresh cadavers. I miss a breath, not wanting to inhale any of this. I sidestep and dash out to the track, only a few metres in front, and then hop the ditch, chest pounding. The passing place was here but now it's gone. I look back, then in front. I absolutely do not want to be here. I stagger towards Hoarder's house and pass a bend that I've never even seen before, and then I find the passing place and my bike. I drag it out to the track but weeds keep tugging it back to the darkness; fronds and thorns tangling in the front spokes and curling round the pedals and holding on to the brake cables. I yank it free and jump on my saddle and ride back towards asphalt.

33

I'm driving to work. The sun isn't quite up and my hair's wet and I have a limp piece of toast in my right hand. My phone rings as I'm pulling into my parking space.

'Tuva Moodyson.'

'Hello Tuva, this is Doctor Schenker from Karlstad hospital. I'm calling about your mother.'

My heart flips over in my chest and my tongue pulls tight as if something's yanking it down from inside me.

'Is now a good time to talk?' she asks.

'Is she okay?'

'It's nothing terribly urgent, but I wonder if we could talk in person. Are you planning to visit your mother in the coming days?'

'This weekend.'

'Ah, well, I'm not in this weekend. Will you be calling in before that?'

The doctor has the tone of an aunt who doesn't want to appear blunt but does want to tell me what to do.

'I'm coming down this weekend to see Mum and spend some time with her. I'm working until then.'

'Very well,' she says. 'Then the telephone will have to do. Mrs Moodyson's treatment is now in its final stage and she's weakening rather quickly, I'm sorry to say.'

My heart stops beating.

'Her doses have been increased somewhat. We're managing the pain. I think it's a very good idea if you visit her this weekend.'

'Well,' I say. 'That's what I'm going to do. I'll absolutely be there. Is there something specific you need to tell me?'

'I just wanted to keep you informed, Tuva. I know it's a lot for you to deal with.'

My voice starts to crack. 'Is there any other treatment you could try?'

'We're doing all that we can for her.'

Tears are coming but I stop them in their tracks. 'Thanks, Doctor. Thanks for calling.'

I end the call and stare through my chipped windscreen at the brick rear wall of the office, and at its black door and three concrete steps. I rub my eyes and drag my fingertips down my cheeks until they're resting by my lips. I look up at the sky. It's my way of looking at Dad, even though I don't believe in heaven or God. I look up into the sky, or even at a white ceiling at a push, and get a jolt of reassurance, like I'm not alone with all of this.

Once this is all over, once the Utgard killer is caught, maybe I could take some time off work, go part-time for a while. She'll need me. Just to be there. I'm not sure weekend visits will be enough to cover all the things we need to get through. We have to talk about what's happened, for her sake as much as for mine. I turn off my heated seat and switch off the ignition and wipe my eyes. Everything goes quiet.

I go into the office and there's a fresh stack of *Postens* on the front counter. It's even taller than last week. Murder's good for business.

At my desk I scan the Kommun memos for new stories but my mind's on autopilot. My heart and my stomach are draining down all my energy so my brain's left with just a trickle. I'm at that point where everything is almost too much but not quite. I'm not at the quitting stage or the running away to Bali stage; I'm at the tired and empty plateau I reach before pulling myself back from the brink and getting on with it. I sit and twiddle my mouse cable in my fingers and wonder if my hair could turn white in a week like Mum's did. Maybe if I was in love, and that love was ripped away from me. Maybe the colour in my hair would go and my warmth would go with it. Maybe I'd go beyond the plateau and sink to the bottom like Mum. Sink down and down and sit at the very bottom and care only for myself and not really live ever again. Maybe I'd just exist and never come back up and just wait down there to die. Maybe I would. Then again, maybe I wouldn't.

The office is comforting somehow. At least it's that. Nils is annoying Lars, teasing him about last night's football match. Lena's door's closed and she's probably reading *The New York Times* or *The Guardian*, something landmark and international, because that's what she normally does on a Friday morning after a print run.

It's quiet. Aside from familiar voices and the hum of computers, and two people who walk in to buy papers and deposit coins in the tin box, it's pretty quiet. My hearing aid beeps its final beep and I remove it from my left ear and open the battery compartment and pop the battery out. It's the size of a flattened pea. I throw it in the recycling box and take a new one from my key fob and pull off the tiny sticker and place the battery inside and close the lid. I hook it back over my ear and switch it on, and then I hear the manufacturer's jingle.

I haven't done much with my morning. I've scanned emails and checked the local websites I always look at but what's the bloody point. Having an unknown murderer loose in Toytown is difficult to ignore. There's no new information. No news on the strip club barman. I make a note to visit the owner again, and I'll to try to meet Savanah when she's back up from Karlstad. The barman seemed nice enough to me, but then maybe serial killers usually do.

My stomach rumbles because one piece of underdone toast isn't enough. I grab my coat and my boots and head out into the street. It's windy; leaves tumbling along the pavement and magazine pages flapping and flipping down the drainage gulley. I spot Frida stepping out of the haberdashery.

'Tuva, fancy seeing you here.'

'Hi,' I say looking at her perfect make-up and her immaculate hair and wondering why she bothers. Nobody else in Gavrik does. 'I'm just popping out to buy a sandwich from the newsagent.'

'Do you know that guy?' she asks.

'What guy?'

'There's been a guy watching you through the window. I saw him when I was paying for my ribbon. He left a minute ago, went that way.'

She points towards ICA.

'Probably an admirer,' she adds, with a glint in her eye. 'Can you bunk off and join me for a coffee? We can go to the hotel, they're open every day at the moment, what with all the new custom from out of town.'

Murder's good for business.

'Sure. I've got time.'

She smiles with her eyes and we walk towards the steaming brick chimneys of the liquorice factory. The wind's blowing hard to the east so I can't smell the place at all but I can smell lily-of-the-valley, it's coming off Frida in wafts.

'After you, beauty before age,' she holds the door open for me.

The reception is silent. This really is a mausoleum of a hotel. There's a living room, home-sized, and a thermos of coffee, with UHT pots of milk, and paper sachets of sugar and sweetener, and plastic spoons. I can see a bin with an ICA carrier bag lining it. There are six hospital-style chairs, all upholstered in 1970s fabric, and a display case of tourist information leaflets. There are probably forty plastic slots in the display case and only six are filled. The owner's spread them out so it looks better. Tours of the liquorice factory all of thirty metres away. Camping. Fishing. Summer caravans. An official Kommun welcome leaflet. Hunting season information complete with dates and maps.

'You look pale, Tuva. Are you getting enough sleep with all the work you're doing?'

'I'll catch up on the weekend.'

Her handbag is next to her foot and I can see there's a novel in there, next to some new cotton bobbins. The book looks second-hand and the cover shows a man and a woman on horseback.

'I read every one of your articles now that I know you. You write very well. I never really noticed them until I met you in person.'

I realise she's the first person outside of the *Posten* to say this to me about my writing. I heard it a lot in London from friends and acquaintances, but never from a local reader and never from Mum.

'Thanks, that's kind of you to say. But how are you managing with all the press coverage right in your own backyard.'

'My own backyard?' she looks aghast.

'Mossen, I mean. Utgard forest.'

'I'm okay with it all, doesn't really affect me. But Hannes isn't so happy and he's not sleeping well either. He looks haggard and I think he needs a mini-break. I was thinking of Barcelona, get some winter sun.'

'I can imagine all this pressure,' I say, looking straight at her, 'with a killer out there somewhere, can put a strain on a marriage.'

'Well, not really. I hope you don't mind me saying, but you can't really know about these things until you've been married yourself. Is there a suitor on the horizon, some dashing young carpenter or businessman?'

'Nah,' I say. 'Married to the job.'

'Well, you'll need a man sooner or later. It's a big bad world out there Tuva and we need protecting. And that clock's always ticking.'

She points to my midriff and I almost spit my coffee in her face.

'I imagine that Hannes . . .' I say, trying to stay calm. 'I imagine he's a good protector?'

Frida pours a second cup of coffee for us both and smiles warmly.

'The best. He'd take a bullet for me, that one, and I would for him. Ever since we were itty-bitty, he's kept an eye out for me. Anyone tried anything, he'd see them off. Men don't mess with Hannes, they know it won't end well for them.'

'I did have a boyfriend in London,' I say. Frida lights up and sits up straight and slaps her palms down on her knees.

'I knew it. Tell me everything.'

'Nice guy, we had fun. But he had a problem.' I look at her closely now, I focus in on her eyes. 'He liked strippers, dancers, escorts, that kind of thing.'

She looks down at her coffee and then looks back up at me.

'Well,' she says, 'Well, I'm sorry to hear that, Tuva. You deserve better than him, I can tell you. I guess this so-called man is still in London?'

I nod.

'Well, good riddance to bad rubbish, sweetie. You find yourself a good local man who'll take care of you.'

'Hannes has never . . .?'

Her eyebrows shoot up, stretching her face. Frida's flawless foundation cracks slightly from the tension and I notice the crows feet around her eyes.

'Hannes? Wholesome as they come, that's what my dear mother used to say. He's a big oaf sometimes, sure, gambles too much, but none of that dirty stuff. You think I'd put up with that?'

I can't work out if she doesn't know about Hannes's little pastime, or if she's in denial and too scared to upset her perfect marriage, or if she just thinks it's none of my business.

'You did well to rid yourself of that dirty London boy,' says Frida. 'I'll ask around and see if anyone's single at the moment. What's your type? I heard you had a thing for,' she pulls close to me and looks around conspiratorially, 'Thord.'

'Thord's like a brother, that's all. I guess I don't have a type as such.'

'Oh, everybody has a type, Tuva.'

DARK PINES

'Well, I guess,' I scan her eyes again, 'I guess I like everyone. A very broad spectrum.'

She swallows whatever words were coming out of her mouth and looks me up and down as if searching for an obvious sign she's missed.

'You mean?'

I nod.

'Oh,' she says. 'You mean?'

I hold her gaze. I can feel her brain whirring behind her eyes.

'I see, well, okay. One of my schoolteachers was like that and she was actually quite ...' she tails off. 'You're keeping your options open, I suppose.'

'Yes.'

She laughs a little, then places her hand on my shoulder. 'I'm sorry, I sounded like my grandmother just then. I'm just, you know, a little out of touch in this place.' She takes a deep breath and rubs my shoulder gently. 'I'm pleased you told me, I guess it's not easy being different, especially here. Now, come on, let's get out of this dusty old trap.'

We walk out, me holding the door open for Frida this time. She looks at me warily as she passes, and the wind eddies up from the pavement. It's cool but dry and its changed direction. It's liquorice wind now, all sweet and aniseed. Frida gives me a hug, a hug with a great deal of air between us, and says goodbye and heads back towards the supermarket. I'm light-headed after my coffee and my stomach feels more empty than ever, but I'm glad I told her.

210

34

I walk back to the office and stand in the doorway for a moment, watching Frida's perfect hair as she saunters off down the street and turns back into Mrs Björkén's haberdashery store. Then I turn and walk towards the police station.

Inside, it's warm and smells of disinfectant. There's a ticket-tape machine in the centre of the room, and above the pine counter the number seven is displayed on a screen. I take a ticket and ring the electronic doorbell button that's screwed down onto the counter.

Thord walks out and smiles at me. He's got a nice jaw but I reckon he could probably floss with a baseball bat.

'You here to report a crime?'

'Thank God, no. I think we've had enough. I was wondering if you might have a minute for a chat, though? Fancy getting lunch? Burger?'

'Would love to, but I can't abandon this place. I'm home alone, you might say. But I could let you come back here for a coffee if you'd like? Not strictly supposed to but you won't tell nobody, will you?'

I walk through the heavy door with the key-code lock and back into the inner sanctum of the police station. There are five desks and two of them are completely empty. Filing cabinets line the walls just like they do in my office. They're the exact same models by the look of them. At the back of the room, there's a corridor leading away to the left.

'What's back there?' I ask.

'The cells.'

'Can I have a peek?'

'Don't see why not, there's nobody in them.'

We walk around the corner. Three cells side by side. I expected bars and three adjoining cages like you see in the movies, but it's just three distinct rooms with walls and toilets and doors.

'Which one was Holmqvist in?'

Thord points to the cell on the right.

'You think he's innocent?' I ask.

Thord taps the side of his head. 'Open mind. Dave's stranger than a blizzard in June and the Chief can't stand the sight of him, but my gut tells me he ain't one to kill nobody.'

'Not what the media thinks.'

'Well, pardon my French,' says Thord, 'but what the crap do they know about anything? Present company excepted, of course. Ain't a scrap of physical evidence.'

We walk back to the main office and he brings me a mug that reads *Protect and Serve Coffee.* The inside of the mug is stained brown and bears the scars of a thousand stirs.

'You seem relaxed,' I say, 'considering there's a killer on the loose.'

'I'm not relaxed, I can tell you that. This week I've accrued more overtime than any week in my career to date. I'll be needing a vacation soon or else I'm gonna hit a wall.'

'Any developments on the Utgard bodies?'

'Direct as ever. The Chief told me to be careful what I say around here, he's stuck between you writing God-knows-what in your paper, and the boys from Karlstad homicide breathing down his neck every five minutes. They're taking the lead on this now although Chief reckons they don't know one end of a Scots pine from the other. We're still talking to people of interest, but could be that it was just a wanderer that's been and gone like the last time. Trouble is, killing in a hunting forest in October – with guns going off left, right and centre, with no good tracks, with no witnesses or CCTV– it doesn't give us much to go on, now does it?'

'You must have something.'

He bites his lower lip. 'Chief told me to keep this discreet but I reckon you'll need to know about it sooner or later. Ballistics got back to us. They reckon the rifle that shot the bullet that killed Freddy Malmström was a Mauser 8mm, old World War II bolt-action thing.'

'World War II?'

He nods. 'Five-round clip. Karabiner 98k is the proper name for it. Made them by the million, still pretty common as hunting rifles, not bad guns if you got a scope on 'em.'

'Are there any registered around Gavrik?'

'A few but none that have been fired anytime recent. We'll keep looking but they're compact rifles, about a metre long, easy to hide.'

'Were all the victims shot with the same gun?'

'I reckon so, but the white coats'll need a few more days before they can tell us.'

'Do any of the registered owners have a motive?'

'Well now, if you look hard enough then just about everybody in this town has a motive to kill just about everybody else. Freddy and Rikard were two straight-talking, hard-working, stand-up fellas. They were both family men who paid their taxes and went to church and never caused no trouble. So to kill them and then do that to their . . .'

He blinks three or four times.

'What about the villagers? What about Viggo Svensson?'

'I gave him a good talking-to after what you told me, I don't think he'll be bothering anyone like that again.'

'Apparently, Viggo can outshoot just about anyone around here. Have you checked his weapons?'

Thord shakes his head. 'He was home with his kid both times. If he'd left we'd have seen it on his CCTV.'

'What about the others? You've got an ex-soldier who hates meat-eaters, you've got two sisters who could probably use a few human eyes for their more expensive trolls, and you've got David Holmqvist who the whole goddam Kommun, except you, thinks did it. And then you've got Hannes Carlsson.'

'Hannes ain't no person of interest, if that's what you're getting at. And we ain't just looking at the village. Coulda been someone from outside.'

'Shouldn't he be, though?' I put my mug down on Thord's desk. 'Hannes? He can hunt, he's in the right location, he's a good shot, he knows the woods, and it seems he can get very jealous of other men, men like the two that were shot.'

'I know Hannes Carlsson a little bit and Björn's real good buddies with him, poker buddies even. Wasn't him, Tuvs. He's a tough old bastard, a good fighter, but everyone knows Hannes and everyone likes him. The boys up at the mill just love him cos he makes sure with the union that they get paid the best in the whole of Värmland.'

Thord's radio crackles into life. I hear some codes and jargon, and then Björn's voice saying he'll be back at the station in five minutes.

'Best you be leaving now, if you don't mind.'

I nod and thank him for the coffee.

'Watch your back, Tuva. Let us do our job and you get on and do yours.'

I walk over to my office and spend the afternoon trawling through the '90s Medusa files for information, and trying to mentally draw the spider's web of allegiances and family ties that binds Gavrik town together. I knock off work ten minutes early and drive down to Tammy's van.

There's no queue.

'What's this? On a Friday?'

She grins down at me.

'Sweden v France in the football. Thought you'd know that being a sports reporter.'

'I'm an everything reporter, my beat covers it all. Seriously though, I thought there'd be a queue.'

'Hey, I'm not complaining here, business is pretty good. They all ordered before kick-off, they all left work early for the game. So then they pick up their bags of food and I've hit my sales target early and I get to take the rest of the evening nice and easy. Hacked *Game of Thrones* off some website and watching it back here on my iPad.'

'Nice life,' I say. 'Is it paused?'

She smiles and nods and takes an empty plastic container and a pair of big chef's tweezers.

'Can I get a chicken with cashew nuts, hot as you like it, with steamed rice and a few crackers, please.' I pause. 'And a favour.'

She smiles and spoons the rice and then the chicken pieces into a container. They're steaming and glossy and smell of everything that Gavrik is not. I breathe it in and close my eyes.

'That's the chicken,' she says, passing it to me. 'Now, what's the favour?'

'I need you to drive me to Mossen village and leave me there. Then pick me up in a couple of hours at whatever time suits you.'

'Hot date?'

'Hardly. Just need to do some research for work.'

'You going in locked and loaded?'

I frown at her.

'Are you invited to somebody's house or are you snooping? If you're snooping, do you have something to protect yourself?'

'You know I have.'

'My old bear-spray?'

'And I've got a catapult.'

'You'll most likely lose your own eye with that. Wait there a second.'

I eat out in the cold clean air and the food tastes amazing as always. The freshness of the ginger, the crunch of the cashews, the heat filling my stomach and tingling my lips.

'Let's go.'

'You can shut up now? You sure?'

She climbs out of the back of her van and closes the metal grill protecting the food-service hatch. She hangs a blackboard sign saying, *Back at* 7 on the metal grill.

We walk to my truck. Tammy holds out her hand for my keys, and I let her open the driver's door and climb up into the driver's seat.

'God, I love your truck,' she says, settling into the seat. 'This isn't a redneck wagon like the locals drive, this is quality engineering right here.'

We drive out of town and into Mossen village and a fine drizzle starts and it looks more like gas than liquid. We go past Hoarder and then Taxi. Tammy accelerates up the hill and I tell her to stop.

'When do you want picking up?'

'Ten okay?'

'Sure, if that's what you want.' She brings the truck to a halt and pulls on the handbrake.

'But I'll have my phone on me the whole time. You call and I'll be back here in twenty minutes.' She looks at me. 'I got something for you.'

She takes out a gun, some kind of revolver or pistol, from her coat pocket and places it next to the gearstick between us.

'That another starter pistol?'

'It is not.'

'Tammy, what are you doing?'

'Trying to help a stupid friend. Now, you gonna take it or not?'

'Why do you own an actual real gun?'

'Well, now, let's see. I'm twenty-two years old and work at night from a crappy food van on the edge of Shitsville. I work from the dark end of a deserted car park and once the supermarket's closed I feel as alone as the man on the fucking moon. I've got cash in the van and everybody knows it. Most people round here, whether you think it or not, whether you want to believe it or not, don't like or trust anyone that's not as white as an aspirin. You think you're an outsider, well you don't know the first thing about it. So, how many more reasons do you need?'

Her voice has an edge to it I haven't heard before. The windows are getting steamed up and all I can do is stare at the gun.

'So I take your gun and then you go and get held up tonight, or worse. No way. I can't take it.'

'I got more. Take it.'

I look at her and then I look at it. I feel like if I even touch the damn thing then somebody will die. Probably me.

'Thanks, but no. You keep it and I'll see you at ten. I appreciate this. Thanks Tammy.'

I grab my backpack from the rear seat and wave her off. As she does a three-point turn and drives away from me, the light levels fade. But I'm alone on a track and not alone in the woods and that is a very important distinction. I'm about three hundred metres away from the sisters' workshop and I can smell their woodsmoke. All the uphill residents have motive and opportunity. The sisters own their own rifles. Holmqvist is still a suspect in my eyes, no matter what Thord wants to believe. He could have a rifle hidden somewhere, maybe his late father's, an old gun, it's possible. And Hannes is a man with as many secrets as he has connections. I reach into my left pocket and stroke the leather sheath of my knife. I reach into my right pocket and touch the plastic case of my phone and switch it to silent. I'm going to be fine.

35

The forest is turning. The three-quarter moon makes the woods as grey as the blood you find under a cooked salmon fillet.

I walk along the verge of the narrowing track, my boots satisfied with the gravel and the dry ground. The thistly verge begins to narrow. On my right is a steep-sided ditch and then a layer of grey trees and then a wall of spruce. It's colder now, about zero, perhaps less. My clothes are good and my nerves are alive and I have a belly full of chicken and cashew nuts. I feel warm. I trudge up the track and there are no more passing places and no landmarks to show where I am. It's either birches, skinny all the way up to the fine branches at their very tops, or else it's thicker pine trees, each one as straight as a ship's mast.

I hear something in the distance. My aids are picking up music, some kind of polka folk music with an accordion, or is it called an organ, I never remember. It's the kind of tune that girls with head-scarves and traditional regional dress dance to. It's shit, to be honest. I turn a gentle bend and see the lights of the sisters' workshop and their house, smoke rising from their metal chimney in the centre of their metal roof. My hands are still in my pockets; left one, knife, right one, phone. The workshop is open to the road, a feature I never quite understood. Do they like the fresh air? Or, do they like to see who's coming?

The ditch is shallower on this side so I step over it and walk one tree deep parallel with the track. An owl hoots. I think it's behind me but then it hoots again and it sounds like it's up ahead somewhere; hidden and cocky and happy with its place in the order of things. The ground's so uneven I have to look down and focus on not tripping through brambles or falling down holes. I get closer and I can see one of the sisters, the quiet one, working with her back to me. She must be carving another grisly troll. I move away from the track nice and slow so I'm two trees deep. The music's louder now and I'm grateful to it for disguising my clumsy footsteps. I have a ski balaclava in my backpack but I can't put it on. I'd look like a burglar or something. I reckon it's more likely I'll get shot with that thing on than with it off.

I pull myself in closer to a tree. This one is a mature, white birch split near the ground, growing up as if twins. Could I get shot here? I cannot because I need to see Mum on Sunday, and I'm already overdue a visit. She has only me. But then I pull myself together and think like Dad for a minute. I look up to him and collect the facts. It helps. No woman has been shot in Utgard forest. I loosen my grip on the birch as the song the sisters are playing ends and another one, this one with a mouth organ, begins. Nobody has been shot on or near the track. This is going well, it's a reassuringly long list. Nobody has been shot not carrying a rifle. Only hunters have been killed.

I decide my vantage point is good enough even though I can only see two-thirds of the workshop. I'm looking into it at an angle as if from a cheap seat at the theatre. I slowly remove my backpack and take out the binoculars, and the bag of wine gums is right there next to it. So I take it and it rustles and I curse myself for not opening it before I got out here. No way I can rip it apart now, no way in the world. I place them back carefully and bring the binoculars up to my eyes. I rest them against the broader of the two birch trunks. Then I change position so my face is between the trunks, and it feels good. It feels like a natural stance.

They're both there. Cornelia and Alice, both holding knives with short blades, both working on a troll or something with their backs turned to me. I imagine them carving, shaving slivers of pale pine away from its ugly body with gentle caresses of steel blade, carving breasts and a pot belly and knees, and armpits stuffed with their own armpit hair.

Money's a fine motive for murder, and who knows what kind of prices their bespoke made-to-order trolls could fetch if they had human eyes. They both shoot. They live apart from other people, and from what I've been able to glean from locals, they have no friends, no partners, no ex-partners.

The song's quite upbeat and they're not exactly dancing but they're both working to its rhythm, swaying and head-bobbing in time with the violins. I increase magnification. The binoculars are excellent, but every time I breathe or move a little, the image shakes and I lose them. I slow my breathing like a marksman in the movies. They both step away from the troll, one to the left and one to the right, as if to admire their handiwork.

But it's not a troll, it's a hare or a big rabbit. No, it's definitely a hare, I can tell by the out-of-proportion hind legs. My stomach groans, not from hunger but from something else. They have it pinned up on the wall of the workshop. Its hind legs and feet have been nailed to a horizontal stick and its head and tiny front feet are hanging down against the vertical post. It's like a hare Jesus, but upside-down.

They're skinning it. It's definitely dead, I tell myself. It is dead.

They've skinned it from its knee joints down to its asshole – which is positioned directly in front of the centre of the cross – and then half way down its torso. Behind the fluff, its body is dark like red wine. It looks like I imagine a skinned human must look like. I can see its muscles in its back legs and its pelvis and they're like the carved muscles of an athlete, all sinew and tight stringy tendon. It also looks like the lamb I tried to roast when I was fifteen. I was trying to bring back some normal to the home, something nourishing for Mum. But I ruined it.

The sisters come back together but leave a space between them for me to watch. The quiet one yanks down on the pale brown fur as the talking one cuts it with her knife. It takes them seconds to tug down the skin as if pulling a woolly jumper over the head of a child. The fur hangs low at the base of the cross, the red torso taut and shiny above it. The talking sister uses her knife to snap the front legs and they look like frog legs compared to the hind ones still pinned to the top of the cross. The sisters stand apart and the quiet one swipes her hand and the hare's head falls to the ground.

I take a deep breath. So now it's two huge bunny feet, still furry, pinned to a cross with a dark red, headless body hanging beneath it. Both sisters look around and then they get to work. I'm guessing they always work in the same order and they each have their special-isms, their favourite tasks. The talking one runs her knife down gently in one smooth line from the hare's ass down to its neck. My stomach growls and I bite the end of my tongue. I'm not scared of wild meat, I like it, I'm scared of these two and how they're doing what they're doing.

The internal organs look small but I can see them easily; the carcass is well-lit by the fluorescent striplights of the workshop. The quiet sister steps away to the fire and pushes in a couple of logs. The talking one uses her bare hand to pull out intestines and other soft, gloopy tubes of flesh. Then I see the liver, glistening and almost black. They leave it in. The quiet sister tugs out the lungs, throwing each one into the darkness of the pines. The talking sister joins her and they walk to the entrance of their house. They're talking but I can't read lips from this distance in the dark. They close the front door.

Business or pleasure? Troll parts or dinner?

I try to look through the windows but they're lit by dangling pendulum lights which blind me from seeing anything beyond the bulb. I let the binoculars hang around my neck. Then I walk past the workshop, the folk music still playing, me two trees deep, and past the discarded organs and on towards Ghostwriter's house.

A cobweb hanging between two trees hits me square in the face. I pull it from my eyebrows and eyelashes, spitting and gurning even though nothing went inside my mouth. I jump out towards the track and hop the ditch. It's full of stagnant water. I walk along the track pulling fine strands of spider wool from my hair and my chin. Even when it's all gone I can still feel it, and I'm sure strands are lodged on my nose or somewhere behind my ears. I walk faster now. It's cold. The topography changes towards Holmqvist's house. On my right, on the side where he lives, it's still wall-to-wall spruces, but on the left there is a steep escarpment lined with pines and beech trees. It's quite scenic in the daytime, relatively speaking.

I hop the ditch and climb up the escarpment. The trees are smaller and more sparse, with rocky outcrops in between them. I see the corner of his house and the edge of a veranda post; there's something shiny wrapped around it.

The ground's more slippery up here, wet rocks and mossy crags. I hear a noise like a howling beast caught in a trap. I think it's a wolf and I fall to the ground in a ball, my chin between my knees. I haven't pulled my knife or my bear-spray, I've just given up. Just like that. The howls carry on. There aren't many wolves in Värmland, but there are some. I bring my binoculars to my eyes. Outside Holmqvist's house is a wire fence, a chain-link barrier running from one veranda post to the next. It's a dog pen and there's a massive Alsatian, or German shepherd, I forget the difference, and it's looking out and barking. The noise is enormous and it's booming through the trees and travelling up the escarpment.

Okay, so he bought a big dog. But it's fenced in. I'm fine. Maybe I'd buy a big dog if the whole damn town hated me and if everyone I met in Gavrik whispered behind my back the moment I walked away. I stand up and it keeps on barking, its whole body rigid and ready. I touch the knife in my left pocket and the phone in my right. I have no idea what time it is. I reach back and pull the balaclava out from the backpack's side pocket. I pull it on, no reservations, and start walking across the escarpment parallel with the road. It doesn't feel like Utgard forest just here, it's lighter and more open. Less cover, but less menace too. It's almost normal. Almost. The dog never stops barking. I walk to a broad beech tree and its bark is plastered with moss, and with pale patches of lichen like photographic negatives of the liver spots on Mum's hands. I lift my binoculars.

Holmqvist has fenced in the entire ground floor. He's surrounded himself with a ring of steel, a wall of twenty-four hour Alsatian protection. The dog can run around the entire house, it has three hundred and sixty degrees of freedom. It's stopped barking now. It's lying down where I first spotted it and gnawing on a bone the size of a table leg. The bone has a hoof.

It's an elk bone. The dog's chewing on a moose shin. I look around. Holmqvist's windows are all mirrored so I can't make out much. I can hear the dog moan with pleasure as it chews the bone inside the skinny leg, silvery dribbles of saliva reflecting in the moonlight. I scan from left to right and see Holmqvist's car connected to an outdoor post: a device to keep the battery charged during winter. Useful if you don't drive often. My face is warming up a little in the ski balaclava. It smells musty from skiing because I don't think I've ever washed it.

The dog goes quiet. I can just see inside the ground floor and there's no activity, no movement at all. I move the binoculars up to the first floor and aim them at the window I think belongs to the second guest bedroom, the one I never had time to look inside. From this angle, the mirrored glass reflects everything. I scan right and see another window. Nothing. I scan right to the final window and pass a blur as I move the binoculars. I move them back a little and it's him standing on the veranda looking straight back at me.

36

I don't flinch and I don't curl up in a ball like before, I just watch him watching me. He's wearing a pink polo-shirt under a grey jumper, and beige chinos. He's holding a large glass of white wine and he's looking right at me. The dog's chewing fuck-knows-what downstairs and he's drinking white wine upstairs and I'm about twelve kilometres from the edge of the forest. He's watching me down the optics of my own binoculars. I look him up and down. For some reason he's wearing plastic shoe covers on his own veranda. And then he looks away and up at the sky. My heart starts working normally again and I blink, and then I drop the binoculars and let them hang by their string. I look up as if Holmqvist's staring at something specific, but it's just sky. And it is beautiful. I can see more than I've been able to see since entering Utgard forest with Tammy. A ceiling of milky sky, dazzling puddles of stars and soft-focus splodges of galactic light. I'm looking at what I think is the Milky Way and it's the first time I've ever seen it and it really is milky. It's calming. So, as the dog chews, it's me and David Holmqvist, the man arrested not once, but twice, for the Medusa forest murders, staring up at an unreal sky. Then he turns, walks inside, and closes the door.

I think I see another man in there with him, someone his height, but it's just a reflection from the mirrored glass.

I stumble through the trees, the steepness of the slope causing me to trip and rest against stumps along the way. The damn dog starts to bark again like it wants to kill me. I stagger through and the slope flattens out and then I'm past Holmqvist's house and back on the track again. My hearing aid beeps.

The dog stops barking and I worry maybe both my aids have died. But no, just paranoid, my other aid has a good battery. The dog just stopped barking, that's all.

I keep the balaclava on because the temperature's fallen. I walk down the track to Frida's house and it's barely wide enough for a car. It loops back on itself like one of those ski slopes for people like me who can't really ski. It's more twisty than the main track, it sweeps over rocks and down between old Scots pines, their trunks sloping away to find the sun. But it's darker here. There's less sky to help me out. I walk fast, almost a jog, left hand on the bone handle of my knife, right hand on my phone. I can see eyes, or maybe they're just bits of wood, holes in trunks where birds might nest. I'm heating up and my breath is collecting in small puffs in the air in front of me. I'm leaving scared clouds of cashew-scented breath along the last bit of track in Mossen village. Something rustles but I think it's the wind. Left hand, knife.

I walk up towards their house and see the security lights on in the garden. Their plot of land is larger and flatter than the neighbours' – with a hill directly behind and a lawn in front. One house with a mansard roof, and one hut on the right-hand side. Two cars. His and hers.

The ground's wet. I skirt the edge of the garden and squelch through boggy grass and the foul water around my boots is starting to make my feet cold. I hate not being able to see what's beneath me. It's shitty land and I don't know what I'm walking through. I want a thousand ceiling spotlights right now, a helicopter overhead with searchlights, a dozen torches, and an asphalt runway lit up with landing lights, thank you very much. I want lights to lead me to the hill at the back of Frida's house. Because Hannes's study is at the back.

I get to the rocky slope, and although my feet are wet from the deeper puddles I'm happy to be on solid ground and approaching the one house I feel almost comfortable with. I perch on a grey granite rock the size of a blue whale, a vein of sparkling quartz running diagonally through it, mirroring the Milky Way above. I take a breath, suddenly thirsty from all the walking and all the breathing. The lights are on in every room of the house. It's not a scary place, with its well-maintained garden and modest conservatory and security lights and tasteful furnishings. There are no wolf-dogs here.

I scan the ground floor quickly and see Frida with an apron tied around her cinched waist. She's washing up in the kitchen, scrubbing saucepans and leaving them to dry on a rack beside the sink. Then she unties her apron, and I notice the light go out in the kitchen. I scan up and see Hannes in his study, sitting at his desk. Then I see Frida crack open the study door and say something to him. Then she leaves, closing the door behind her. I see her in the bathroom, slipping out of her clothes, and suddenly I'm a guilty pervert wearing a mask, so I look away.

Hannes checks his door. I think he locks it, but he has his back to me so I can't be sure. I watch him bend over the sofa in his room, the one next to the stuffed brown bear. He pulls on it and it turns into a bed and suddenly I'm shocked. More shocked than I was about the hare guts or Holmqvist on his balcony or the pile of dead mice near Viggo's wall. Hannes is a man who sleeps in his study.

He turns his light off and then from the corner of my eye, I see Frida's bathroom light switch off as well. I feel like a kid looking into a doll's house. He moves to his desk, the stark glare from his computer the only thing lighting the room. His monitor is as big as a flat-screen TV and it's pointed right at me. I watch Hannes sit at his desk and pull on a headset, the kind you see telemarketers wear all day long, microphone at his mouth, earphone against one ear, metal band across his silvery hair.

He types something on the keyboard and a woman appears on his screen. I wonder if it's Daisy, but I've never met her or seen a photo. I adjust my zoom. Could just be a porn movie but it doesn't look like it. The woman's sitting on a bed. I can see it all clearly: Hannes oblique at his desk and her on a bed. She's good-looking, brunette, maybe my age or a little younger. I watch as he puts his socked feet on the desk and spreads them apart. I see her laugh at this. His socks are white and they glow bright in the glare from the screen. I see him unzip his jeans and then I look away.

All the lights are off in the house. The only thing I can see is screen-glow from the centre of the first floor. I bring up my binoculars and he's changed position thank God, so I can only see his back now and one foot with its white sock. He's shaking. But I can see her pretty clearly on the monitor. She's still dressed from the waist up. She's sitting up on her bed with her knees up by her chest and there's a noose tied around her neck.

My right hand leaves the binoculars and finds my phone in my pocket. I call the police now, right? He seems to be controlling her and this must be illegal in some way, conspiracy to murder or incitement or something? But before I even touch the phone, I know this is not what I should do, or what I will do. This could be a recording or it could be a staged porn thing. I look back and Hannes is shaking more now. I watch as his foot slips off the desk as the girl on the screen starts to pull at the rope around her neck. She's turning red. She's writhing around. Hannes stops shaking. She pulls off the rope and throws it on the bed and then she closes her legs and opens her legs and then closes them again and blows him a kiss. He removes his headset and turns off the monitor and goes to bed on the pull-out sofa.

I want to get home. I've seen too much and I want my truck and I want Tammy and I want to get out of this hellhole. I walk briskly, my ski mask still on, and then I trudge through the wet boggy edge of the garden again. I'm thinking about what I've seen and what I can do with it all and who I can talk to. My mask stinks. I take a short-cut just two trees deep to re-join the track because I've had enough of wet feet and weird marshy ground. I walk and it's dark. It's very dark now and I'm being stalked by a cloud of midges. I

turn back to the garden and it's not there. It's just trees. I turn around
to get my bearings. I can't be lost here, I'm just two or three trees
deep in the forest, and this must be still officially Frida's garden. But
it's all the same, every point on the compass is dark vertical tree
trunks. I look up and there's no sky at all, no stars or moon or Milky
Way, just branches hanging down one on top of the other, sagging
low in a hundred shades of black.

I rip off my ski mask and breathe. The midges come closer. I stare
into the gloom and see something, the top of a wall maybe. I swat
my hand around and walk towards the wall and within twenty paces
I'm back in the main garden. I can see a house and two cars and
that's pretty fucking magic right now, signs of life, human life. I run
down the track towards Ghostwriter's house. No mask, I just sprint
as fast as I can. I outrun the midges and get out my phone. Barely
any reception. Four missed calls. I call Tammy as I run.

'Where are you?' I whisper.

'I'm here. I'm where I dropped you off. Where are you?'

'Drive up to meet me. I'm on the track. Drive up.'

I keep sprinting, cursing myself for not being fitter. I'm twenty-six
and I'm fighting for breath like Mum. I run straight past that dog,
barking at me every second I go by, and I run up towards the sisters'
workshop. Headlights. I don't really care if they're from my truck
although I know they must be. Just lights is great. Lights and engine
noise and the ground vibrating beneath my feet.

The truck stops.

37

We reverse at speed up the track and Tammy seems to have no problem with this at all. I tell her what I've seen and she cringes and screws up her face like she's smelt something awful. She looks behind with her right hand gripping my headrest, driving my truck backwards with one hand on the steering wheel like a pro rally driver. My feet are damp and cold.

'You been here before?'

'Pick most of my mushrooms here,' Tammy says. 'Free produce from about July until November every year.'

'You don't mind the woods. You come here alone?'

'There's nothing scary in these woods unless you're a man and you're a hunter. I saw the wood-carvers once, they were shooting rabbits or pheasants, but we gave each other a wide berth and I was fine. Mum used to come here a lot before I was born and it saved her a fortune when she set up the food van, so she said. She used to get the same bullshit from locals that I get, only ten times worse. No idea how she managed. Threats, stalkers, dogshit in her postbox, people following her home at night. Cops never listened to her back then, never took her seriously. So she'd come to Utgard all on her own to get away from all that and to forage. Nothing bad ever happened to her here.'

She looks up at me.

'You need to confront it one day, go deep inside.'

I turn to her and she looks small driving my truck; she's low down in the seat with her hands gripping the top of the steering wheel.

'I used to hate lakes,' she says. 'I mean, I liked lakes but I really hated swimming out deep in them, you know, to where my feet couldn't touch the bottom. So I decided I needed to face my fear. I packed a tent and went out to the reservoir, the one with the tourist caravans. Next morning, I psyched myself up, then swam right out to the middle. I was treading water out there, must be ten metres deep or something in the middle, that's what the locals say, all leeches and pike and God-knows-what down there, and I was pretty much fine. You should try it.'

'Tammy, if I wander off into the middle of a forest and just "let it happen" you'll never see me again cos I'll get lost. That's the difference. With a lake, you know where you are and where you need to get to. Tonight I managed to get lost in someone's front fucking garden.'

'I'm not saying you do it lightly and I'm not saying you do it at night-time, you idiot.'

We pass under the motorway on the way back to Gavrik.

'Go in the daytime. Let me know where you're setting off from. Take your phone, some food, use a ball of string if you need to. Tie it to a tree on the edge of the wood and walk as far as the string lasts. Then you're in but you know you can get back out.'

When she says string I think of wool, a ball of brightly-coloured yarn, and this makes it all seem possible. Nothing too bad can happen if you're holding a nice ball of yarn.

I can see the town's twinkling lights now, a dull glow against a clear sky. I've still got my backpack between my cold, wet feet so I reach back and put it on the back seat and that's when I see the rifle.

'What's this?'

Tammy bends her neck to look back.

'What does it look like?'

'Why do you need a rifle?'

'I thought we went through this. I'm a cute young Asian woman living amongst Neanderthal men who see me as sub-human yet still very much fuckable. So that's why I carry it. It's just Mum's old gun.'

I stare at it lying across my rear seats. Dark varnished wood and a matt-metal barrel with a scope. It has a weight to it. It looks like an older version of the rifle carried by that man who walked into the office, the brother of the '90s victim.

I turn to face forward.

'What's the news on the ghostwriter?' Tammy asks.

'Nothing new.'

'I had the ambulance driver pick up some food earlier, the one with the limp. Reckons he saw the ghostwriter and Hannes Carlsson in a car on some road. He was out on a call, lights flashing, and he saw them on some little side road and they looked like they were arguing.'

'Not those two,' I say. 'I doubt it was those two.'

We drive up *Storgatan* and past my office. Everything's locked up and the lights are off. A year ago, Ronnie's bar on the corner would have still been open and people would have been falling out of it right about now. But it's being renovated, and rumour is that Ronnie's run out of cash. I doubt it'll reopen, and this town feels like it's shrinking around me. Options are narrowing.

We pull up to my apartment building.

'I'm gonna walk you inside,' Tammy says.

I open the truck door and step into the street. The smooth, flat, predictable asphalt feels good under my boots, but my legs almost collapse from under me. I'm tired as hell.

We climb the stairs, me first, my keys held out in front of me. The light bulb still hasn't been fixed. It's dark. I unlock my front door, Tammy's warm breath grazing the back of my neck.

'Shit, you get burgled?'

I close the door, smiling.

'Y'know, I've been tied up these past weeks what with all the dead eyeless bodies and all. Housework hasn't been a priority.'

We sit on the sofa side by side sipping tea from white Ikea mugs. 'How's your mum?'

I just shrug. I feel even more exhausted thinking about Mum and about my Sunday visit and about how she will focus on why I haven't been to see her recently and how Dad was always there for her, and how if I moved back to Sweden to be near to her I could have at least lived in the same goddam town.

'Not good. She's in decline, that's what the doctors call it. Hate that word. They say it's in her bones, in her blood, in her brain.' I drink the last of my tea. 'They're not really treating her, just looking after her.'

'She knows you're close by. She knows if she needs you you'll be there.'

I look at her. 'I'm not good at this.'

Tammy says nothing, she just stretches a hand to my head and strokes my hair. She strokes slowly like you'd stroke a scared dog, her fingers moving softly over my head.

'Whenever I look in a mirror, I always see her for the first split second and it scares the shit out of me that I look so much like her, that we have exactly the same expression, so I always change my face to one that's clearly not natural to me but that I'm happy with. That first glimpse is real, and then I change it to a pose more like how I remember Dad.'

She continues to stroke my hair.

'Some daughters would be there three days a week, home-baked cinnamon shortbread and family photo albums and anecdotes. Maybe I would be that kind of daughter if she ever looked pleased to see me. Not pleased, she's too ill for that, I don't need her to look pleased. Just not disappointed. She's so disappointed, Tam. Because I'm not Dad, I suppose. I'm not him.'

38

The sun wakes me. I look around the living room and stretch like a cat under my blanket. I guess Tammy put it over me. The room's tidier than I remember it. It's not estate agent tidy or dinner party tidy, but it's been cleared up, clothes piled on top of my set of drawers. I grab my hearing aids and put them both in and switch them both on. Tammy's cleared away the pots and pans. Without her I'd have moved out of Gavrik within a single calendar month.

There's a tightness in the back of my thighs. I drink a carton of UHT orange juice, the cheap stuff like coloured water.

It's hot. I can't regulate the heating, it's the same for the whole building, and they've clearly now moved into winter mode. I pull off my robe and throw it on the sofa. Then I look at it a while in this semi-tidy room and pick it back up and walk into my bathroom and hang it on the door hook. It takes me fifteen minutes to get ready because I let my face enjoy the shower for a while. A thousand droplets beating down on my skin like a bargain spa treatment. Steamed and warm, I emerge with rosy skin and a calm pulse. I get dressed and rub my hair with a towel and stick it up in a ponytail, semi-wet, and pull on clothes from the wardrobe. I need food and information in that order.

I put on my coat and boots near the front door and unlock it. As I walk out I almost trip over something at foot level. I look down and see the troll. It's the same one as before. It's facing away from me, sun striking its front, the side I can't see, from a stairwell window.

How the fuck did it get back here? My pulse isn't calm any more.

I kick it and then curse myself. Stupid. Coward. I pick it up. Hard pine body and rough sackcloth trousers. I step back into my flat, nudge the door shut with my hip, and turn it around.

It's not the same troll. It's similar, it's the same shape roughly, the same size. But this one's face is worse. It's not so hairy, it's almost bald, no nose or ear hair. But it has eyes, little black eyes. And it has a soft tongue hanging from one side of its carved little mouth. I can't touch the tongue. I can hardly even look at it.

But that's not the worst part. I thought its rough trousers were rucked when I picked it up, but they're not. This one's breasts are bigger than the other one's. They're heavier, like a breastfeeding mother or an ancient fertility sculpture. I tug at its trousers, like a child undressing a Barbie, curious to find the secret parts. The fabric is sewn onto it or glued on but there's a fly. I separate the two sides of the fly, there's no button just a crack in the fabric, and an erect wooden penis nudges past my hand.

I place it down on the kitchen counter next to the dirty dishes in the sink. Its little phallus is still poking out. It looks like a stick. It is a stick, I guess. But the whole thing's evil, it's an abomination, some abstract cruelty I could never have imagined. I rub my eyes and stand there sweating in my boots and coat.

I remember what Tammy said last night about facing my fears. I sniff, then walk up to it. I hold it firmly around the shoulders. That tongue. It looks drunk with its little tongue; drunk or the victim of a seizure of some kind. I reach out to touch it, then pull back. I rub my fingertips together as if about to appraise an expensive vase in an antiques showroom. Then I touch the tongue with the end of my right index finger. It moves. It's stiff, but it moves. Like my tongue, it has tiny bumps all over it. They're taste buds, I suppose. It is animal. I squeeze it gently. It's firm. I pull it and more comes out from the mouth. Suddenly I feel unsteady on my feet, my empty stomach not up to this. The tongue comes out and then stops. It reaches the top of the troll's chest; it's about as long as my middle finger.

I want to take the troll to Thord and have it arrested and locked up in a jail cell. Or maybe I should drive to the sisters' workshop and throw it in their log-burner. But I just stand and sweat and look at it. I reach up and open a cupboard, the one where spare table mats and a broken kettle are crammed on the bottom shelf. I bite my lip and pick up the troll and stretch to place it on the top shelf, facing the darkness of the cupboard. The thing's ass, complete with a little ginger tail I hadn't noticed before, points at me. I open my front door to walk out but it doesn't feel right. I can't leave this in my flat, I'll never sleep again. But part of me knows it may be evidence of some kind. Might be important. I check that my basement key's on my key chain, which is stupid because it always is, always, along with my spare batteries, always, and walk downstairs with the little bastard hidden inside my coat, its cock firm against my ribs.

I pass the laundry room and its meadow-fresh scent and unlock the solid door to the storage lock-ups. Where do I put the troll? I place it in the centre but it looks like a sick art installation, so I push it to the far end facing the wall but now it looks like a naughty kid who's being punished. I bring it back to the centre and position it at an angle and then both its eyes fall out and roll across the polished concrete floor. I slam the door shut and run up and out into the cold Gavrik air.

There's a white taxi parked right outside my building. But it's not Viggo. It's Saturday, 11am, and there's nobody on the streets, no smoke from the liquorice factory, no shoppers walking down *Storgatan*. I jog towards work and I can taste blood in my mouth, but I'm not sure where it came from. The shops don't open until lunch and then only for two or three hours. They'll all be at handball practice or hockey training or grocery shopping at ICA Maxi. I say grocery shopping, but people here in Gavrik buy pretty much everything they ever buy from the supermarket. Clothes, garden supplies, fresh flowers, prescription drugs, small pieces of furniture, toys. And food. With only a few exceptions, this is why everyone dresses, smells, eats, and looks, roughly the same, albeit on different days of the week.

The office is locked. I think about the eyeless troll incarcerated in my basement. Two people cycle up towards the McDonald's end of town. It's a kid I recognise from a school feature I wrote on a local art exhibition, and it's his mother who I recognise because she comes into the office every Friday to buy the *Posten*. She nods almost imperceptibly as she cycles past wearing the same coat I'm wearing. There's a killer loose somewhere around here and people are still cycling around Toytown like everything's okay.

The only places open apart from the supermarket are the news-agent and the hairdresser and the police station. I head for the station.

It's unlocked but empty. The ticket-tape machine says 15 on its label and the screen above the counter says 15, so I ring the bell.

'Thord,' I shout. 'It's me.'

No answer.

I ring three times.

'Thord, it's me, Tuva.'

The door opens and Chief Björn Andersson walks over with a face like someone's just kicked his grandmother.

'Can I see your ticket?'

I reach back and take ticket 15 and pass it to him over the smooth pine counter.

'What can I help you with this morning?'

'Sorry to disturb you, Chief. Is Thord here?'

'I made the constable take a day off, he wasn't looking well. Do you need to report anything?'

He looks hungover. Maybe he's just as tired as I am after the past few weeks. His sleeves are rolled up and I can see his tattoo real clear, it's a faded red heart above a capital 'K', first letter of his wife's name. Katarina works in the optician's across the road from my office.

'Cold outside,' I say.

He licks his lips and I notice that the corners of his mouth are red raw.

'You should see it in January,' he says.

'I have.'

He snorts at this, like the last two Januarys don't really count, like my Januarys will never really count.

'If you need a scarf,' he smirks at me. 'They sell wool down the road.'

'Any progress with the Utgard killings, Chief?'

'Well, I'd say you'd probably already know if there was.'

'One of my sources thought it'd be a good idea to search Hannes Carlsson's house for an unregistered rifle. Thought he might have the motive and the opportunity.'

'Did they now.'

I nod.

'And who is this source of yours?'

I shake my head.

'Well, let me see here if I'm understanding you straight, young lady. Mr Carlsson, the upstanding member of the local community, governor of the local high school, family man, regular attendee of the local church, and generous donor to the annual Gavrik *Sankta Lucia* parade, is this that the same there Mr Carlsson that you are referring to?'

'It's an unsolved multiple murder. I just think you might want to check out his house and office, that's all. Would be uncomfortable for you if he was the perpetrator all along and you were warned and you never acted on it ... theoretically speaking.'

Chief Björn grips his side of the counter with both hands and I can see his tendons through his skin, tight as piano strings.

'Is it complicated because he's your cousin?' I ask.

The sides of his cheeks throb as he grinds his molars.

'Carlsson isn't my cousin and if you were from around these parts you'd know that. He's my second cousin. And for your information, young lady, if that's even what I should call people like you, my mamma had eleven cousins and my pappa had nineteen. So in this town pretty much everyone worth knowing is my second cousin.'

I force myself to be professional even if he's not.

'Well, do you have any new suspects?'

I can see the pulse throb in his temple.

'I think maybe you should leave professional police work to me, as I have thirty years' experience under my belt, and I'll best leave story writing to you and your Stockholm pals.'

'Can you just ask him in for questioning, then?'

'Not the way it works around here, not even close.'

'Well, could you—'

The door opens behind me and the Karlstad homicide cop with the Bluetooth earpiece walks in.

'Björn.'

The Chief nods to him.

The Karlstad cop walks straight past me, talking on his phone through his earpiece, and then he disappears through to the back office. Björn looks at me and chews his teeth and shakes his head. And then closes the key-code door behind him.

39

My phone vibrates in my pocket; a text message from Savanah asking me to meet her at the petrol station again. Asking me if we can meet this afternoon. I type back that I can be there in forty minutes. My phone vibrates in my hand. She says thanks, she'll see me there.

I switch off both aids and drive. There's a dead animal splayed across the line separating the slow lane from the hard shoulder, and the black and white of the road matches its markings so well it looks like it's been placed there. I think it's a badger. A white Volvo drives past with its sign up on its roof and I wonder if Viggo's inside. I indicate and pull into to the Q8 petrol station. There's nobody here yet because I'm five minutes early. I park up and turn off the radio and switch my aids back on.

A face in my wing mirror. It's a thin girl, long hair with a fringe cut at an angle. She's gripping her hands around her torso as if to hold herself together. I press a button and my window winds down.

'Tuva?' she asks.

'Yes.'

'I'm Daisy. Savanah called you to set this up. So I could meet with you. She said you'd be okay about that.'

'Savanah's not coming?'

'She'll pick me up when we're done. Can I get inside? It's freezing out here.'

She opens the door and climbs into the truck. I look at her. She's a pretty bird next to me, her coat wrapped around her like an extra-large hotel robe. I feel like a giant. I realise she's not the girl from Hannes's computer, the girl with the noose. She rubs her slender hands together and breathes on them so I switch on her heated seat and turn the blower to max but it's too loud for my aids and I get feedback. I turn the blower down to medium.

'Savanah said you were a good person,' she looks at me, her hands over the air outlets. 'Can I talk to you in confidence?'

'You want this off the record?'

'God, yes. I don't want anyone to know we talked like this about him.'

'Him?'

'Can you promise?'

I nod.

'Hannes,' she says. 'I'm his girl.'

'This is off the record,' I say, showing her my palms. 'You can talk freely.'

She shakes her head as if about to change her mind, as if she's about to sprint into the petrol station and hide inside a toilet cubicle.

'You need a minute? You want coffee?'

She nods to me and smiles. She's a beautiful girl, like a young Kate Moss, but with an asymmetrical face and a shit hairstylist.

I go inside and buy two cappuccinos that bear no resemblance to cappuccinos and two Danish pastries. I pay cash and jog back to my truck and hand her a cup and a greasy paper bag that's now almost transparent like tracing paper.

'He's got a problem,' she says, like she's been rehearsing while I was inside. 'Nobody knows about it, not even his wife.'

I wait.

'It's his eyes.'

Didn't expect that. I take a sip from my bitter coffee and look at her.

'He's got some kind of degenerative eye disease. It's awful really, for a man like him. He's known about it since his twenties. He wears contacts so you'd never know, but his eyes have gone from medium to severe, from about minus five when I met him to about minus ten now, maybe worse. You know what that means, don't you?'

'What?'

'He'll lose his hunt permit. He'll lose his gun licence to hunt his own bloody land. They tried to take it away from him this year because he failed the test; but him and the police are good friends so they let him have it, but they told him it's his last one. This is his last season.'

'Okay.'

'It's not okay, not for a man like Hannes. He's been shooting all his life, since he was about eleven years old. He'd killed and skinned and gutted a bull elk before he'd even kissed a girl. Aside from poker, it's his whole life. It's what gets him through the summer months, the thought of hunting all autumn and all winter. And this is his last. And that's turning him crazy.'

I gesture with my cup in my hand for her to continue. She's not drinking and she's not eating.

'He's always looked after me real nice,' she says. 'But now I'm scared. The other girls have always bitched about how well he takes care of me, not to my face, but I know. And now he's got more jealous. A lot more. He doesn't want me talking or looking at any other men but him, professionally or outside of work. Gets staff to keep an eye on me. And that's just not practical, you know? He's my client and he was always kind of my friend, but he's got a wife. I have to have my own life, you know? So I'm . . .' She stops talking.

'Go on.' I gesture with closed fingertips, zipping my lips like a schoolgirl keeping a secret.

'I got this friend, right, she's from Gothenburg and she's working in London and she's doing real well. Good money. She says I can visit, I can stay with her, she'll help me out, introduce me to her club. I've got savings so I reckon there's nothing much keeping me here.'

Now I'm the one who's jealous. In my head, in the blink of an eye, I see her flying to London and starting fresh and working in Mayfair, in some fancy bar, and having drinks with this friend of hers, who in my mind's eye is Tammy somehow. She'll be living the life I should be living.

'Great idea,' I say, taking a bite of over-sweet Danish pastry. 'Which part of London?'

'Don't know exactly, but real close to Heathrow airport so that's pretty convenient for getting back home.'

Suddenly I'm not so jealous. The yellow slime of the Danish pastry glues my tongue to the roof of my mouth and I take a swig of coffee to wash the whole lot down. 'Heathrow. Nice.'

I look at her and brush flaky crumbs from the fine blonde hairs on my upper lip.

'You're not telling Hannes, are you?' I ask.

She clenches her teeth, turns her head to face forward, to face the motorway, and takes a tiny sip of coffee.

'I'm already packed,' she says, still facing forward, staring at the E16 and the lorries streaming from left to right. She takes a deep breath and looks at me. 'I got to be careful cos he's said before if I leave he'll come after me, he has some fantasy we can make a life someplace new, him playing cards seriously and me dancing. So, I already talked to the police on the phone and they totally ignored me. They don't take the word of a stripper real seriously. Their ears just close over. To them, I'm not really worth listening to. But, you ... That's why I wanted to talk to you. I think you need to look into Hannes and what he's ...' she pauses. 'What he's been doing.'

'Been doing?'

'I don't know nothing for sure.'

'But what do you suspect?'

'Well, he's mad as hell these days, he's boiling. He thinks his life in Värmland is over, nothing left here for him if he can't shoot on his own land. You have no idea how serious he takes his hunting, how serious all the men round here take it. It's like their freedom and their manhood and their childhood all rolled into a ball. It's what their daddies did. I'm worried he's doing something real bad or maybe he's just about to.'

'Do you know what?'

She opens the door on her side of the truck and starts to step down.

'Daisy, wait one second, please.'

'That's all I know really, I gotta go. Just . . .' She pauses again, her hair splayed across her face in the wind, and lifts the collar of her raincoat. 'Just get them to check his stuff. The police will listen to you.'

She disappears into the warm petrol station shop. I sit thinking for a while, rehearsing how I'll present all this to Thord, tapping the fob of my key as it dangles from the ignition. I watch a Renault pull in and stop right outside the pumps. I see Savanah in the front seat. She looks different, she's wearing glasses. Daisy gets in and they drive off. I have an urge to follow them but I let them go. Then I pull out onto the E16 and head south.

Utgard forest looms on the other side of the road. But it's not night-time and it's not raining and I get excited for a second. I make the decision. I will drive to the woods and I will step inside and then I will step out again. Well, a little more than that, I'll go in for a while and I'll face it. I'm not scared by this. It'll be okay. I'm a woman and I'm not a hunter and I don't have a rifle. I am not the target. I'll be fine. I think through what Daisy said. I don't like Hannes one bit but now part of me feels almost sorry for him and the other part wonders what he's capable of if he's so desperate. And how safe is Daisy? And Frida?

I head into Gavrik first and park right outside the haberdashery store. I'd go to the cop shop but Thord's not there and I don't trust Chief Björn with this new information, he's too friendly with Hannes. There are a few shoppers milling around on *Storgatan*, people heading into Benny Björnmossen's shop with its wild boar metal sign squeaking in the breeze. I step inside the haberdashery and the bell tinkles above the door.

Coloured yarn. I need something sturdy and bright. Mrs Björkén comes in from the back room and her face drops when she sees me like she's just spotted dogshit on the till.

'Hej,' I say.

She just nods and then stands there and crosses her arms across her huge strapped-down bosom.

This fucking town.

I pick out a ball of red wool with a little angora in it, furry and thick. I place it by the till on the counter.

Her nose is twitching. 'Think it's easy doing business in Gavrik?'

'I'm sorry?'

'You got no real roots in this old town, eh?'

I pass her a hundred-kronor note.

'What are you talking about?'

'Always thought you were okay. Well, more fool me.'

'Sorry?'

'In times of struggle we pull together round here, we're Christian family people round here. I buy from them and they buy from me and we try to keep it all local, to keep each other going. But, oh no, not for Miss Stockholm City, you write your clever stories, telling the whole world Gavrik's business and then what? It's a betrayal is what it is. Everyone's been talking about what you're doing, what you're writing. Everyone. You shouldn't write bad of this town. We've got to live here. You'll write bad of this town and then you'll leave us in tatters.'

I take out my purse. Maybe Lena was right. Maybe my principles and my writing make people anxious. I should have listened. 'Patriotic to the community' is how she put it. Maybe, no matter if I like it or if I don't, the rules are different in a small marginal town, a cut-off place fighting just to stay alive.

'I'm sorry,' I say. 'I don't know what—'

'You ain't got no roots around here so you ain't got no reasons to stay once you've gone and ruined things,' she says, her nostrils flaring. 'There are jobs on the line.'

I watch her put my wool in a cheap white plastic bag, and then I watch her open her till and place my change on the countertop.

'I think you misunderstand. I write the—'

'Of course you do, you don't think we got two brain cells to rub together. And then you go and slanderise my nephew and my cousins, well you can find somewhere else to buy your wool for all I care.'

She's red now. I can see hives, some kind of rash spreading from her chest up her neck.

I collect the change, each coin scratching across the counter as I pick it up, and I take the wool.

'Sorry you feel that way. I just write the news.'

She's shaking her head. The rash is spreading up her jowls now and up to her cheeks. She's crossed her arms again and she's as red as the yarn.

I step outside, a dozen barbed unused insults queuing up in my head, and the bell tinkles. I look back through the window, my mouth slightly open at what just happened. She's staring at me and I look at her face and read her lips.

'Leave us be.'

40

I'm approaching Utgard forest from town. I've already passed under the motorway and I know I can do it. I feel high like I've just downed six espressos. I scroll down the contacts in my phone.

'Hi Frida, it's me, Tuva.'

'Hi sweetie, how are you?'

'Not bad,' I say, the flavour of a green wine gum lingering on my tongue. 'I don't need to work tonight so do you fancy catching a film at the cinema?' I need to ask her about what Mrs Björkén said and maybe, somehow, about what Daisy said. I need to find out what is going on. 'You said you liked movies and that new George Clooney film is on.'

'Well, now, that is tempting, but you see,' Frida's voice quietens slightly, 'Hannes is home tonight so I can't get out. But, would you like to come here, maybe? It'll just be the three of us, but I've made enough wild mushroom and walnut soup to feed an army. Rye dumplings, too. No Clooneys, just Carlssons. What do you say?'

My fingers are tapping my steering wheel and I think it sounds like the best chance I'll get to work out what's going on around here.

'I'll be there. If you're sure it's not an imposition.'

'Don't be silly, it's always lovely to see you. About seven okay?'

'See you then.'

I end the call and dial Tammy. Her phone's not switched on, or else she's using it because it goes straight to voicemail. I ring again. Voicemail. Where is she, and who the fuck still leaves voicemails? I

246

ring again, my hearing aid battery beeping in my ear and I make a mental note to change it this afternoon. Her phone must be off. I'll try her later.

The forest edge is a dark cliff. I see birds flying above it and out of it, black birds like crows but they look bigger. Ravens, maybe. I pull off the road and head up along a farmer's lane I've seen on Google Maps. It's bumpy. Piles of horse shit. I drive further and pull onto a dirt track and thank myself for renting this truck with its brake horsepower and its all-wheel drive. I park up just outside the tree line. Backpack and half a bag of wine gums and wool and my phone. I stand by my bonnet, still warm at my back, still humming, and face the woods. Tammy said I need to confront this and she was right.

I'll give it two hours and leave well before the storm comes in. That should do it. I'll head up the foresters' track: the avenue they keep clear for quad bikes and hunting trucks. I'll go into the trees a bit. I'll go deeper in than I've ever been before, and then I'll make peace or something.

The sun's low, like a torch sitting on the floor. I can't see it but light's piercing through the trees in beams. It's quite picturesque just here, with my truck still in view and a blue sky above. It's okay, just here. I walk up the track for half an hour or so and I notice piles of dung, but have no idea what kind of wild animal left it. Badger? Elk? Lynx?

There's somebody else here. Someone's ahead of me in the trees close to the track and they're carrying something. This is a thousand-hectare forest and someone's here when I need to face the loneliness of nature and I resent them so much I want to scream. This was supposed to be my slot. I have two hours to do this before I need to get home and shower and dress for dinner with Frida. The person comes out of the woods and hops over a ditch. It's a woman of fifty or so with black hair and a red coat. It's the woman I saw in town, the woman on the bike. I think. She's wearing black tracksuit bottoms and she's carrying one of those huge blue IKEA bags. She looks like an older version of Tammy. As we pass, she looks down at the floor. I glance inside her bag and its half-full of mushrooms, hundreds of gold nuggets sprinkled with dry moss and soil.

'Congratulations,' I say. 'They look delicious.'

She just walks on straight past me. I think she mutters something as she walks away but she says nothing to my face.

I stand there staring at her broad back as she trots off in the direction of my truck. I've heard that locals are protective of their best picking spots but this dismissal takes me aback. Or did she recognise me? Is this Mrs Bitchface Björkén of the haberdashery store all over again?

I'm sweating a little and my boots are suddenly tight around my toes. I pause, staring into the trees. They're not so dark now in the daylight. It's probably three degrees above zero and I hop a ditch and stumble into the shadow of the pines. I walk three trees deep and then turn back. I can see the track so I could just turn left and there would be my truck, no problem. My escape route. I reach back awkwardly and pull the red yarn out of my backpack. It feels soft in my hands. It feels like Mum before Dad died; like Mum before she gave up all her hobbies: her bridge and knitting and baking and birdwatching; before she quit her job as an optician, before she gave up on life, before she gave up on me. The soft wool, springy in my fingers, feels like the good years before everything changed. It feels safe.

I slip off the cardboard ring and pull out the frayed end of the yarn and loop it around a rough spruce trunk at about waist height. I loop it three times and tie a strong knot and pull on it to make sure it's secure. And then I turn and walk into the woods, my lifeline unravelling in my hands as I go in deeper like a potholer down a cave. It gets darker and cooler and more uneven but I have my wool. I have to slap my own cheeks every now and then to kill mosquitoes, and the buzzing of their tiny wings near my hearing aids drives me crazy at times but I'm not scared just annoyed like any normal person would be, like you would be.

Sweat's beading on my neck. I turn and the thread is there strung over granite rocks and mossy fallen branches like a fine trail of blood back through the wilderness. It looks fluffy where the sun catches the angora strands. I'm okay. I'm in the woods and it's actually fine. There's a slight incline ahead, more birches than before, their fine branches all high in the sky and more delicate than the pines. It's wet underfoot. I look down to check where my boots are and see something under my right boot just as I start to put my weight down on it. I lift my foot and stand back and see the bird.

I crouch. It's a normal-looking bird, maybe a blackbird, I don't know all their names. Its wings are flailed like a feathered angel and its head is pointing in the direction I'm walking, its shiny beak like a triangular marker on a compass. Its eyes stare up at me, black as gemstones. There are flies buzzing above it, and a few ants crawling around. I don't think it's been here long. It's a recent victim of something or other and it's quite fresh.

I step over it and walk on. The mosquitoes are worse now and they're fucking huge. One lingers in front of my face like it's looking for a fight. The thing that hangs down from its body, its stinger thing, is long. It's like a refuelling airplane, with a hose dangling down mid-air to refuel a fighter jet. I swat it away but it is persistent. I hear something behind me and look back, but there's nothing there. I'm a woman and I'm not a hunter and I haven't got a rifle. I am not the target. The wool unravels behind me and I keep walking up and over the shallow hill. At the top, I face a valley. It's quite pretty with a clearing in the middle and some kind of chimney standing all on its own. I walk down, red angora spilling out from my hands, the ball shrinking smaller and smaller.

It's a torp ruin. A stone foundation and a chimney stack and little else. There's a sign the size of a newspaper with a laminated sheet stapled to it. Apparently this place belonged to a Mr Ahlberg, a smallholder who lived here from the 1850s to the 1880s. That's all it says. I walk up into what would have been the house. The chimney stack is as tall as a double-decker bus and it looks absurd all on its own, but I suppose everything else was timber and rotted away over time. The stack has a fireplace at its base, and the upper section's held up with planks and branches and it looks like it could collapse at any moment. The torp foundations are covered in soil and leaves and saplings and moss but there's one thing left here. So I touch it. A rusty skeleton of a narrow single bed. It has some of the frame left and some of the springs. It looks smaller than a modern single bed, almost child-sized. I hear a bird noise above my head and look up. Two birds of prey, eagles or buzzards maybe, are circling around high above the treetops. A cloud moves overhead and everything darkens and the birds fly away squawking as they go.

I climb off the torp and out of the clearing and up the next hill. The air's ripe with rot. I look back and see the torp's chimney stack, alone and kinked halfway up like an old man's finger. On the other side of the slope, my wool's running out now, it gets steeper, not quite a cliff, but a boulder as high as a house. I perch on top of it and pull out a handful of wine gums. I put them all in my mouth at once for a fruit cocktail effect. The sugar hits me. Tutti-frutti deluxe. I look down into the trees and see nothing. It's me sitting on this rock with my feet dangling over the edge, and a thousand spruce trees in front of me and each side of me. The wind picks up. The treetops are rustling but it's perfectly still down here. I stash the rest of the wool, a loose little ball, into my backpack, and bring out my bottle of Coke. I open it carefully because it fizzes and hisses and I drink half the bottle. It's warm, but it is good.

This is it then. I turn my hearing aids down. I want to hear things if they come, but I also want it to be quiet. I sit cross-legged and stare into the trees. I'm the same height as the dead lower branches, but I'm above where the trunks sink into the wet ground. I think of Dad and look up, and my chest tightens. I stare up at heavy rain-clouds the colour of dolphins as they scroll through the sky. I force myself to remember. I think back to the feel of his rough cheek on mine and the sound of his voice just before I used to fall asleep and his way of bending down and opening his arms wide for me to run to him. I blink and my eyes begin to prickle.

I can hear almost nothing now. My head is all Dad. The smell of Vosene shampoo and boot polish and cigarettes. I can hold on to his scent for a tiny fragment of a moment if I focus hard enough, if I really try. He had rough hands, not big, but rough, with sore nails and jagged cuticles. He used to stick plasters on my knees the way I liked, blowing on the cut, then separating the plastic strips and placing it down softly. Then a hug. My eyes are changing now. I stare up and scan the clouds, then reach back for that loose remainder of soft red wool, and then Mum joins Dad in my eyes and tears fall down the sides of my face and stream over my temples. They're together and I'm safe and she's happy. But she's not happy and I'll see her tomorrow and she's as far away from happy as she could ever be.

The tears come faster, but I know deep inside that I have a thousand crisp layers to break through here on this mossy rock before it's all out. I'm getting through but I'm still close to the surface. I look up. The birds have gone and the grey clouds are rolling by faster now, cold air bristling through the trees in front of me.

There's one memory I have of them kissing and it's stupid, really. They were kissing in the kitchen, a grown-up sort of kiss, lingering and full, and then I walked in for a glass of milk and I saw them. They looked at me and I ran off. I was annoyed with them both, and annoyed with myself. But now I treasure this hazy image. They were happy before Dad died, before that elk came along and broke his neck.

My mouth is dry. I reach up with wool in my hand and stroke my cheek with it and smell the angora, and my eyes burst open with tears, spraying and pouring as my chest convulses and my stomach tightens until it is just a stone. My neck is straight and I'm looking up at the sky at Dad.

Mum has white hair in my memories, but she was blonde before he died. She was happy, too, reclusive and awkward, but still happy in her own way. I resent the newspapers for ruining all that, and I although I hate myself for it, I resent Mum for a hundred different things. And now I'm here on this rock and she's two hours' drive away and all on her own in a hospice receiving palliative care and dying on her own. And I'm here. On my own. The wool in my hand is wet and it smells stronger now. I hold it up to my eyes and mop them and look through its crazed angora threads to the grey sky, now almost indigo in its heaviness. Mum failed me and now I'm completely failing her.

Gunshot. My head bolts forward. My eyes are full of tears, like lenses of water I can't quite see through. The shot's muffled with my aids turned down this low, but I feel it. I blink hard and look out.

And there it is. I can hardly see it at first because it's so perfectly still, standing between two bold spruce trees. It hasn't flinched. Not like the one on the road. This one looks older and more distinguished. It's lower down than me, its antlers lower than the rock I'm perched on. I'm looking down at an elk and it's looking up at me and neither one of us moving and in a single breath I forgive it completely. It didn't mean to take my Dad with its own life. It didn't want to do that, there was no plan. The elk shakes its heavy head, the grey beard under its jaw swinging into my vision as it evades a horsefly. Then it bends down to chew berries or saplings, I can't see from this angle. I'm just up here staring down at its antlers and they're as wide as my truck, maybe wider.

The tears come and come, along with noises, animal noises that stir him from his munching and make him look up at me again. I sob. I retch. I crack through more layers and I ball and my whole body shudders, but I am not afraid at all. Not one bit. I look up at the sky and away from him even though he's just metres from me.

I look up and cry out and try to smell them both one more time, the way they were back then; the Vosene and the knitting, and I manage it for just a blink. I can actually smell them. The sobs start to ebb. My chest aches and my collar feels wet against my neck. I look down and the elk's disappeared back into the woods. I stand up and turn around. There's movement near the chimney stack. I can hear the rustling of branches, and then I notice a man dressed in grey and he's holding a zip-up rifle case.

41

My mouth's so dry my lips are stuck together. I wait. I can sense everything moving, the living things all around me, nature getting on with its business; me frozen and out of place. The man's gone, I think. I only saw his back and now he's disappeared through the pines. I'm still not moving, no way, not yet. He looked like Viggo, but it could have been anyone, could have been any random hunter from Hannes's team. But it did look like Viggo. A little broader at the shoulder, perhaps. Thank God it's daylight.

I stay perfectly still. I've made peace in a way, with nature and with Mum and with Dad. Not completely, but in some small way. I feel lighter. I wait for another five minutes and then I follow the red yarn back to the tree and back to the path, and then I walk to my truck and get in and drive the hell away.

I get home and rest and shower and put on the smartest non-funeral clothes I own: a pair of fitted dark blue trousers and a white long-sleeved T-shirt and a navy merino wool cardigan. The cardigan's got a moth hole from my London years but it's under my armpit so it's fine.

Storgatan is quiet for a Saturday night on account of the wind. I'm driving out of town. It's twenty-one metres per second and strong enough to blow your wig off, as dad used to say. Bengt would know. Hanging baskets of heather are swinging wildly on their chains outside the hairdresser, and the boar sign outside Björnmossen's hunting shop has fallen flat on its face.

I stop at the lights and glance over towards Tammy's takeout van on the outer edge of the supermarket car park. There's a crowd of people queuing on the far side of it. My truck sways a little as I crest the small hill out of town and drive under the motorway and past the digger yard. I'm okay in my warm driving seat with the truck's sturdy chassis all around me. They use this model in the deserts of Africa and the mountains of Alaska, at least that's what the rental guy told me.

I'm not going to drink tonight. This is work. I need to investigate and work out if Hannes is involved, and then I need to write it up accurately, because nobody else will. And I need to help end it. I can do all these things. I'm not drinking tonight but God knows I need one.

And then I see the tip of Utgard forest and the trees swaying hard in the wind. The birches and pines lurch at different tempos. The weight of their needles and branches must be distributed differently. The pines look solid and strong, whereas the birches appear bendy and loose, and they whip about, and then when the gusts hit, they thrash wildly like headbanging teenagers. The sky's thick with dense clouds that look so low they're almost stuck in the treetops, but they're moving fast, speeding as if to get the hell out of this damn storm. I put my wipers on low speed. It doesn't feel like it's blowing itself out, it feels like it's working itself up.

I turn onto the Mossen village track and the rain comes quicker now, almost horizontal squalls like someone throwing buckets of water at me from offstage. The rain is thick and sticky, it's sleet really. Hoarder's home, and his optimistic solar lights are blinking faintly and they look like eyes in his garden. Taxi's home, Volvo in the driveway, TV on. Up the hill, and I see water flowing back down the other way, rivulets of ice-cold rain gushing back down the slope. At the top it gets darker. I notice the temperature on the dash fall from two degrees to zero, but it's not snowing. I can smell the smoke of the workshop before I get to the sisters' place, and they're both there, carving and sanding and lathing and not looking my way as I drive past their demonic little operation. But, no. I brake and reverse. I can do this. After today, I can do anything. I back up and stop right outside their workshop. If I can face the woods, I can face them.

The run from my truck to the sisters' workbenches takes about ten seconds and I keep my hands over my ears the whole time.

'What you looking for, girl?' the talking one asks.

'I'm looking for no more trolls turning up at my apartment.' I've got my hands on my hips and I already feel better for saying it. I feel like how Tammy and Lena must feel every day.

She looks over to her sister who's gouging out slivers of pine with what looks like an apple corer. 'We lost any trolls, Alice? Any gone missing? Any escaped?'

'Nope,' says Alice.

'Not our trolls, girl,' says the talking sister.

I look at her and she holds my stare, and then I have to look away. It's the eyes with no lashes that does it. They don't look quite human.

'If I find another troll I'll call the police on you, and I'm not talking about the Gavrik police.'

'You call whoever you want, girl,' the talking sister says. 'Now . . .' she moves towards the back wall where two identical rifles rest against the rough-sawn siding. 'We got work to do for the craft fair in Munkfors, and you ain't helping Alice's concentration one bit. I reckon you'll be swinging your butt back in your pickup and driving away right about now, wouldn't you reckon so, Alice?'

'Yep.'

They get back to carving.

I don't budge.

'Why did you leave Norway?' I ask.

Cornelia, the talking one, looks up at me with a steel gouger in her hand.

'Maybe you need new hearing aids. I said you'll best be driving away about now, girl. We'll be seeing you.'

I get in and turn the key and switch my wipers up a gear and set off. My pulse is racing and my lungs feel like they might burst out of my chest, but I fucking did it. I was fourteen again standing up to that shitbitch who bullied me for having no pappa. Stood up to her and now I've stood up to them. I turn my heated seat down and then I see there's something in front of me so I slam my right foot down and the truck skids as it stops. I'm pushed tight into my seatbelt. Deer on the track. It's the spotted-Bambi-cutesy variety, and it's standing still and looking straight at me. Legs like matchsticks. Idiot. I focus on its head. It looks dead still, like it's been stuffed, all except for its ears, they're very much alive, two furry radar dishes, spinning in the wind this way and that. It looks away and walks across the road like it's not scared at all and then another deer follows close behind it, seemingly oblivious to me or the howling gale or the sleet or the villagers. They jump the ditch and disappear into the trees, me stalking them with my eyes like they're a celebrity couple crossing Oxford Street.

I scratch my lip and set off again, this time much slower. I drive past Ghostwriter's house. There are lights on inside but I can't see the dog. There's a line of sawdust on the track up ahead from where Hannes has cut up the fallen tree, and it looks like some kind of marker, some sort of boundary. I drive over it and along the twisty final stretch to the very centre of Utgard forest.

Frida's house looks welcoming, always does. Maybe it's the roof with its dainty protruding windows, or the fact that the lights seem to be on all of the time. And that little grey hut makes it feel more like a hamlet in a strange sort of way, it feels less isolated than the neighbours' houses.

Their cars are parked side by side. The flagpole's bending and it looks like it could snap like a toothpick. As I get out of my truck with a bottle of Chilean screw-cap merlot in my hand, I rush past it with my chin pressed to my neck to avoid the worst of the sleet.

I approach the double front doors and they swing open and Frida pulls me inside. She hugs me awkwardly and dusts the sleet off my hair. It's turning to snow now.

'You look smart,' I read her lips. 'Can I get you a towel or a hairdryer? Don't want you catching a chill.'

'I'm fine,' I say, one eye keeping lookout for Hannes. 'It's my hearing aids that hate water, not me. I reach into my pocket and hook them over my ears. Frida looks both intrigued and somehow embarrassed as I switch them both on right in front of her. Music fills my ears. It's coming from the living room. 'The Leader of the Pack' is playing softly on the Carlssons' Bose stereo.

'Glass of wine?' she asks.

I pass her the bottle of Merlot and the wet label is starting to peel off.

'Can't tonight, I have to drive back through this storm later. You have one and I'll drink water if that's okay.'

She cringes sympathetically and I hear a new rock and roll love song start up in the other room.

'We're out of mineral water I'm afraid. Tap water okay?'

I nod and we walk into the kitchen and it smells amazing. She hands me a glass of water that's not quite transparent. It's pale brown, which is pretty normal in a village like this one. No municipal supply. Each home has its own well in the garden and the iron in the acidic forest soil makes it brown. Centuries of decaying organic matter. Rot. I take a swig and the water's cold and it tastes like screws. The windows are fogging up. The floor's warm under my socks. Frida offers me a plate of little crisp things topped with crème fraiche and gravadlax and lemon zest and a curl of red onion and a frond of dill. I eat seven of them without even realising.

'I hope I'm not prying,' she says, turning her head from the saucepan of soup on the hob. 'But are you feeling okay, sweetie? You look like you've been crying.'

How the hell can she see that? After hours and a nap and a shower and make-up and a torrent of eye drops, how can she tell?

'Hormones,' I say, waving it away with my hand. 'Where's Hannes?'

'Oh, didn't I say? Hannes has one of his migraines. He works so hard you know; a lot of pressure in that kind of position, lots of late nights. He's gone upstairs early. I'll take him up a tray. It's just you and me eating down here tonight. He says hello, though.'

'Hope he feels better soon.'

'Just popping out for my secret ingredient, I'll only be a jiffy.'

'Can I come with you?'

She smiles and then frowns. 'No, no. You stay in here and keep warm. Won't be a sec.'

I watch out of the window as she bends down and walks to the grey hut, a fleece jacket thrown over her head against the sleet. The weather vane on top of the hut is spinning this way and that. In the white glare of the security light, she looks almost heroic, the brightness picking out each fat droplet of sleet as it falls.

She comes back inside and pushes three ice cubes into the bubbling saucepan and then puts the rubber ice cube tray into the dishwasher. She stirs for a while, adding coarse sea salt and cracked black pepper, and six large herb dumplings from the oven.

We sit down at the table. She's at the head and I'm adjacent to her like two lovers on a date. The wild mushroom soup's incredible; rich and doused with cream and flat-leaved parsley. It's gamey and even better than the last one. And the dumplings, huge rye dough-balls really, taste like being a kid again. Soft, bready dough with a crusty shell, each one soaking up broth with tiny chunks of chopped walnuts attached. I can't eat it fast enough. I feel nourished with every spoonful.

'This is delicious,' I tell her. 'So delicious.'

She smiles and tells me they're all Utgard mushrooms and then she ladles me more soup and takes up a tray to Hannes, along with a bottle of beer.

I've finished the second bowl by the time she comes back down. I butter a piece of flat Norrland bread and as I pull the wooden knife out of the butter, it catches on my cardigan sleeve and leaves a smudge. I dab it with a paper napkin but the smudge stays.

Frida walks to me.

'Give it here and I'll bung it in the washer. I've got a special cycle for delicate woollens.'

She holds out her hand so I slip it off and pass it to her.

'That way the stain won't have time to catch hold, if you know what I mean. I'll take care of it.'

She walks through a door to what I presume is her laundry room and then a moment later she walks back.

'I was watching a deaf man on television last night and he didn't talk nearly half as well as you do. I thought to myself, it's impressive the way Tuva speaks just like a normal person. I wanted to tell you that. It's impressive. Well done.'

I almost spit the bread out of my mouth

'I endured years of painful speech therapy. It was hell, actually.'

Frida clears away the soup and brings out two smaller bowls from the fridge filled with thick creamy liquid.

I continue. 'After school, every day, all my childhood, special classes so I could intonate, so I could pronounce words like a hearing person.'

'Well, I'd say it was well worth it, you sound lovely.'

This isn't going anywhere good. She doesn't know how God-awful her words sound right now. But I need to stick to my plan.

'Can I ask you a question? I'm thinking of building an outbuilding for my mum. Not actually building it myself, of course, just instructing a carpenter. For when she moves back home.' This lie tightens my stomach into a knot. 'I don't know much about it and your hut out there looks so smart. Do you think I could take a look with you, just for inspiration?'

'What does your mother want a hut for?'

Her tone isn't aggressive, just curious.

'Storage mainly, and perhaps a guest room in case she needs a live-in carer. It's quite a nice spot, her place, close to Lake Vänern.'

Frida looks at me.

'You know, it's all Hannes's private stuff in there. We shouldn't go in without asking him. It's all his tools and things, he's quite protective.'

'Just a peek?'

She smiles, her eyes glancing through the window towards the hut, then back to me.

'Oh, come on then.'

She pulls out an umbrella from the stand in the hall. I pop out my aids and place them in my coat pocket. Frida can hardly open the front door, the wind's so strong. We go out and for the first few metres our heads are covered by the porch awning, but then as we emerge from underneath it, we run. Frida's umbrella snaps violently inside out, the metal struts spiking out like a porcupine under attack. I see her hair blow across her face and she's trying to say something, but I can't read her lips out here in this weather. I go to the hut door but she doesn't come with me, she heads to the corner of the building and reaches under the lowest part of the timber and pulls a key from a gap in the stone foundation. She joins me, sleet freezing my cheeks, and unlocks the door. We fall into the hut and the door slams shut on its own.

I dry my hands on my trousers and put my aids back in. Frida switches on the fluorescent strip lights. We stand together, half-drowned, looking into a garage with no car in it. There's a lot of pine shelving with paint tins and chainsaws and boxes of screws and nails. The floor's chipboard and it's sagging in places. There's a mousetrap poised by a low shelf, a small piece of Marabou milk chocolate balanced on one end. I can see the raised *M* letter on the dusty brown surface. There's a chest freezer humming against one wall and it looks like the one Mum used to have. The far end of the space has looped electrical extension cords hanging from long nails, and a sleeping bag and a pack of razors and a camping lantern. I can see car-cleaning equipment, and a series of padlocked wooden boxes screwed to the wall. One of them has a shamrock or clover symbol etched on the front.

'Gun storage?'

Frida wipes the sleet from her eyelashes, mascara running down her cheeks like black tears.

'Just weedkiller and that sort of thing. Fertiliser. When Peter lived with us Hannes had to lock all this up as a precaution.'

'Peter?'

'Our boy,' she smiles and sighs. 'We haven't seen him for almost twenty years.' She pulls a cross out from her sweater and holds it.

'I'm so sorry.'

She smiles at me. I can't tell if the water on her cheeks now is sleet or tears but she looks gaunt of a sudden.

'Where is he? What did Peter do?'

'Oh,' Frida says. 'He was an engineer, had real promise, but he left us a few years after college. Gambling problems. Ran off with some girl from Karlstad and now they live in Spain, or did last time I heard anything. Your mum's lucky to still have you around.'

I swallow hard.

Frida wrestles with the misshapen umbrella, cold slush turning her hands red.

'You'll have to excuse the mousetraps, Tuva, it's the only way we can deal with them.'

I assume she's talking about the chocolate trap but then I follow her index finger and see a glue trap under a workbench. There's a mouse in the centre of the trap, which looks like a paper plate, and it's trying desperately to escape. It's glued to the spot and exhausted and it looks like it'll pull its front half away from its back half if it can get any traction.

The storm outside is intensifying, the metal loops rattling where the flag meets the pole. I look at a stack of *Gavrik Posten* copies, with last week's issue on top. There must be thirty of them. The mouse-trap with the chocolate bait goes snap and we both jump. Then the lights all go off.

42

'It's okay,' says Frida.

But it's not okay at all. I reach out for objects in the room but I can't remember where things are clearly, I just got in here. I need to see. I need to be able to see things because seeing's what I've got.

There's no light at all. Nothing.

'Wait one second,' Frida says. 'There's a torch on the wall.'

I move like a zombie, arms outstretched, and bump into the chest freezer with my hip bone. I hold on to it like it's a raft. There's a draught at my neck. The wind is inside now.

Frida knocks something over and then clicks on the torch.

'Come on, let's get back to the house before Hannes comes out.'

Frida points the torch at the ground so I can see where I'm walking and we jog holding each other. The forest, I can see it in my peripheral vision, is black as black and it feels too close to us. I think about that poor sticky mouse. We get to the front door and Frida opens it and pushes me inside.

The house is dark but 'Be My Baby' is playing and it sounds louder than it did before the power cut.

Be my little baby.

'Oh, the stereo's battery-powered,' says Frida, like that makes it all fine now.

Everything is blackness. I'm in the bullseye of a fucking murder forest and there are no lights on anywhere.

'I'll get off home now,' I say. 'I need to go. I don't want to be a nuisance.'

But I can't hear my own voice properly. My aids got wet during the dash over to the house, the sleet must have got in. I pull them both out and blow on them.

'Hannes,' Frida shouts, I can read her lips clearly in the torchlight. 'Hannes.'

I put my aids back in my ears and one's stopped working altogether. The other one's better now, some interference like a badly tuned radio station.

'I need to go,' I say, icy water dripping down the back of my neck.

'Shhh,' says Frida. She switches her torch off. 'Listen.' We're standing about an arm-length apart where the hall meets the living room and there's no light and 'Be My Baby' finishes and then it starts over again from the beginning.

I hear a knock at the front door and Frida throws herself at me and clings to me.

'Frida. Let me in, woman.'

She apologises and moves away from me. She switches on her torch and unlocks the door and there's Hannes, rain dripping down his face.

'Damn electric company, why don't you write about them in your paper? Cutting corners, not maintaining the cables. This is what we get for living at the end of the line. Power cuts all the bloody time.'

'How's your migraine?' I ask him.

'What did you say?' he looks big in the torchlight, not tall especially but almost as broad as the door. And he's blocking my exit.

'Frida said you weren't feeling well.'

He looks over at her with a disappointed expression.

'I'm fine.'

Frida glances at me and her eyes say, 'indulge him.'

'No toilets, now,' she says, standing close to me. 'We can light a fire, we have plenty of wood, but the well pump's electric. No toilets, no showers, no dishwasher, no laundry. Oh,' she covers her mouth with the palm of her hand, her diamond wedding ring twinkling in the torchlight. 'Your cardigan, the cycle won't have finished yet.'

'I'll get it some other time. Thanks for the dinner, Frida. I think I'd better head home.'

'Don't fancy it out here in the woods with no creature comforts, do you?' Hannes says.

'Not especially, no.'

'Thought as much.'

He stands aside and I see the door.

'Thanks again, I'll see you soon.' I touch Frida's arm and make a move for the exit but Hannes gets to the handle before me and makes some kind of chivalrous exhibition, holding it and bowing slightly and pushing it open.

'Mind yourself,' he says. 'Nothing good out there tonight.'

I run as fast as I can to my truck. I get in and breathe and my aids are both malfunctioning now so I can't hear anything. I pull them out and place them on the passenger seat. They'll need to be in desiccant all night to fix this. Maybe that won't be enough. I turn my key in the ignition, my fingers shaking from cold. Nothing. I start to pant, strands of my hair plastered over my eyes, my hands slippery on the wheel. I turn the key and nothing happens. Everything is dark and completely quiet. I peer down at the ignition on the side of the steering column and lick the sleet off my upper lip and focus. The gearstick. I left it in drive, not park. But I never do this, I've not done this for five years at least, not since I started driving automatics. I stare at it, at the illuminated 'D' symbol. I pull it to park and turn the key and the engine starts. My lights come on and bathe the wall of the grey hut in sleet-speckled light. I'm exhausted. I reverse and turn and drive away from the dark house that I can no longer see.

I want to be somewhere in a big city right now, in midtown New York or central Madrid or anywhere. I want lights and cars and people and shops and late-night comedy clubs, right now, everywhere around me; I want noise and hubbub and electricity.

I drive slowly, remembering that baby deer. Unlike me, it won't be spooked by a power cut. That deer won't give a shit. I drive through the twists and come up by David Holmqvist's place. No dog, but I can see his house, the mirrored windows reflecting my headlights. There are puddles on the track as big as paddling pools now, and potholes filled with ice-slush and mud. The sisters aren't in their workshop but the log-burner's still smoking. The whole fucking village is dark. Down the hill and I can see nothing but pines. I can't see houses and I can't see the sky.

Viggo's home is filled with candles, little tea lights and candlesticks on the kitchen window sills. Bengt's caravan looks like it normally does. I get out of the woods and breathe. My seat's warm and it feels like my clothes are steaming from the inside. The truck shakes in the wind and I grab a handful of wine gums from the passenger seat and stuff them into my mouth. There are no other cars on the roads. None.

Then I see lights. The motorway has a few trucks on it, their long wipers scraping back sleet as they push forward to make their deliveries on time. The town's lit up, there's no power cut here. On my left, behind McDonald's, are Saturday night hordes of teenagers: beautiful girls and boys who will all kick themselves in later life for a thousand different reasons. Then there's the hockey rink. Floodlights. I've always liked floodlit matches. Sport at night, whatever the weather, illuminated to the max. I can't see the rink itself from the road but I can see the lights beaming down through the weather from their steel struts. The sponsor's logo is lit up on one side of the stand. Hannes Carlsson's employer, SPT pulp mills.

He seemed on edge tonight, spooked, desperate. I didn't get a chance to search his hut properly but at least now I know where Frida hides the key.

43

I wake up and take my aids from the desiccant jar and shake them and hook them over my ears and then I switch them on and open my bedroom window. Icing-sugar snow on the ground. I feel good, warm feet and cold cheeks. The air smells of liquorice. I watch a drunk-looking wasp buzz around the closed part of the window searching for a way in. It seems weary. I half turn the window latch and then I hear a sharp scream from the street below. I look down and see an old lady on the ground clutching an ICA Maxi shopping bag. Four red apples roll away before settling in the fine snow. Then someone helps her up.

I can't remember my dreams but I know I've been thinking about Mossen village and the dead hunters. It's like my thoughts have been reorganised for me, highlighted and ordered and filed in the correct places, like the research archives in David Holmqvist's spare room, the one I saw. I shower and put on long-johns for the first time since Easter. And then I get too hot and look out of the window and the snow's gone. I can see just a few patches of white left in the shadows of hedges and walls and cars. I pull off the long-johns and feel a static crackle as the material brushes past the fine hairs on my autumn legs. I make a portion of microwave porridge and take a swig of Coke.

It feels like a Sunday. I can hear church bells ringing and the town's shut for business apart from the liquorice factory, which only closes on Christmas Eve and Midsummer.

I'll spend some quality time with Mum today, some real 'her and me' time. I bought her a cashmere blanket for Christmas, a supersoft thing with a herringbone weave. Risky to wait. I'm going to give it to her today.

I mumble my little speech to myself as I walk from my apartment building to the police station. The door's locked so I buzz and Thord walks through with a mug in his hand. He holds up his splayed fingers and mouths 'five' to me and walks back to the rear office.

My hands are cold. The air's thick with moisture, brief glimpses of sunshine through cloud like the day hasn't decided what it will be yet. *Storgatan*'s deserted so I walk towards Hotel Gavrik with its off-centre sign. A candle sits either side of the front entrance but they're not the usual garden candles the hotel and Tammy use to show they're open for business. They're graveyard candles, little white things with rain guards designed to burn for twenty-four hours. They're expensive. I guess they ran out of the usual ones.

I turn and head back to the police station. The door's unlocked now. I walk in and the ticket machine reads 21 and I pull out the paper ticket and hold it in my hand.

'Hi Tuva. I don't have long – you've caught us at a busy time.'

I smile and look around the empty waiting area.

'Back in the office, I mean. We're very busy today. What is it?'

I put my hands on the counter.

'Can I speak with you and the Chief at the same time, please?'

He laughs. 'No chance. You got me and you got me for about one more minute.'

He's looking at his watch as I start talking.

'You need to visit Hannes Carlsson. Did you know he has gun cabinets in that hut next to his house and they're hidden behind shelves? You haven't found the murder weapon yet, I'd say that's the place to start looking. His eyes are failing him, he won't be able to hunt much longer, he's getting desperate. Now, if you and the Chief don't get over there and check out what I just told you, I'll have to call in the Stockholm police. I've got a few contacts down there.'

He smiles.

'You done?' he says, still looking at his watch.

I nod and he looks up at me.

'Chief knows all about Carlsson's eye problem. Who do you think authorised his last permit? You don't think we know much about much, do you? And he has licences for three firearms, as I remember: two rifles and a shotgun. Either way, ain't a law forbidding gun cabinet ownership, in fact I wish more people around here would store the weapons responsibly. Now, I'll give you a tip-off, an exclusive for your newspaper. The TV appeals worked. Back in there, we're meeting to discuss it all. Fresh info. We now have a prime suspect.'

I raise my eyebrows.

'You'll have to wait and see like all the others.'

A plug-in air freshener wheezes artificial pine scent at me from the wall behind him.

'You can't follow up on two leads?'

'You're not in possession of all the facts, Tuvs. Now, if the suspect we're looking into isn't our man, we'll talk to Hannes Carlsson. You have my word. I gotta go.'

I didn't quite hear the last few words, my aids are still playing up from last night. The desiccant removed most of the moisture but I'm still getting interference. Luckily for me, Thord has a big old horse mouth and I can lip-read him from the next street.

He types in the key code to his door and walks back to the office. I see Björn standing there, and three or four others. As the door closes Björn turns to look at me and he rubs his nose with his hand and I see the tattoo again. A 'K' and a heart. All red. And then I get an image in my head and it is not the face of his wife.

It's a playing card.

My heart rate accelerates. I step out into the cold, my mind whirring, a riddle solving itself, and then I walk around to the police car park. I count seven cars, four of them unmarked or civilian.

I march down *Storgatan*, my hands tucked into the ends of my coat sleeves. Need to think this through and I need to get some supplies, especially now it's turning wintry. Maybe a miniature rose in a pot for Mum. I'll plan my next move in the supermarket cafe although God knows it is the most depressing place this side of the crematorium. Black plastic seats and a TV screen for betting on horse racing, and cling-wrapped sandwiches that were soggy well before they got chucked behind the glass counter.

I walk up to my office building and the lights are off. A white taxi drives past me and I see its reflection in the office door. I push my face against the glass. Locked, but I think Lena's in, her door's open a little. I knock three times and she comes out.

'You working on a Sunday?' I ask her. 'Why aren't you home?'

'What are you, my mother? Jesus.'

I walk in and take off my boots and hang up my coat. The office is nice when it's empty; it has the familiar stuffiness of a well-loved university room. It's warm and it smells of coffee and printer ink.

'Had an argument with Johan,' she says, holding up a hand. 'Don't ask.'

We walk into her office. She's reading *The New York Times* from last weekend because I think someone there still sends it to her.

'Nothing as exciting as here,' she says, pointing down to the front page.

I clear my throat. 'Tell me more about that gambling ring.'

She frowns.

'The poker club. You said the rumour was that a council official was a member.'

She sniffs. 'Years back, talk of a four-player club, high stakes, kinda thing you imagine in a gangster movie. Lots of liquor and girls, macho bullshit, some weird code, maybe some shady real estate deals. People around here called it "the game".'

'Any ideas about who was in it?'

'The council guy people gossiped about died in the '90s. I haven't heard it mentioned for years.'

'I think maybe it still exists and I think Björn is a member.'

'Okay.'

'And Hannes, too.'

She frowns at me. 'Go on.'

'I don't know. Could be that Hannes is Medusa and Björn's protecting him. Hannes's eyes are failing and this is his last year of hunting and it was drilled into him and every other boy around here that if they can't kill and butcher then they aren't men and they won't be able to support their families through a tough winter. He has a son who moved away, and a wife, Frida, well I don't think they're really together, I think they live separate lives in the same house. It's a front. And he's a great shot, Benny Björnmossen told me, one of the best he's seen.'

'Any actual evidence?'

'Or it could be that "the game" itself is Medusa, I've heard about S&M stuff, high-risk bets with huge stakes.'

'This is what the stripper told you.'

'What's that got to do with it? Listen, we all went after the ghost-writer bogeyman, but I think the respectable, rich guy at the end of the road maybe did it out of frustration. Or envy. Maybe with his poker mates, or maybe they just helped him to never get caught. Hannes had everything and yet the only things that mattered to him have left or are leaving.'

'Interesting theory. Now, tell me, how much do you know about Holmqvist's parents?'

'Just that they're both dead. Why?'

Lena scratches her cheek. 'They died with David at the wheel. It was the day he passed his driving test, and he took them out for a drive in good weather and managed to crash into a tree. They were both killed instantly and he walked away from the accident. He was unscathed.'

'I did not know that.'

'Well, now you do. He was the only one in the car wearing a seatbelt. It's likely not relevant, but I thought you should know. Just because the cops don't have evidence doesn't mean Holmqvist isn't Medusa. You've told Thord or one of the Karlstad cops about your Hannes research?'

'Thord's busy on a lead and won't even consider Hannes as Medusa. It's as if Gavrik is standing together like a human wall guarding him.'

'He's well liked.'

I raise my eyebrows.

'So, what's your plan? There might be something to your story, but so far it's all conjecture and about as libellous as can be.'

'I'll get you copy and something concrete and I'll follow up on the poker thing. Might need to liaise with police from another force once I've worked it all out. But right now I have to head down to Karlstad.'

'Ooh, bright lights, big city.'

'Bed-ridden mamma. Can't put it off.'

Her expression softens.

'Be careful, Tuva. Don't get too exposed, and don't get tangled up in old myths and legends. Remember, I'm happy you're here, but I want to see you working somewhere like this,' she taps *The New York Times* on her desk. 'Before you get too old for it, you hear me? Check out Hannes by all means, but keep your mind open.'

I put my outdoor gear back on and walk out. I head past the haberdashery store and the hunt shop and the hairdresser and the newsagent and it feels like it could snow. I walk up to ICA Maxi and its vast car park and it's busy with early shoppers. It is windy here because there's nothing to stop the breeze. I see Tammy's takeout van and jog over to it. She's sometimes here early, prepping food and cleaning up after the busy Saturday night shift, but not today. All locked up. I walk to the supermarket and the doors swoosh open and I pick up a basket.

There's a calm inside. It's climate-controlled and predictable and clean. I've been doing the weekly shop since I was fourteen, along with paying bills and cleaning and picking up prescriptions and everything else Mum couldn't manage. People here are buying pick'n'mix for their Sunday evenings in front of the TV. I smell fresh bread, and then one of those ride-on floor polisher things drives by and my aids scream in my ears and the feedback makes me cringe.

I get my groceries and a gift for Mum, and then I approach the tills. There are three open. I see the pretty girl's working on till 1 so I head over to her. I place my items on the conveyer belt and she bleeps them through while I bag them up.

'Eight hundred and thirty kronor, do you have a loyalty card?'

I shake my head. 'You see Hannes Carlsson, the mill boss, come in here?'

She looks at me with a careful smile showing just enough white teeth to make it perfect.

'He's like the only man in town who doesn't need the coin, that's what they say.'

'What do you mean?'

I hand over my card to pay.

'I mean he just leaves his trolley next to his car after he's done. He's got a good economy that one, so he never bothers to bring the trolley back to get his ten kronor. That's what they say, anyway.'

A woman bumps into me after she pays at the next till. She's with her friend and I recognise them both from the haberdashery store. I've seen them buying knitting patterns and wool in there.

'Deaf and dumb,' one of them says to the other, just loud enough for me to hear. She has a mole on her cheek with a kinked hair growing out of it.

'And a dyke,' the other one replies. 'Deaf, dumb and homo. I'd call that a hat-trick.'

'Pin code please,' says the pretty girl before I can berate the women.

273

I turn, agitated, and enter my four-digit code. I want to bite them both. When I've finished paying, I scan around for the women but they've gone.

I walk home subdued. Clouds overhead. I head up towards the monolithic liquorice factory and take a left turn to get home. The handles of my plastic shopping bags cut into my hands like cheese wires and I keep adjusting my grip. Is this poker club the victims or the killers or both, and how the hell do I find out? I get home and unpack my bags and as I reach up into the cupboard above the sink to put away a box of macaroni, '30% Extra Free', I remember the troll, the one with the surprise in his pants, the one locked in my basement. I make a cheese sandwich and it tastes amazing. It's cheap white bread, and as I chew it turns into sweet paste on the roof of my mouth. I grab my handbag and the rose plant I've bought for Mum and walk out to my truck.

44

I pull out of my parking space and dial Mum. No pick-up. But that's pretty normal now, it usually takes her a while to get to the phone, or for someone else to hand it to her, so I end the call. I drive up *Storgatan*, past a line of people filing into the Lutheran church and then I drive past another crowd walking out of the evangelical church. I reach down to call again and there's a message on my screen from Frida. Do I want anything from the department store in Karlstad? I reply that I'm heading there myself later so I'm fine and then I thank her. I redial Mum.

'Hello, who is this?'

'Mum, it's me. You know I said I'd come by today, well I'm on my way.'

I wait for her to answer but there's nothing.

'Mum, you there? I'll be with you about three, traffic permitting.'

'It's Sunday,' she says. 'There won't be any traffic.'

'How are you today? Is it a good day or a bad day?'

'Oh, I'm all right.'

I sweep past ICA Maxi and the car park's really filling up now. Most people are wearing woolly hats and gloves.

'Well, I'm coming over to cheer you up. Anything you need?'

I can't hear her answer, just the crackling on the line.

'Mum, I can't hear you.' I overtake a cyclist. 'I'm bringing gifts and I'm looking forward to seeing you, it's been pretty busy up here.'

'You mean the writer killing those people?'

I grab a wine gum and put it on my tongue without looking at it. It's a red one. Third favourite. Not bad.

'Mum, I'll see you at three-ish, and I've got a surprise for you. Gotta go now, I'm joining the motorway. Bye.'

I indicate left and pull into the lane taking me southbound towards Karlstad and Gothenburg. I switch the radio on but something catches my eye in the truck's wing mirror. It's lights, flashing lights, police cars speeding past me towards the underpass. I swerve right without thinking and push my foot down to catch up with them. Then I check my mirrors and half-swerve back to the E16. Two cars honk their horns. I can't leave Mum all alone today, I can't. But I can delay the visit by an hour. Maybe they really do have information I don't have, a gun dealer who remembers selling a second-hand rifle to Hannes. Or maybe Daisy called them up on her way to London. Or the wood-carving sisters made a deal too far. Or Viggo's been doing more than just target practice.

I follow the cop cars. I'll drive to Mum straight after this, one forty all the way down to make up time and then I'll stay longer with her. I'll stay until she falls asleep. I drive under the E16 and check my back seat. I have my ski coat and my backpack and more importantly, I have my camera. The battery's probably quarter-full. It'll do.

They're driving pretty fast. Police Volvos are supercharged in some way, at least that's what people say. By the time I see Utgard forest, they've turned onto the Mossen track and the woods have swallowed up their lights in one silent gulp. I take a right turn off the asphalt and my truck's suspension judders as it joins the rough gravel at speed. Maybe Hannes has an accomplice? Or an apprentice – maybe Viggo? Could be the whole village is infested or even the whole fucking town.

I drive towards Hoarder's house and see the flashing lights have stopped right outside his caravan. I slow down and find three cars parked in his garden and one on the far side of the vegetable patch with its tyres flattening a neat row of cauliflowers. Two more cars are over in the ditch. I stop my truck thirty metres or so before the house itself and grab my camera off the back seat.

The lens is long enough so I don't need my binoculars. Four or five police officers, maybe two guys and three women, are standing outside the house itself. Wait, no, they're going into the house and taking out stuff from it. It's a dry day, so I guess Bengt's stuff won't get too damaged, whatever it is he stores in there.

The cops are wearing face masks, like surgeon's masks, and they've all got thick rubber gloves and boots. I can make out stacks and stacks of magazines on the lawn and a big cardboard box full of Christmas decorations. A man walks out. It's Thord and he's carrying a kid's doll's house, one of the cheap '70s plastic ones. He sets it down near the newspapers and magazines but the ground's uneven and it topples into the ditch. I photograph it all.

I know there are people in the caravan because I can see it wobble and shift, but I can't see any faces from here. Two officers drag out a sofa covered with old detergent boxes and large cardboard containers. Then someone walks out with a neon sign, the glass smashed, I can't make out the words. I can tell by the speed that they're going in and out that they're still working on the entrance hall. A cop pulls out a plastic sheet – no, it's a deflated paddling pool, and it's filled with photo albums, the front covers blistered and curled with damp.

I drive forward slowly and see Thord walk out. He's holding a roll of blue-and-white police cordon-tape. As I slow down, he starts to tape across the front of the garden, using blackcurrant bushes and the henhouse and boulders as taping posts because there are no trees just here and no telegraph poles. The tape looks ridiculous, all saggy and loose.

I wind down my window and stop and take more photos. Thord is walking towards me but I ignore him. I can see through the caravan window from here. I can see Bengt crying. He has his head in his hands and he's crying. I drop the camera to my lap.

'You've got enough,' says Thord. 'Now, back your truck up please, you're obstructing the road.'

'It's not a public road, Thord, and I'm not quite done.'

'Move along.'

Two policewomen walk out from the house with what looks like a shrine, one of those roadside shrines to the Virgin Mary you see in Italy or Spain. This one's made of painted pine complete with little shelves for candles.

They're throwing it all down now, no more careful placing. They're dragging it out and chucking it on the vegetable patch, boxes squashing cabbages, and broken pieces of furniture leaning up against delicate pea sticks. And Bengt's still crying. I get out of the truck.

'Thord,' I call him over with my hand. 'I'll leave in two minutes, just give me a quote or something for the paper. Give me something I can use.'

He looks at me and shakes his head.

'Just something. Please.'

He glances back to the house and to one of his fellow officers, wiping something off his boots. The something came from indoors, not outdoors.

'Anonymous caller says there's a body inside. Says it's upstairs in the master bed. Some sex game thing gone wrong years ago, I don't know. If there's one house in the world I do not want to be inside on a Sunday afternoon, then it's this one. But I gotta. So let me do my job and you go back to your neat little office and do yours.'

I climb back in the truck and look up at the upstairs windows through my camera. Ivy. I can't see much more, the window panes haven't been washed for years, they're covered in birch pollen. I look at the caravan and see Bengt dabbing his eyes with a white hand-kerchief. He's pleading about something with his hands held out in front of his face.

I wind down my window.

'Thord. I'm going to Hannes Carlsson's place. I know you don't want to hear what I'm saying, but you know something's not right. Spare me one officer for thirty minutes.' I point at Bengt's caravan. 'He's not going anywhere. Thirty minutes.'

He walks over towards the truck and ducks under the loose tape.

'Didn't you hear what I said, Tuva? Could be there's a man's body in this house. Could be there's Bengt's old army rifle hidden in there somewhere. It'd be from 'bout the right era. Now, drop your theories and your ideas and leave Carlsson in peace.'

I close my window and drive on deeper into Mossen village. It is empty. Taxi's not there. I guess he's at church. I call Mum again and she picks up on the third attempt.

'Who is it?'

'It's me, Mum. I'm on my way but I'll be an hour later than I said, I'm sorry, it can't be helped.'

I can feel her smile down the line like she's pleased she can be disappointed in me.

'Pity.'

'I'm coming, Mum. I'll make it up to you. I'll see you at four.'

I hear a hiss on the line.

'I can't hear you,' I say.

'I said . . .' But the line goes dead. I'm driving up the hill now and reception always cuts out completely just here. There's fog, little patches of it dotted along the road. I'll call her when I'm back on the E16.

The sisters must also be at church, and Ghostwriter's not home either. No car and no dog. I drive up the track, smooth grey lines under my tyres and a rough grassy strip in between. I pass in and out of fog like I'm flying through clouds. At the entrance to Hannes and Frida's drive, I see the house and it's all lit up.

It's okay. There are no cars in the drive. I speed up to the front door and my nerves are hot and my palms are clammy. Nobody at the windows and nobody comes out of the house. The blue burglar alarm light is on. Nobody's home.

I drive back out and park in Ghostwriter's parking area. I take my camera and backpack and coat.

'What a pleasant surprise,' says David Holmqvist from beneath his veranda. He's framed by his open front door. Opera music plays behind him.

Shit. How come his car isn't here?

'Hi,' I say. 'Do you mind if I park in your guest space for a few hours?'

The hairs on his arms are standing up from the cold. His polo-shirt is pale yellow and he has no shoes on.

'Be my guest,' he says, moving his arm in a sweeping movement to indicate I should come inside.

'Sorry to be rude, I'm on a deadline and I need to get into the woods.'

'Just five minutes, humour me,' he says. 'I'm writing a short story with a deaf protagonist. Perhaps a novella, I'm not sure yet. We'll call this research. Come inside and I'll make you a ristretto.'

'Ristretto?'

'A quick coffee to fortify you,' he says. 'Ethiopian beans. Please, come inside.'

I step towards him and the wind pushes me inside. He shows me where to hang my coat and place my backpack and my shoes. He uses his iPad to turn down the volume of the opera music.

We walk towards the kitchen. I'm relieved to find no calf head on the stainless steel worktops. It's all gleaming and clean and there's nothing cooking so far as I can tell.

'I'm pleased you came by.'

'Well, I just have a minute, I have to follow up on a lead.'

He looks at the steel espresso scoops hanging above his industrial machine. He stares at them for a while, before selecting the mid-sized scoop and lifting it off its hook. He's wearing cashmere socks, I can see the feathery weave, hairy socks and hairy calves. If there weren't police nearby I would not be standing in this guy's kitchen right now.

'Where's your dog?' I ask.

'He's been a bad boy,' David says. 'Ate half of my car interior so he's gone to school to learn some manners. He'll be back later.'

Holmqvist hand-grinds coffee beans into a steel bowl and then dips his scoop into the dark powder and levels the scoop with his index finger. He breathes in the aroma as he does this and I see his shoulders slump with pleasure. He taps the scoop and fills the machine and pushes down the powder and presses a button and places a pair of tiny white cups under the split spout.

'Here you are,' he says. 'Do tell me what you think.'

I take the cup and sip. It's strong.

'Very good,' I say. 'Can I ask you a question off the record? You've lived here all your life, have you heard anything about a secret poker club, some kind of high stakes thing?'

He smiles and the scar on his lip stretches. 'You mean "the game".'

'Do I?'

'I'd say it's ninety per cent fiction, but the myth goes something like this: a four-man elite club has existed in these parts for decades, maybe fifty years. It's a strictly one-out, one-in, invitation-only affair and when I say "high stakes" I don't just mean kronor. The club's rumoured to make or break careers. My lawyer, Oscar Krevik, was approached some time ago. He declined and he had enough dirt on the other members for him to be able to walk away.'

'Who's in the club?'

He stares at my ears, behind my ears, taking mental notes for his new story.

'I have absolutely no idea, Oscar wouldn't tell. It's legendary around these parts but the present members are rather discreet. I did hear of girls being used as poker chips – and some kind of initiation ceremony – but like I said, it's ninety per cent fiction.'

'Any guesses who's in the club?'

'No, but I'd be quite delighted if the town starts probing into that myth and leaves me well alone to write in peace. I should sue for harassment, I've already discussed it with Oscar.'

I drink up and put on my shoes and coat and take my backpack.

Holmqvist points at me and says, 'May I borrow one of your hearing aids?'

'What for?'

'Research.'

I shake my head, touching my left aid defensively. 'Thanks for the coffee, David. I have to go. Thank you.'

'My pleasure,' he says, staring at my ears, and then as I close the front door, I hear, 'see you later.'

I speedwalk away from the house and up the road towards Hannes and Frida's place. Halfway along I spot someone through the trees. Is he following me? But it's just a shadow cast by a gnarled old oak. I walk and focus ahead and the fog is less solid on foot. I can see through it pretty well. As I get to the house itself, I check my phone. No reception. I'm by the hut. My left hearing aid beeps its final battery warning. I jangle my key fob in my pocket. All good. Then I reach down to the stone foundation of the grey hut and work my hand into crevices and cracks and find the key. I stand up and check that nobody's coming and step up to the door of the little grey hut.

45

I'm inside the hut and it has two windows. The blinds are down but they're thin enough to let some daylight in. I don't have to switch on the lights. First thing I do is walk over to the big chest freezer.

But then I turn to the window facing the house, and lift one corner of the blind. Nothing there. Waterlogged lawns and mist and trees, but no Hannes and no Frida. He's God-knows-where, probably the strip club, and she's in Karlstad like always on Sundays. Best chance I'll get. I go back to the freezer and open the lid. It smells of old fish. It's not a bad smell, it's the smell that all old freezers have. Frozen burgers and boxes of peas, tubs of ice cream and rubber trays of ice cubes. But the larger compartment is filled with bodies, I can see that now. Pheasants and turkeys and rabbits. There are loins of bigger creatures. I think they're parts of deer and elk, long dark sticks of frozen lean cuts. I rummage around, sharp ice crystals sticking to my fingertips and melting as soon as I look at them. Then I close the lid and face a wall with no window.

Looking from left to right, I scan the things hanging from long nails driven into the chipboard walls. The room smells of damp cardboard and petrol. Between the sheets of chipboard cladding, little fluffs of insulation sprout out like baby chicks. A fan heater. Lots of extension cords. I count five. A row of hammers, all types, three carpenter's claw hammers and four heavier hammers, maybe they're mallets, wooden handles with thick rusting metal heads. Then a row of screwdrivers and chisels, all in size order. I'm looking for a mid-twentieth-century rifle and anything related to poker, a club rulebook or something. I know it's a long shot. There's a basket of paintbrushes and then a tool bench. Hannes must have built it himself. It's two pallets, each standing upright, with an old door bolted on the top to make the work surface. Vices hang off its sides and an electric saw sits on the top, its cord dangling down into the space beneath like a cat's tail. Next to that, there are three chainsaws, a strimmer hanging on two nails up near the ceiling, and a green plastic container of fuel.

Then the other wall, the one with all the shelves and cabinets. I see rolls of insulation and gaffer tape, new padlocks in their hard plastic cases, ceramic flowerpots and gardening implements, trowels, and piles of gloves with floral patterns. The floor creaks as I move. The chipboard must be damp, it's warping, and I feel like one wrong step and I could fall through to whatever's underneath.

The cabinets are a hotchpotch of reclaimed kitchen cupboards with padlocks, and home-made wooden boxes wrapped in bicycle cable locks. There are so many types of lock in here. I rattle a few doors and try to look through the gaps left by the amateur joinery, but I can't see anything. The air's musty. My hearing aid beeps and I pat my jeans pocket to feel my key fob.

I count sixteen locked cabinets, ranging from two the size of shoe boxes, to a row of three tall gun cabinets at the very back. My hand reaches for a hacksaw off the wall without me even telling it to. I pause. There are enough new locks on the walls for me to replace any I break. Hannes will find out but not straight away. Best I can do. I approach the wooden box I saw last time, the one with the leaf motif. It's secured with a small padlock so I start sawing through the little metal hoop that's stopping the catch from opening. The blade slips left and right and I almost never hit the same scratch twice. I look back over my shoulder and find a pair of wire cutters or maybe they're bolt cutters, two long arms leading to two short, squat blades. I open the arms wide and place the blades around the padlock and squeeze. I squeeze so hard my arms start shaking, and then the blades snip through the lock and it pings off and falls between two containers. I open the box and find three spray bottles of weedkiller.

I look back to the larger secured units. The gun cabinets are locked with a key and made out of metal, no way I can break through those, I'll leave that to a professional, if you can call Thord that. I move a few heavy wooden lock-ups and get to a trunk of sorts with a lid on the top. My eyes dart to the hut door as a gunshot fires outside in the woods. I try to swallow but my mouth is as dry as the sawdust under the workbench. I open the bolt cutters and snip the lock and open the chest.

Porn. Magazines and VHS tapes. Looks like old stuff, things Hannes doesn't use any more but keeps here because how and where do you dispose of this kind of collection? I pick up a magazine and open it. Hungarian, maybe Romanian or something, eastern European writing and pictures that I feel obliged to look at but then instantly wish I never had. Naked bodies and blood. But I look and I flick through and I look some more, and it all appears to be make-believe, all make-up and poor craftsmanship. This isn't violence, it's cartoons. It's disgusting but it doesn't look remotely real. The videos appear to be more mainstream, some Swedish, but mostly foreign. I stick it all back and close the lid and wipe my hands on my trousers and move to the final wall. Thord's useless, but he has a gun and he's close by. He knows I'm here. And then I realise for the first time that the police, Thord and Karlstad Bluetooth and the others, are armed with smaller guns than every other fucker around here. But still, it's something. They're ten minutes away. Max. The police are just down the road if I need them.

I can hear something above my head. It's mice or rats scurrying in the loft space of this damp, little hut. And they're in the walls, too. I've noticed droppings and I've seen more glue traps, paper plates with sticky torture glue and bait. I move a stack of carefully folded and bound tarpaulin sheets to see what's underneath. Clear plastic boxes with lids. Clothes. I open a lid and it's full of children's clothes, for a boy of twelve or so. The other boxes are the same. One of baby clothes, bonnets and booties, and one of toddler stuff, little shoes and wellington boots. I feel uncomfortable. I move the boxes back and notice something behind them. Pushing the clothes box to the left, I see a glue trap and there's a mouse in the middle of it. A little shrew or a mouse on his back with his legs in the air. It's dead, I think, or almost dead, four large teeth sticking out of its open mouth, and the teeth look too big for its head. Long whiskers sprout out from each side of its face. And then I hear the car.

My breathing speeds up and I look around. Why didn't I think of an escape route? Or a hiding place? I peel back the bottom left corner of the blind. It's Hannes. Do I run? He leaves the car unlocked so maybe he's here to pick something up and then drive away. But do people ever lock their cars when they live in a place like this? I walk to the other window, my belly pressed against the freezer, and move the blind a fraction. He's gone inside. He's upstairs looking out of the window. He's tipping his head back and he's pointing to his eyes. No, he's putting in contact lenses or drops. I watch him pull on a jumper and then he moves away from view. A minute later, he walks out of the front door with his rifle in his hands.

I jump back from the hut window and look down. He's Medusa, I can feel it, I know it. I look everywhere, probing and scanning the hut walls for the right place. I squeeze down under the workbench, between the two vertical pallets and pull myself into a tight ball, my knees tucked under my chin. The door opens and I hear him but I can't see him from under this workbench. He steps in and the floor bows under his weight. He steps closer and I can see him now and he steps past me to the wall of shelves and picks up a small-blade knife and puts it in his camouflage trousers. I half close my eyes, scared that my marbles – that's what Dad used to call them – will give me up. I have perfect twenty-twenty vision and they might set him off. His boots are almost touching mine and his knees are level with my face. I can't see the freezer from down here but I know I left my backpack next to it. Shit. Hannes, don't look that way, just stay focussed on your weird fucking cabinets. My toes scrunch tight in my boots. He's opening something but I can't see what it is. I pray my hearing aids wont bleep. No noise. Please. No breaths right now. He's an arm-length away from me.

And then he walks off. He's carrying a rifle in one hand and a small cardboard box in the other. The box looks like the ones I saw in Benny Björnmossen's shop. Ammunition. Around his right shoulder, he's carrying a loop of coiled rope. I hear the hut door slam and then everything's quiet again.

I should watch him from the window but I don't, I just stay under the workbench, under the horizontal old door with its handle still in place and a key still slotted in the useless lock. I'm scared to move an inch. I am pathetic, and the scurrying's getting louder now. It's coming from the wall closest to me, and from underneath me, under the chipboard. I can't hear his car. He's not driving off. I squeeze out from the two pallets with my heartbeat echoing in my ears. I nudge the blind. He's walking away into the woods to join his hunting buddies. Or not. He's holding his gun facing up to the sky and he's trudging off through muddy grass into the thin wispy mists of Utgard forest.

Hannes must have seen the police cars at Bengt's house as he drove past. What did Björn tell him? The hut feels small now and humid and I'm amazed Hannes didn't find me hiding here like just another glue-trapped mouse. I take out my camera and photograph everything but there is nothing to photograph. Everybody else around here owns a shed just like one this one filled with stuff just like this stuff.

More scurrying. I can hear little claws scratching the chipboard looking for food and sex. Why can't I find anything that'll put a stop to all of this? I pull out my phone and there's no reception. I hear a noise outside, it's very close. It's coming from the other side of the window. He's coming back. I dive down into the hole under the workbench again and pull myself in and fold myself up like a penknife. I'm holding my camera facing out with my hand covering the lens. I knock the pallet a little and try to steady it with my hand but there's something on top, a vice or maybe it's the electric saw, and it's not screwed down tight and it's rattling. The door opens slowly and I hear him step back inside.

The floor creaks. Maybe he senses something's wrong? The door's still open so he'll be gone soon. I hear him lift up the lid of the chest freezer and rustle around. I'm breathing shallow, quick breaths, as quiet as I can manage. It sounds like he's moving frozen things out of the way, maybe ice-cream tubs and loaves of stiff bread. I imagine the food piling up on his right-hand side. I imagine his tanned face and silver hair lit from one side by the freezer's internal light. The machine hums. I imagine him lifting out a whole salmon, stiff as a plank of pink wood, and placing it on top of the other things. It's quieter now. Has he found what he was looking for? I must be silent. No beeps, no stomach grumbles. Then he pulls out another thing and has to tug on it to get it free. I hear him throw the other bits and pieces back into the freezer and shut the lid. What has he found? And then he steps away from the freezer and I catch a glimpse of his boots and then I hear the door open and he steps outside and the door slams shut.

I stay where I am for at least a minute. What if he comes back again? I stay still but allow deeper breaths. More noise. And then I crawl out and check the window and it's just gravel and puddles and rain. He must be back in the woods already with his ice-cream or whatever the fuck he took out from the freezer.

But he didn't take an ice-cream. I look at the freezer and there's a deer lying on the lid. It's a baby, or maybe a smaller deer species, with no head or feet, just a long, dark torso and four stumps. The mice have stopped scrabbling now. I check the window again, both windows. The house is quiet and Hannes's car is still in the driveway. The deer has a cut lengthways along its stomach. I presume it was made by Hannes when he gutted it and now there's a cavity inside. The deer is as long as the freezer and the cut is as long as the deer. There's something shiny inside the carcass. I can see it glint. The thing inside the deer looks like metal, brass maybe. I touch the deer and then pull away and then peer inside and pull out a bullet the size of my middle finger.

46

My lips fall apart. A bullet stored inside a dead deer? The deer is on the freezer lid, lying on its side like a sow suckling her piglets. I stand up, brain whirring, trying to focus on it. The deer is red and lean like a duck hanging in a Chinatown window. I have an urge to open the freezer and put it back inside, some absurd domestic impulse. But I check my phone instead. No reception.

I step to the door and open it but the wind takes it from me and it bangs against the hut wall. The fog has lifted a little but it's drizzling now, rain falling in a fine spray. Can I just walk out of this? There's a hunter with a rifle not far away and maybe he's out to kill some other hunter. I stick half my head out of the door and see nothing. Just puddles and a rusting snow-blowing machine I never noticed before. I step back inside the hut for my backpack and realise I forgot to take a single photo of this corpse. The air is heavy. I pull out my camera and take a few shots of the deer without touching it, keeping my flash off the whole time.

There's something sticking out of the cavity at the neck end of the carcass. A blue triangle. I don't want to contaminate what could be evidence, but what the hell is it? Blue. Rigid. About the size of a big toe. I push at it but it's stuck to the frozen flesh of the deer. It's plastic. I hold the rigid carcass and push the blue triangle hard until it comes unstuck. Then I reach inside the long slit down the belly of the deer and pull. It's larger than I thought and the cold burns my hand. I get a grip on the blue thing and tug it out. It's an ice-cube tray, one of the bright blue rubber ones Frida uses for stock. I breathe and then I flip it over onto the freezer lid. I stop breathing and taste sick in my mouth but I do not make a single sound. I look at them in order, in rows and columns. No noise. I look down at them and the hut's very cold and the draught's catching the wispy hairs on the back of my neck.

There are twelve of them. Each eye sitting neatly in its own ice-cube socket.

They're looking straight up at me. Four brown and two pale green and six blue. There are two empty ice-cube sockets at one end of the tray. Then I notice a tiny bit of sinew, a millimetre of red human tissue next to one of the brown eyes and I throw up in my mouth. Burning acid from inside me but I hold most of it in. I swallow it down and clench my teeth and look away. It burns. Time has stopped. It's just me. And a freezer humming gently in a hut. And a butchered deer. And twelve eyes.

I hold my camera and point it and look at the screen on the back. It feels intrusive, like photographing car-crash victims on the side of a motorway. I'm looking at people, not at corpses in body-bags. I'm looking into their fucking eyes. I'm looking at six people.

Six pairs. But they only found five bodies. Three in the '90s and two now. Somebody else is lost out there in Utgard forest. From back in the '90s or now? A body trapped in the never-ending pines; a body deprived of a burial and deprived of their family's tears and certainties. Who the hell is Hannes? Does he think he can use the eyes somehow, or are they just souvenirs like the antelope head in his study? Is this the price you pay to leave the poker game? Do I put them back in the freezer to preserve them? I can't touch them. I can't and I won't.

I stagger out into the hazy drizzle. I breathe in hard but it does little to take away the vomit taste on my tongue. Then I dash back inside the hut. I feel like I'm in a sniper video game on level seven with no lives left and no cheats and no fucking clue what I'm doing.

He could be out there, standing in the driveway or hiding on the rocks at the back of the house. Waiting.

I take my bag and stick the camera in it and grab a big steel wrench from the wall. I have bear-spray and a knife but this thing's weighty and it feels good in my hand. I sneak to the house wall and peer around it. I look at myself in the window of the grey hut. A big pale face in the middle of a black wood. I pull on my balaclava and that's when I see him. Through the eye holes of the mask I see the trees move by the rocks behind the house. I see his broad back.

My eyes dart around for clues. I am not okay. An image of Mum waiting in her hospice room flashes into my mind. I shake my head and walk towards the back of the house. Then I keep walking. It's a story. I'm doing my job. I'll follow Hannes from a safe distance, and then as soon as I get phone coverage, I'll call it in. I can use my phone's GPS. I can photograph him – my lens is long enough. I remember Freddy Malmström's son playing *Call of Duty*. He'll grow up with no dad. Then I see Rikard Spritzik's wife in her doctor's office. No husband. I can't allow the last two sockets in that ice-cube tray to get filled. Is it just him out here or the whole fucking poker team? How does this work? If Björn is the King of Hearts, then what's Hannes? What are the rules of this club, of this game? I skirt past a bird table on the lawn and then clamber up onto the rocks, my boots slipping on the slimy granite.

Gunshots. I freeze and look around, my knife in my left hand, Hannes's wrench in my right. Two more gunshots in quick succession, the echo of the first melting into the boom of the second. I look back and I can't see the house any more. I turn to where I last saw Hannes and it looks the same, every fucking direction looks exactly the same. Pine trees. Fully grown and ready for harvest. More than ready. Overdue. Too big and too close together. I can see footprints in the mud beside a hollow stump. I follow them.

I walk faster because there's a ticking clock in my gut like the one in Peter Pan's crocodile. I'm tired but I have to keep going, I have to find out what's going on and I have to help stop it and I have to write about it. That's just the way it is. Can I trust Thord? There are little ribbons tied to some of the trees, red ones and yellow ones and blue-striped ones; flimsy bits of plastic tied to branches and around trunks. I think they're for orienteering or for hunters to find their shooting towers. I see glimpses of Hannes. He's walking through a valley beneath me. I'm too close to him so I hold back a while. On this muddy ground, I can follow him pretty easily if I keep looking down. There are lots of boot prints on the paths, so I have to be careful to follow the right tracks. A mosquito flies close to my ear. I flick it away, then pull out my phone. No reception and battery at 14%. The mosquito comes back. There are more people on Mount fucking Everest right now than there are in this forest.

I move and keep close to his tracks and walk from tree to tree using as much cover as I can. My left aid plays a little tune and then switches itself off. I'm down to one but I've got spare batteries and I can change them with my eyes closed in about twenty seconds flat. I'm getting bitten. I keep glancing down and finding big mosquitoes on my wrists. I can't feel them at all, they're experts, pumping anaesthetic into my system before my brain even registers them sucking. But I'm getting bumps now, red bumps on my hands and they're beginning to itch. I want to scratch my neck. Two more gunshots, but they're distant and from the direction of the house and the track. I think.

The trees are unending. Un-fucking-ending. It's an ocean, a spacewalk, a nightmare. Who planted all these? They're so dense that the lower branches – the grey needleless dead ones – are almost touching each other. There is no sky today, just drizzle. And the animals are quiet. No birds and no rustling. But I know they're all out there.

I need to pee and I need to eat and I need help. I need Tammy and Benny Björnmossen and the Karlstad cop with the Bluetooth earpiece, all here now, all locked and loaded. The ground's so uneven; I'm just trying not to fall into a badger sett or off the edge of a slippery boulder. I see Hannes every now and again, camouflaged and broad as he steps through the birches. This is his habitat.

I look down to check the time but there's a tick on my wrist. It's further up my sleeve than the leather strap of my watch and its body is already half-full with blood. I look up to the sky, to Dad. Without stopping, I reach in and pinch the tick with my finger and thumbnail, and pull. It's not what you're supposed to do, I know that, but I can't just leave it, can I? Its pale grey sack comes off in my fingers, my own blood smearing on my nails. I pull off a leg and then I see the fucker's head burrow deeper into my skin. I scratch at it with a nail and make myself bleed but it is inside me now and it's biting or whatever it does. I am not okay. It's tunnelling. I can't feel it exactly and I can't reach it but I can see it.

My phone vibrates and I check the screen and it's a text message from Lena. She says a forensic pathologist has found traces of coffee in both of Rikard Spritzik's eye sockets. My lungs deflate. I stop walking. It's Holmqvist. Those espresso scoops. It's not Hannes. But, the frozen eyes. It is both of them? I call Lena but the call fails. No reception. They're working together, Holmqvist and Hannes. Medusa twins.

I see Hannes sniffing the air and checking the ground. He's running his fingers over the moss and the dirt beneath him. He's hunting. He heads off in a slightly different direction, over a sharp rocky slope. I follow and my feet catch in exposed tree roots and in deep cracks filled with leaf mould and needles. I'm rubbing my skin continually now, scratching under the balaclava, trying to crush any bugs that might be eating my face. The Velcro strip on my coat sleeve is already a graveyard of wings and thoraxes and stings.

I get to the top of an incline, where a large spruce has fallen in an earlier storm. Its flat root system stands erect on the ground like a brown satellite dish, and it's taller than I am. I clamber past it and the woods thicken. Brambles ping back at me and sweep up to catch my thighs. They're animals, not plants. Their thorns are teeth and their wiry stems are muscle and cartilage and ligament. I'm starting to bleed from head to toe, from a hundred pinprick wounds. Bites and burrowed ticks and midges and fucking bramble thorns.

I take out my phone and look at it. I stand on tiptoe and wave it around and get one bar of reception. I call Thord on speed dial, but the call fails. I call 112, but the call fails. I come out of the brambles to a long clearing with birches scattered around and piles of rocks like someone once arranged them here for a reason. I can see Hannes in the centre of the space with his silvery hair and his strong back. He aims his rifle at something and tracks it as it heads deeper into the trees at the far end. I want to stop him. Then I remember the insignia on the butt of Hannes's rifle. It wasn't a shamrock or a clover, it was a club symbol. Hannes is the goddam King of Clubs. And then he lowers his gun and stands up and walks on like it's the most normal thing in the world.

I don't trek through the clearing, it feels too exposed. I skirt the edge of it, squelching through brown water and sphagnum moss as deep as my knees. There are ant nests. I've spotted at least four the size of dome tents. The forest floor is alive. I get to the far end of the clearing and see Hannes through the spruce trunks. The rain comes down thicker now and I've given up trying to swat away mosquitoes because there's a constant cloud of them. They're with me. I walk into the treeline and step on a splintered pine branch just like I've done a hundred times before. Except, this one snaps.

Hannes and his gun turn to face me.

47

I'm perfectly still and I have a knot in my throat. The dark eye of the rifle's staring straight at me and I'm staring straight back. It's like I've swallowed a lump of crusty bread without chewing it. I'm vulnerable – ridiculously, laughably, pathetically, vulnerable. I can't move, but even if I could, I've got a sheathed knife and a phone with no reception and a steel wrench. I've got a catapult and a can of Tammy's Canadian bear-spray that I'm not sure even works.

If I could stop breathing, I would. I'm that deer I saw from the car. I'm caught in time, paused by my own realisation of what's about to happen. I'm facing a man I don't really know, and I'm facing his rifle loaded with bullets nobody ever knew existed.

And then he turns slowly and sniffs the air and walks away in the same direction as before. I want to sprint away as fast as I can. I'm pretty quick. I'll get lost, hopelessly lost, but I'll be away from this unknown thing that I'm following, this unknown potential event. And anyway, I'm already lost.

I start walking again, the wrench gripped tight in my bite-covered fingers. My hand is shaking. I check my phone, I walk, I check again, I walk. The afternoon is drifting into early evening and the brown and green colours are dampening all around me. I make out owl boxes high up in the Scots pine trees. They look like baby coffins up there, baby coffins fixed half way up trees. Who put them up there? Miniature coffins in the forest canopy with little holes for owls to fly into, or for babies to stare out from.

My stomach's not growling, it's too tight and too hard for that. I pass little clumps of lingonberries and cloudberries growing in amongst the pine needles and birch leaf carpets. They glisten like wine gums, or more like midget gems really, little red and orange sweeties on the soft, green floor. I taste wine gums on my tongue. I taste them from memory and saliva floods my mouth from nowhere as the taste clarifies behind my front teeth. Artificial strawberry and artificial pear. I check my phone. Nothing. As soon as I get reception I'll call this in.

He's speeding up. The way Hannes moves through trees and over fallen branches and trunks is spellbinding. It's elegant, like he's water passing through a forest stream. I walk and scramble and do little semi-jogs to keep up, touching trees as I go.

I removed my left hearing aid a while back to stop it getting damp, no point risking it if the batteries need changing. So that ear's open, unencumbered; it's naked. I can feel the wet in that ear and the soundless touch of the breeze. My right ear's screeching and whistling, the wind causing feedback. He stops. I can see him hiding behind a tree like he's just been spotted. I move behind a birch to mirror him. My tree's inadequate for the task, it's half as broad as I am. It's not white and clean, but grey and half rotten. Patchy bark spotted with lichen. He's watching someone. Or something. But his gun's down.

A mosquito flies into my left ear. I can't hear it but it is vibrating and I feel its buzz and its bloodlust. I smack my ear with my left hand like I used to do sometimes as a child, as a frustrated six- or seven-year-old. Back then I wasn't annoyed that I was deaf, I was annoyed I was pitied. Kids would give up trying to tell me stories when I asked them to repeat parts. No malice whatsoever, just easier to say, 'I'll explain it later, gotta go,' or 'doesn't matter, wasn't that funny anyway.' But it did matter, it always did. Still does.

I push myself closer to the birch, its papery bark curled and striated like dry winter skin. I don't mind pressing my face against trees as it turns out, I seem to trust them. You know where you are with a tree. It's what's hiding behind the tree, what's waiting up in the tree, what's buried under the tree that's the problem. It's getting darker. The drizzle's collecting in the branches, and dribbles of rainwater are finding paths down the trunk to the soil, some touching my lips or my eyebrows as they stream by. Hannes is bringing his gun up again now. A small part of me, the part that's sometimes tempted to step over cliffs or spin the steering wheel on the motorway, yearns for him to shoot. I want to see him shoot that rifle and for it all to be over even though I don't have a clue what he's aiming at.

But he brings it down slowly and adjusts his footwork. My neck itches like chicken pox. Gunshots. I hear three in succession, then a break of a minute or so, then two more. Five bullets discharged. Not close to here, but somewhere in Utgard forest. It could be Bengt. Or the police. Or an unknown hunter bringing down a calf elk and then its mother. That's something Lena told me about hunters, they never shoot the mother first, they never leave a child without its parent, not even for a minute between shots. The kid gets it first, never the adult.

Hannes is just waiting there by that Scots pine and he's completely focussed. I try to maintain the same kind of unwavering concentration on him but peripheral movements snatch at my gaze. I notice a blackbird in a spruce tree skittering from branch to branch like a busybody, and then I think I see a mouse, but it could just be leaves moving in the damp murk.

I'm standing perfectly still behind this birch and the bugs seem so fucking appreciative. I have mosquitoes and midges slipping inside my jacket like boys' hands at a cinema. I've counted three ticks on me including the one now living in the subcutaneous layers of my wrist. And that's just the things I can see. My mind flashes words and I swat them away like I want to do with these damn bugs. Leeches. Centipedes. Woodlice. I'm not afraid of spiders but there's one abseiling down from fuck-knows-where on an invisible thread so I back up and let it pass me by. It's lime green or even brighter, not huge, but lime-fucking-green, so it must be poisonous, right? It's warning predators with its colouring because that's what we all learnt in school.

Hannes is bringing his rifle up and resting the barrel against the trunk, his elbow cocked into a triangle, his feet planted well apart. My focus is zooming in and out. I see an ant walk across my hand. I'm breathing as quietly as I can and then I notice red toadstools behind Hannes and then he lowers his gun and he walks away towards a hunting tower at the far end of the clearing. I stay where I am and watch him climb up the ladder of the rough pine tower with his rifle over one shoulder and a coil of rope over the other. I can't see him any more but I know he's up there.

Gunshot. A piercing boom travels to my one functional hearing aid. It's much louder than any shot I've ever heard. Very close. It's harsh and scraping and metallic and it is right here. Birds I never noticed before squawk and flap and rush away from the nearby trees. Something just died. I don't know how I know this but I do. The air has changed around me.

I step through dung and my boots squelch and then I step through moss and it's deep and clean and soft as candyfloss. I'm walking more slowly and making sure Hannes can't see me. I wonder how far away the edge of the forest is because I have no idea whatsoever if I'm in the middle of Utgard or near the end. There's a fly or a mosquito or something inside my balaclava and it's buzzing its last, desperate buzz to escape and I just let it be.

The clearing is perhaps ten metres wide but it's as long as a football pitch. I'm closer to the hunting tower now, a little shack built up in a birch tree. The tree itself is split above the ground, three separate trunks growing up from one root. The tower looks like a big pallet resting maybe four metres up on the three trunks. There are a few horizontal planks higher up acting as guard rails, and a makeshift roof made from corrugated plastic. I'm behind a decent pine and I must be close to invisible here in my mask. I stare at the tower and then I see something move beneath it. No, behind it, on the far side, there's someone else here. The air is sickly with fresh rot. I swallow. There's another hunter here. I stay behind the tree and my mask is partially covering my eye but someone is walking towards the tower now. And he's bold, he is not afraid. Looks younger than Hannes. Looks like David Holmqvist.

I move slowly, hidden five trees deep, into the woods. I have a partial view through the trunks to the hunting tower, and in between me and it are a scattering of hedgehog mushrooms. They're not glowing in the sun like you see in the tourist magazines, and they're not perfect either. These ones are big and spongy and days past their best, and they're probably riddled with worms but I'm transfixed anyway. Me, then mushrooms, then Ghostwriter looking up at an elk hunting tower. Is Holmqvist in the game? He's rich enough. Is he Spades? Diamonds? Do they play in that second guest room? He's climbing the rough pine ladder up to the pallet platform. He's dressed all in black. I'm hungry, my stomach loosening a little now that the gun's been fired, and it wasn't so bad after all. Right? Hannes and Holmqvist. The Medusas.

I check my phone. No reception and 7% battery. I try to fit the wrench into my coat pocket because I'm tired of carrying it around but it won't fit even if I stretch the material. A crow squawks some-where behind me. I briefly get one bar on the phone, and then it goes. I move the phone up to my eye level to see if I can get the reception back and that's when the body falls out of the hunting tower.

48

The body hardly makes a noise as it hits the moss. It's like a silent movie. The body's just there. I'm not sure if I saw it fall or if I just saw it land. It bounced a little. It's face-down in deep moss and I think it's Hannes. I think Holmqvist pushed him.

He climbs down the ladder of the hunting tower. He's wearing black. Something tight. He arrives at the bottom of the rough pine ladder and turns towards me for the first time. He's wearing Lycra covered with green marks. He pulls off his cap. It's not Holmqvist.

It's Frida. It's Frida. My friend.

I can't get my breath.

Frida?

I'm staring at her and I'm numb. My legs feel weak and my brain's a mess, I can't form thoughts. What happened? Frida found out about Daisy and followed him home and stalked him and then this? She found Hannes's ice-cube tray slowly defrosting on the chest freezer? God, I don't want to think about what that ice-cube tray looks like now with those dozen eyes coming back to life in that damp little hut.

Hannes moves. His head moves just a fraction, and Frida bends down to look at him. He's facing away from me and the moss is too deep for me to be able to see much. I can make out hair and the hump of a shoulder and his hip and one edge of a boot. Frida stands and looks down at him and she's perfectly still. And so am I, completely motionless as I watch her watch him.

The noises of the forest muffle and crackle as my last hearing aid malfunctions in the drizzle. I watch Frida start rolling Hannes over. He's bleeding from a chest wound. He's been shot. Frida shot him? That was the bang. She shot him from the other side of the clearing, from deep in the trees on the other side of the hunting tower. I see Frida heave and push Hannes towards me. She's rolling him and I can see his face. He's looking straight at me. I freeze but in a second he's over onto his back and facing up at his wife.

My malfunctioning aid switches itself off without even a warning beep. I remove it and push it down deep into my bra because that's the best place to dry it out.

My ears are naked. I'm staring at a wife staring at her husband about a million fucking kilometres from anything good. I don't know which way is north or which way is south. Gavrik could be anywhere from here; the police could be a kilometre away or twenty kilometres away. I think Hannes is dead. He looks dead. There are two rifles leaning up against the elk tower birch. His and hers. My phone has no reception and 6% battery. I need to do something, but I don't know what. How did I get this so wrong? I can read people, that's my job, I'm good at it. How did I not read her? Maybe I should creep away to find reception but is there any reception in Utgard forest? I'll call Thord. Will his phone work at Bengt's place? And is he still there? Must be. There's five ton of crap in that house to sort through so they must still be in Mossen village.

I pull my backpack open and slowly take out my camera.

I'm six trees deep from the edge of the clearing. I know I can't use my flash but I don't even want Frida to see my lens reflect her way. I don't want to move fast and I don't want to step on a twig or breathe too loud. I want to take a photo silently and then retreat slowly and then run like hell. But it's not so easy to judge how well I'm being silent when I can't hear anything.

There is blood on Hannes's hunting jacket. Chest wound. The blood looks like a black reflective stain in this light. Frida's still standing over him and looking at him and maybe she's praying or maybe she's just taking it all in. Very slowly, I bring my camera up to my eye. It takes maybe three minutes for me to move it forty centimetres. I check the flash is off. I take a burst of photos, my eye trained on Frida's face, half waiting for it to snap round and snarl at me. But she stays still. It's fine. I get my images and I'm getting my story. All of it. I pull the camera down to my backpack just as slowly as I raised it. I'm okay. Frida's unzipping a small pocket on her sleeve – one designed for joggers to store a phone or an iPod. She unzips it and I see something metal glint in the moonlight.

She wouldn't. Fuck, I can't watch this. She's holding a small knife tight in her hand. She's going to take his eyes now and I cannot watch this. Crouching on all fours, I take a slow step back. I can't see where I'm stepping, and I hate that, but I need to keep looking forward and keep moving back. She's still holding the knife and she hasn't leant down yet. I will take ten, maybe twenty big paces back, and then turn and run.

It's the fourth step back that's the problem. Up until that fourth step back, I'm okay. It's moss and granite covered with pine cones and it's Frida growing smaller in the distance. But my fourth step lands on something quite different. I reach my boot back, my confidence growing, and place it down on something wet. I can't get purchase. My boot's sliding around so I look down. At first I think they're snakes but they're not. They're entrails. The innards of some animal, lengths of stringy guts and intestines and membranes. No blood that I can see, just loose sausage skins filled with bile.

I want to panic but I can't. Frida's bending down on one knee by Hannes now. I can see them through the web of trees. But the slippery entrails are behind me and in front of me and to my left and right. They're everywhere and they're sour and they look like human umbilical cords. I take another step back and have to place my hands on the ground in amongst it all to stop myself slipping. I step back again, a giant step back, and my boot hits a rock that rolls away. She doesn't hear. I take another step back and nudge past a dead bush and look down and there's an elk's head right under me.

I look down at its dull eye and its bristly fur and its severed neck. I retch and see maggots and flies and heaving masses of something going to work. I stop breathing so I don't inhale any of it. It's the size of a horse head. Bigger. If I smell it, I'll pass out. I think it's a cow elk because it doesn't have antlers. I look up and see Frida and Hannes but they're too far away now for me to see any detail. And it's too dark. I step back from the elk head and my feet and my hands reach normal soil again, and that's when my pocket shakes and my phone reminder goes off, because, silly me, tonight is laundry night.

49

I silence the phone and look up at Frida through half-closed eyes. She's standing about ten trees away from me with that knife in her hand, that shiny little knife. I can't breathe. She picks up her rifle from the ground.

If I run, she will stalk me and kill me and then ... I blink three times and squeeze my eyelids tight together. She's somehow very good at all this hunting stuff. No point running. I need to do what Hannes did not do, I need to lay low. I thought he'd shot someone from his tower, but *he* was shot in his tower. Frida heard about one note of my alarm tone so it won't be easy for her to find me. I see her do something to the rifle, load it I suppose, or take the safety catch off, something like that. She holds it to her hip and not to her eye.

She's saying something that I cannot hear. I can see she's calling something, probably 'who's there' or 'come out' or 'show yourself' but I cannot hear anything. I can sense someone's saying something but I can't make out words, and I can't lip read from here, not in this murk. So I squat perfectly still. I notice slugs now. Time moves one frame at a time. I see slugs and a moose's eye and entrails and Frida's dyed blonde hair and her pale skin. I can't move my head so I start to notice everything around me in minute detail and there are four or five slugs, each one as big as a lipstick, making their absurdly slow way from here to there. They are black and they shine slick with whatever they are made of. They're like black wine gums after you've sucked on them for a while. And they're so ridiculously fucking slow that they'll never be able to leave this goddam forest.

She starts to walk towards me. There's nothing much between us except the dead bush I'm hiding behind. She's looking around but she walks two, then three trees deep in my direction. She can't see me. Can she see my tracks? No, I never stepped that close to the tower, she's working from her memory of the noise, from the alarm. Wrench. Catapult. Bear-spray. Knife. What a fucking pile of fuck I've brought with me. Against a rifle only a rifle will do, and I've got shit. I hate being this ill-equipped. I want my truck and I want a gun.

Stay perfectly still, Tuva. You can do this. Frida makes a turn past a birch tree, then pulls back towards me. Don't breathe. She holds up her rifle and walks straight to me, stopping just before the elk entrails. I feel like a little kid playing hide-and-seek with the devil. I have no cover apart from a dead bush and I have no escape.

I read her lips. 'Stand up.'

Slowly, I stand. I am very cold. There was never any question that I'd do exactly as she said. How could I not? She steps in the entrails and holds out one hand and pulls off my balaclava.

'Tuva?'

Her make-up is perfect and she looks appalled to see me, like a mother who's just noticed her child hiding in a cupboard watching her having sex.

'What on earth are you doing all the way out here?'

I point to my ears and shake my head.

She nods like she understands. She comes closer to me, her rifle down at her hip again now, and speaks slowly and clearly so I can read her lips.

'Why are you here, Tuva?'

'I knew Hannes was Medusa. Nobody would believe me. I came after him.'

She raises her eyebrows and shakes her head like she's listening to her daughter tell her all about a horror movie she's watched with friends.

'Come on, let's get to open ground, it's not good to be this deep in the woods after dark.'

She holds my hand, my actual hand, and leads me towards her dead husband. Just shoot me now. In a way I just want to get out of this place and that's how she's going to do it so just fucking get on with it. I let go of her hand and look at Hannes. He's dead and his eyes are open and his skin is already turning grey.

Frida passes me a compact thermos like we're out on some kind of Boy-Scout camping trip and I shake my head. She reaches down and unhooks the loop of rope from Hannes's shoulder. She has to heave his arm up by the elbow to pull it free.

'I'll need to tie you up just while I finish. I'm not going to hurt you, Tuva, so I don't want you to worry yourself. I just need to finish what I'm doing and clean up, and I don't want you running off and getting lost out here. Hold out your hands for me.'

I do it and she ties a knot that I don't recognise around my left wrist and pulls me gently towards a Scots pine tree. It's one of the pines bordering the clearing and it's the broadest tree around. She pushes my body to face the trunk as if I'm about to embrace it. She pulls the length of rope around its girth and ties the loose end to my right hand. I'm tied to the tree like I'm hugging it, my face and breasts squashed tight into its unyielding bark.

She comes to stand near me and I can smell her lily-of-the-valley perfume.

'Wait here a few minutes and I'll finish up. Then we can go home.'

I see her knife now in her hand. But it's not a knife at all, it's a silver teaspoon like the one from the fancy silk-lined set we used back at the house that time. Frida's wielding a silver teaspoon.

'Wait,' I say, because, fuck, I can't let her do this. 'Did you? In the '90s?'

She touches the tip of the teaspoon.

I remember her making a quenelle of cream with a spoon back in her kitchen. A perfect quenelle. 'I'm pretty scared out here, can you just talk to me.'

She smiles and puts the spoon back inside the little zip-up pocket on her jacket sleeve. That's where the coffee residue came from. Not Holmqvist. Not Hannes. Her.

'I know this was all an accident, Frida,' I say. 'I'll tell the police this was a shooting accident, that's all. You haven't touched his eyes, so I'll tell them that this was all a mistake.'

'This wasn't a mistake, Tuva,' I read on her lips. 'But you're sweet for saying that.'

I look up through the branches of the pine and I can't see sky and I can't find Dad. I realise she was the one in the grey hut. It wasn't Hannes coming back, it was her. She's been hiding her rifle inside that deer carcass.

'Why?' I ask.

It's still drizzling. She pulls strands of my hair, sodden strands, away from my face and places them on the top of my head where they belong.

'Why what?'

'Why all this, Frida?'

I see a bird fly overhead. Maybe it's an owl and maybe it's hooting, and if it is I'd never know. The owl doesn't care. To that old owl, all this is irrelevant; it's just something down below that'll be over soon.

'Why do I need to clean up?' she asks. 'Because I have to, don't you see? These so-called men have ruined some very sacred things and they've reduced themselves to vermin. Less than vermin. So I have to clean it all up because someone has to.'

Her hand's cold on my scalp.

'What did they do to deserve all this? What have you done?'

'What didn't they do,' she says, shaking her head. 'They've spoilt and tainted the most important things in this life, Tuva, that's what they've done. They were privileged enough to find good women and get married and have their own sweet families. That's quite something. They were lucky. Well, my daddy made sure he was true his whole life, but these men failed. They ruined everything. They chased after whores and sluts and pigs when their wives were back home waiting for them. There's no going back once that's happened so I had to clean it all up.'

My breath feels cold and empty. One breast and one cheek is crushed so hard into this damn tree trunk I feel like I'm growing into it. Frida swats away mosquitoes as they try to feast on my neck.

She looks up to the sky and pushes her palm over my mouth and then she looks back to me. Is it a plane? I can't see anything up there and I can't hear anything. But something's up there. I know it.

'Helicopters won't find us down here, sweetie,' she whispers. 'Can't land a helicopter in Utgard forest, the canopy is too dense.'

She pulls her hand away.

'You sure you don't want some hot chocolate? I didn't bring much, just enough for one person really,' she snorts like this is funny. 'But I'll split what I have with you. It's getting cold out here and winter's creeping up on us again like it does every year.'

I don't want hot chocolate. I want my hearing aids. My whole world right now is this crazy bitch. I can't see much other than her face and I can't feel much other than her hand. I can't hear her. All I can do is read her lips.

'Why did you have to take their eyes?' I ask.

'Oh, they're not really eyes any more, not once they've seen those things, Tuva. Not really. You and I have eyes but those so-called men had, well, I don't know what to call them, but they're not eyes. Those things saw sluts and prostitutes and hard core pornography, so I took them out. Those rotten bits aren't human any more once they've seen all that depravity, all that disgusting depravity, while their wives were at home caring for the children and looking after the house.'

'You kept them in your freezer.'

Frida scratches her eyelid. She must have waterproof mascara on today because her make-up's still in place.

'I had a pause from all this,' she says. 'Between '94 and last year, I didn't need to be cleaning up so much. That was quite a relief, to be honest. Once that cathouse shut down, things got a little better. More clean. Hannes was still not what he should have been, he wasn't the gentleman he was destined to be, but he was better for a while. So every time it all got too much for me, I'd walk over to the hut and open the freezer and look into the eyes – or whatever they are – of those so-called men, those home wreckers, and I'd let off some steam. Those things in that freezer calmed me down no end. I'd stand there and look at them one pair at a time, one so-called man at a time, and I wouldn't feel the need to clean up so much. They were all sorted out and clean and ordered and safe in my freezer. It was a good thing, having them so close by.'

She looks over at her husband and unzips the pocket on her jacket sleeve.

'Speaking of which. If you'll excuse me a moment, this shouldn't take long.'

She takes the spoon in her right hand and moves towards Hannes.

50

'Frida, wait.'

I'm strapped so tight to this damn tree that I'm rooted to the spot just like it is. I can turn my head a little but I can't look directly behind me to where Frida is, and I hate that. My senses are being stolen one by one. She might be talking right now. She might be pointing her deer-carcass rifle at the back of my head and I'd never even know it. She might have changed her mind and run away and I'd never know that either.

But she's back. She's at the side of my face.

'What is it, Tuva?' her lips say.

'Please don't do this. We're friends. Don't do this.'

She smiles at me and checks the ropes on my wrists.

'Are these chaffing? You want me to loosen them a little bit for you?'

I nod and smile but my lips are trembling now. I'm cold and she is too close to my face.

'I'll do it soon, right after I've finished up.'

'Wait,' I say again. I cannot let her do this to him. 'Wait, my hearing aids.'

'Oh?'

'Can you change my batteries for me? I have two more spares. Then I'll be able to listen to you better and we can talk properly.'

'Your key fob?'

'Yes,' I say looking down to my jacket pocket. 'In there. It'll just take a minute.'

Her eyes widen and she shakes her head.

I frown at her but the frown's covered by her handkerchief, now wet with rain and sweat.

'I check his phone,' she says.

What?

'He doesn't think I know much about these things but I check it all the time. Had my coping strategies up till now, but no way I was letting him leave me here all on my own, no way.'

'Change my batteries,' I say. 'Please.'

'No point,' she says, a vague smile on her face. 'No need.'

My tongue stiffens in my mouth. I don't want her hand or her fucking handkerchief anywhere near me. I almost choke on her lily-of-the-valley scent as it fills the damp air. I can't speak. I'm tight up against what seems like the biggest tree in the world with a psychopath patting my forehead.

'Excuse me,' her lips say. 'I'll be just a jiffy.'

She walks away. I pull and strain at the ropes and manage to move about a centimetre around the tree but it's too tight. I turn my head hard until it feels like my neck will snap but I can't see her. I don't want to see her but I hate not knowing where she is. Is she taking his eyes? There's no noise, no squelching. But then I realise I have no aids so of course there's no noise. There's a tick crawling down the tree and it's at my nose level. I pull back, pushing with my pelvis and tensing my arms but I can't get far enough away from the bark. She's behind me somewhere but I don't know how close. And this tick's arching with its back legs and its fat rear end. It looks too big this close up. I don't see it jump but now it's on my cheek. I can't feel it but I know. I peer down as if trying to see the tip of my nose but it's not there or else it's dropped off. Then it moves. I strain and scream and look down and see it on my lower eyelid. I blink manically, thrashing my head from side to side.

Frida's back. She's next to me.

'Tick. My eye. Get it off.'

She holds my head firmly and says something but I can't hear it or read it. She has her fingers at my left eye and I feel a light pinch. And then she's stroking my cheek. My eyes are watering but I can just about read her lips.

'It's gone,' she says. 'Just a deer tick. I took it off and it's gone, Tuva. But if you scream like that again I will shoot you.'

I don't fucking care. Shoot me.

'You're lucky it wasn't a moose tick.'

I scan the bark for other insects and then look back to her.

'Moose ticks see your eyes and they think they're moose nostrils,' she says. 'We used to have them real bad up in Norrland when I was a girl. They see your eyes and they think they're big old nostrils and they want to lay their eggs in there. Nice and moist. So they spray at your eyes, they spray their eggs right at them. And it doesn't feel so bad, I mean, sure, it hurts, but you wash them and you think they're gone. But they're barbed. They are not gone. Those little eggs are designed so they'll stick inside those warm nostrils even when the moose is sneezing and hollering. So they cling to your eyes and that's where the eggs grow and then one day they hatch.'

'You're fucking crazy.'

She shuts her eyes and shakes her head.

'Don't use that language, Tuva. You're a writer so there's no need to resort to cussing. You're better than that.'

She disappears behind me again.

The woods are grey. The moon is shining through brighter now, but I'm faced with the curve of a tree and I can't turn, I can only look left and right and straight up and that's it. Each time I try to squeeze my hands to slip the ropes they seem to tighten up like nooses. Every now and then, cones fall from the trees. I can't hear them, but I can feel them if they're falling from the upper branches of this tree, and I can see them if they're falling from other trees close by. I can see eyes, too. I can see pairs of eyes twinkling up in the trees and down on the ground. Nothing close or big. And the slugs are still shining like gemstones.

Frida comes back.

'I'm almost done here, then we can go home.'

I see her hand and want to scream. She's holding a little transparent freezer bag with a bright green plastic clip. The contents are hidden in her palm, but I can see a drop of blood in the bottom corner of the bag.

I hang my head low and let my chin fall to my chest. I give up. This is not where I'm supposed to be, not by a long shot. I want to scratch my ears and my neck and my wrists. They're covered in red bumps and bites and it feels like the mosquitoes are coming back, coming back to the raised bumps for more like they can't believe their luck. I think about that tick, the one that got inside me. How deep will it go? Is it alive? Is its head still alive?

'Let's have that hot chocolate now, shall we?' Frida says.

'Let's fucking not.'

'Suit yourself. You know, I can't help thinking that if you'd let go of those big city ways, if you'd let that silly phase pass and you'd settled down with a nice man, you wouldn't be here right now. It's a shame, really.'

And then I remember the King of Hearts.

'What about the poker club?'

'What?' she says. 'Just a silly game, so-called men playing like boys. It's not as bad as mixing with vermin and whores.'

She picks her rifle up from the base of my tree and clicks something. I think she's taking the safety catch off.

'What are you doing? You said you wouldn't kill me, you said I wasn't like them.'

Frida bites her bottom lip again and looks apologetic.

'But you screamed, Tuva, and that changed everything, didn't it? That's not my fault. I'd rather you didn't try to blame other people for your own actions.'

She walks behind me with the rifle.

'No. Frida, wait. Please, wait.'

She reappears. First, her scent, and then her face comes close to mine. I can feel her breath against my wet skin.

'I'll tell them it was all an accident, I promise, I swear.'

'Don't worry about that, sweetie, it's too late for all that now. We're leaving together and I promise, you won't feel a thing. This had to come to a head. Two little clicks and we'll both be off to a better place, I'm going to take care of it.'

'Take care of it?'

She reaches close to me and pulls a single hair from my mouth. The hair pulls tight against my lip like a strand of dental floss.

'I'm going to do this the correct way, Tuva. There's a strict code we follow in Norrland, you know. We never cull the cow elk before the calf. It'll save you the trauma. We never shoot the mother before the child. I'll take care of it.'

51

I look up through the tangle of branches and I see sky. She's behind my back somewhere but above me there are a million stars and a million more for every minute I stare. I can't see her and I don't know where she is or if her rifle is loaded. My head's cocked back and fine drizzle is wafting across my face. All is silent. I can't feel the cold any more. I look up at the droplets of rain caught on the tips of my eyelashes, like the ones above me hanging off the tips of pine needles. And my heart gains mass and it sinks deep into my chest and it grows hard as I look up for Dad.

'Hot chocolate?' I say, almost laughing now. 'Last request, Frida.' I swing my head around but I still can't see her. 'I'll share that hot chocolate with you before, you know . . .'

And she's at my face again, her breath warm at my temple.

'Yes,' she says. 'I think we deserve it.'

The muscles in my arms and legs loosen and I slouch and let the ropes take the strain of my body for a moment. The rough cord bites at my wrists and almost pulls my arms from their sockets. Why did I do that? Why did I delay the inevitable? I want to live, of course I do, but I did it for the story. I did it because I can't write the complete piece with what I have, not properly, not well enough. And whether I write it with Dad somewhere else, or with Lena in Toytown, I need to write this story or else what's the point.

She unscrews the lid of the thermos and I watch steam rise into the grey air.

'No cups, I'm afraid,' her lips say. 'Wasn't expecting company, sorry.'

She fills the lid with thick brown liquid and holds it up to my mouth. I look at her as she tips it towards me. I stare at her blue eyes and she's looking down at my mouth to make sure that it doesn't spill. The chocolate fills my mouth with heat. My tongue's covered in silk and my gums are coated with sweetness. Then I swallow and my empty stomach fills from the very bottom. My body warms and my spirits rise absurdly and my blood loosens and my organs feel like they've been jolted into action. I'm coming back. My thoughts are clearing and ordering themselves. Frida takes a sip and wipes away a brown smudge from her painted lips.

'More?'

I nod and smile and she feeds me more. I'm like a baby lamb being fed from a bottle. I feel warm with cocoa and I'm right next to a gun and a demon and a dead eyeless man. And a thousand acres of dark and wild. The police are in the same forest; well it's officially the same forest, but they may as well be in Gothenburg or London. A kilometre anywhere else is a thousand kilometres here.

I drink it up and leave the last gulp in my mouth, tasting it properly before I swallow. I want to savour it, not because it's my last mouthful of anything, but because it tastes so damn good. Maybe because I'm tired and thirsty or maybe because it really is just delicious. Frida knows how to care through food. And then I think of Hannes behind me and what state he must be in right now with his eyes in her pocket in that neat little bag with that bright green clip. He deserved divorce papers and a slap, not all this.

'That's the last of it,' Frida says, sipping down the last chocolatey drips. 'Seventy per cent cocoa, and I mix in a little cream and a sprinkle of fresh nutmeg, that's the secret.'

'It was lovely,' I say. 'Tell me about Norrland, Frida, about your real home.' I need time. Please keep talking. 'Did it look like this?'

'Ha,' she says, screwing the lid back onto the thermos. 'This is a kid's petting zoo compared to Norrland. This is nothing compared to up there. Back home, things are bigger, colder, darker, and much further apart. My dad – this here is his old rifle – he didn't have any whores or lap dancers within a hundred kilometres of him. There were no temptations whatsoever. He and Mum still held hands and kissed on the lips till the very end. They were a couple till the very end, till death do us part. Up there in Norrland, I don't know, it's just cleaner and purer. The water and the air, the people, all of it. Thought my Hannes would be like that, too.'

She's looking behind me at her lifeless husband. Her smile fades and she's tight-lipped.

'First year of our marriage, he changed. He was cold, not interested. Sure, I was presentable at corporate events and I fitted the bill, but that was all it was. It got worse when that stinking cathouse opened. All he wanted was his stupid poker games and his rancid whores and his hunting. I don't know. At least our courtship was lovely.' She turns to me and smiles now, her eyes glazed. 'Dinner dances and midnight walks, drives to the lake, and sparks every time our fingers touched.'

Just keep her talking. More time.

'Mamma and Pappa set me up with him, they thought he'd be perfect. Not their fault, though, they didn't know. He was perfect until that first year of our marriage. He was my Rhett Butler and my Robby Redford and my Paul Newman all rolled into one, and he did save me from that hot dog place. I looked at him through my veil in the church and I saw my parents' life ahead of me; only it would be acted out by me and him. I saw a long stretch of affection and romance and happily-ever-afters. He had a good job, too: apprentice engineer at the mill near here. It was brand new back then. So we moved down, only needed a car for our stuff, and most of that was wedding presents. We had our own place straight off, a little house in Gavrik near the Grimberg factory. And then one night he decided he'd sleep in the spare room.'

'Why?'

'Who knows what motivates slugs and whores, sweetie? You and I will never understand them. I could tolerate it all because I had the eyes to visit whenever I needed but I could never tolerate him leaving me for a slut, no way.'

I look to my right and see blackness. Some grey, some moon on the pine trunks and puddles, but really it's all as black as a nightmare. I've had enough of listening to her disappointments so I zone out. I can't read her lips looking this way but I know she's still talking because I can feel her breath.

I think about the last time I went snorkelling. I was in Greece when I swam out to sea with my mask facing down into the water. It was beautiful, all turquoise and shells. Then the sea deepened. It went from light blue to navy to black in seconds. The water cooled and the seabed just fell away. I was still where I was before, on the surface, nothing had changed for me at all. Except everything had changed because there was nothing underneath me any more, just bottomless dark. Anything could have been down there. My aids were out because I can't swim with them, so it was just like this really. Like now. Cold and wet and dark. I had the exact same feeling because it wasn't my environment. Back then I swam like hell back to the beach but now I'm tied to a fucking tree with a tick boring into my wrist and a lily-of-the-valley-scented killer talking to me about her marriage problems.

I snap my head back to face her. 'Why didn't the police ever question you?'

'Me? Why in the world would they question someone like me?' she says, like she's shocked at the question. 'They talked to the strippers and the losers and the homo hermits in the village, that's who they spoke to. Björn and me were having lunch one time at the hotel in Gavrik, and I told him about my food deliveries to the oldies and about the lids. I'm not like your little Chinese friend cooking from her dirty caravan, Tuva. My food's all home-cooked from fresh ingredients. I don't have any of that sodium glutamate in my food, no way. So I told Björn I was making deliveries to the oldies with their frozen lasagnes and fish pies with mashed potato; proper food that's good for them. And I always write on the lid with a sharpie: the date and time I made it, the cooking time and temperature, and the name of the dish, and the date and time I deliver it. I've always done that. That was my so-called alibi, right there. I planned it all out. They could check the food and they'd see I was delivering. Doing my good deed. But then I never actually needed it because, of course, they never asked me. Why would they?'

I look up at the tree and can't think of another question to ask. It makes no sense whatsoever. It's like trying to interview a toddler. I look up towards the sky. I should be with Mum right now in Karlstad. I should be with my own mother right now who needs me and who's a fucking grade A saint next to Frida.

'How did you find out who was visiting the strip club and the cathouse?' I ask. 'How did you know which men to kill?'

'So-called men,' she corrects me. 'I've always kept in pretty good shape, Tuva, you know that. I've always taken care of myself because I think a wife has a duty to do that. So I would park up somewhere convenient and walk. Simple. I'd walk with Nordic walking sticks sometimes and without sticks sometimes.' She glances at the pedometer watch strapped to her wrist. 'Had some real good workouts. In wintertime, I'd ski, and in summertime, I'd jog. You would not believe the so-called men I saw stepping out of that cathouse and then later on from that whore strip club. All sorts of so-called men who should've known better, and who were lying to their wives and their children and their holy vows. The books get it right on this, the Bible and the romance novels. It's a man and woman for life, that's just what it is.'

She is out of her mind.

I watch as a mosquito lands on my left hand and plunges its stinger into a raised bump. It's double-dipping from a wound and sucking my blood out a second time. I watch it and I can't feel a thing and I can't hear Frida because I'm not looking at her lips.

'There were twelve eyes,' I say, turning to her again. 'Six pairs. Where's the other body?'

'Fourteen,' she says, holding up the plastic bag and I accidentally see the eyes, I didn't mean to. I see them and look away and crush the mosquito feeding from my hand against the tree. I look at Frida's lips and nowhere else.

'He was a millworker. Hannes introduced him to that pigsty cathouse back in the '90s,' Frida says. 'A loser with a family, he had everything going for him. I won't allow home-wreckers to go unpunished, I will not allow it. So I left him close to the stack, that old torp with just the chimney left. He must still be lying there. Suppose he'll be found now, but maybe not.'

I remember the stack and the rusty single bed.

'Tell me about—'

But she pushes her finger to my mouth and the cold tip tickles my top lip.

'No more telling, sweetie,' she says, lifting the rifle from the ground. 'I'm gonna take care of us now.'

'Wait,' I say, my voice breaking. 'Wait, I want to know about your boy, your son, tell me about him.'

I scan up and down and to the right, desperately looking for something, thinking about screaming again, my chest pressed tight against the tree.

She taps me on the shoulder and I turn to face her.

'I said,' her lips say. 'That I just told you all about him.'

I look at her, at one eye, then the other.

'He's down by the stack, the old chimney on its own.'

I look up at the grey branches and feel faint and then I look back to her.

'He took after his daddy.'

I turn right and see a glint. My sweat's stinging my eyes. I squint and strain to look through the murk. It's metal. I can see a figure, no, two figures, both squat. No.

I turn back to Frida.

'Wait, please.'

'I'm going to take care of us now because I've got to.'

I turn my head to the right. I'm stuck between Frida and the wood-carving sisters and one of the sisters has a rifle pointed right at my head. I glare at them and suddenly Frida's not so scary any more and the forest just got a whole lot worse. There's a troll locked in my basement and one of its creators is waving her arm at me and mouthing something. What?

'*Your,*' she's saying. Fuck, I can't make it out. I strain to see her mouth.

'*Move . . . Your . . . Head . . . Girl.*'

'I've got a lash in my eye,' I say to Frida, my voice trembling. 'Lift it out for me before you take care of us both, please. I can't do it myself.'

I see her finger come closer towards my eye. I see her pale fingerprint with its lines and valleys. I take a sharp breath and jerk my head back away from the tree, pushing at it with every muscle I've got, and arching back. I strain against my ropes and feel the gun fire, and I can hear it a little too, it's that loud. The air in front of my face moves and it's hot and I feel a spray of something wet on my forehead.

Frida falls.

I hold the tree, something rooted to keep me upright, something safe. I cling to it, shaking, shivering, my fingernails digging into the bark. It smells sweet like pencil shavings.

There's a hand tapping my shoulder and I spin around, horrified, expecting Frida to be back upright up but it's Cornelia, the talking sister.

'I'll cut you down.'

She takes her knife and slashes at the ropes and I fall away from the tree and stumble and she steadies me.

'Thank you,' I say.

The quiet sister's crouching down with her fingers pressed to Frida's neck.

'Dead?' asks Cornelia.

I look at Alice's face, not at Frida, although I can see blood in my peripheral vision, I can see the wound, but I focus on Alice, just Alice.

'Dead,' she says, her lips hardly moving.

I check my phone and my hands are shaking so much I can hardly see the screen. 2% battery, no reception.

'Best wait here till the policemen come over,' says Cornelia.

'Yep,' says Alice, removing her heavy waxed jacket. She places it slowly, carefully, over Frida's upper torso and head. Cornelia takes off her coat and walks over to Hannes. My God, don't look at his face. And then she covers him over.

52

I'm driving down the E16 in my truck, except I'm not the one driving. The heater's on full and I'm looking out of the window at the forest fringes as they scroll by. I'm curled up with Tammy's sweater tucked over my knees. My wrists are bandaged and my arms are bruised and my aids are working pretty well now considering.

'You've got that police appointment at four, so we have plenty of time, no rush. You need to take it easy.'

I hear Tammy's voice but I'm still dozy from the sleeping pill. I can taste rum on my tongue. My thoughts are separating into headlines and I'm making order from the chaos with margins and quotes and typeface. Tomorrow, I'll write it all up, ready for the next print. It's what I need right now, a string of hours alone with my memories and a keyboard to put them all straight. I can't think about what happened at the tree. Not yet. Lena's already told me she's tripling the print run and I've got an email from my old sub-editor at *The Guardian*. She's offering me a job. A real job, my dream job, but I can't. Not just yet. And I've had a message from Lena to call a prestigious bi-weekly periodical based in southern Sweden.

So, I need to write this story.

'Still can't believe those carpenter sisters saved you. I just can't believe it was them.'

'David Holmqvist, too,' I say, my voice quiet and calm. 'The sisters shot her but Holmqvist found us all. He gave me his coat and had his dog stand guard until the police tracked us.'

Tammy shakes her head and sighs and checks the rear-view mirror. 'And they made that troll, too,' she says. 'And then they went and found you and saved you.'

'There were two trolls, they made them both,' I say, the seatbelt digging into my bruises. 'Last night I asked them about it before the police came with their dogs and their lights. The one you saw was a special order paid for by Frida months ago. But the one with the dick was re-carved, Frida customised it herself. They told me they don't make that kind of filth no matter what price people would pay for it.'

Tammy shakes her head again and overtakes a white Volvo taxi and a truck full of rough lumber.

'All three of them gave up their coats,' I say, and it sounds stupid when I hear myself say it out loud but last night it felt important. 'The sisters placed their coats over Hannes and Frida, and David gave his to me. Everyone thought Holmqvist was some evil monster, all those years he lived with the rumours, the sniggering and the looks.'

'And two arrests,' says Tammy.

'And he'd done nothing. Last night we sat there like some weird family, the three of them arranged around me, shielding me from everything out there, and Holmqvist's big dog shielding them.'

'I still can't believe it,' Tammy says. 'Listen, I want you stay at my place as long as you need to. Let me look after you for a while.'

'Just for as long as there are press crawling outside my apartment,' I say. 'It won't be for too long, they'll soon move off to the next big story.'

'Whatever suits you,' she says.

'Thord reckons Frida tampered with my hearing aid batteries.'

Tammy shakes her head in disbelief.

'He also told me that Frida delivered a month's worth of frozen meals to the elderly yesterday. And she wore waterproof make-up in the woods. She was ready. Frida knew she was either getting arrested or . . .'

'You want to eat first or after?' Tammy says. Her voice is like a balm, it cools my memories and warms my skin. 'That sushi place down by the station opens at twelve so by the time we've found a parking place and paid, they'll be opening up for us.'

'Let's do all that after,' I say.

We find the building and park and buy a ticket and the creeping vine covering the high brick walls has turned red since my last visit. It's turned. We walk in through the revolving doors and the stale heat hits me. We pull on blue plastic shoe covers and walk along the squeaky rubber floors and past artificial pot plants, but she's moved rooms. Tammy waits near some chairs and magazines and a water dispenser. I find her name on a board and then I find her new room. The halls smell of bleach and stale air and incremental dying.

'So, you came.'

I walk in and she's almost gone. She's sinking through the bed now, her body barely noticeable under the sheets, the sheets with the hospice name printed on them to save the laundry company from mix-ups. Nightstand. Pills. A small glass of water with saliva or something floating on the surface. Maybe it's just dust. A photo of her and Dad on their wedding day, and next to it a photo of me on my graduation day. A travel clock and a small tube of rose-scented hand cream.

I pull up a heavy pine chair to the bed. It squeaks as I drag it. My wrists burn and I think of the troll still locked in my basement. I notice the board clipped to the end of the bed with a pen dangling from it by a piece of red yarn.

'I'm sorry I haven't been for a while,' I say. 'I should have come.'

'You had your reasons,' she says, her voice a heavy whisper.

'It's over now,' I say. 'I'll be with you more from now on.' I try not to think about the messages from the other papers, the chance to leave all this. I look up to the white ceiling, at the ventilation grill, and then I turn back to Mum. 'I want to be with you more.'

I move closer to her, to her shrunken face, and she smiles at me. She never really smiles, but now her eyes soften and her lips part a little and I almost collapse with it all. I bite the inside of my mouth and smile back.

'Water?'

She nods. I throw the old water into the sink in the corner of the room and turn on the tap and fill the glass and glance out of the window. This is a better room, it has a lake view. And then it hits me and I know why they've moved her here. I feel unsteady. I sit back down and hold the glass of water out to her and she sips from the glass like an insect might drink from a saucer. Her lips have faded into her skin. A droplet escapes from her mouth and rolls down her chin. The room's so quiet. I watch the droplet roll and hang for a moment and then fall. And I fall with it. My head rests on my mother's hard little chest. It's barely moving, just shallow wispy breaths. Sideways-on, I see a nurse walk to the threshold of the room and she sees me and then she walks away.

Mum's stroking my hair with her crêpe-paper fingers. I close my eyes and feel numb. As I sit up, I see her crying except the well has run dry. Hers are invisible tears. I clear my throat and pick up the hand cream and squirt a little onto the pad of my index finger. I work it into her hands, the life almost gone from them now; they're translucent and cool to the touch.

'Your pappa would have been,' she forces a breath. 'Proud of you,' she says, and her voice is as thin and as pale as her skin. 'Proud. You know that, don't you?'

I nod and the tears come. I wipe them away with my wrists and rub my hands on my jeans and reach out and stroke that area around her cheekbone where the skin's still smooth and young.

'Your pappa,' she waits for a breath to come. 'Your pappa loved you, Tuva.'

I nod and feel a shiver down my neck and see her eyes flash back to youth for a split second. They turn back from watery grey to vivid green and then back again. She's my mamma again for a glimpse with her blonde hair and home-baked cinnamon shortbread and knitting. I place my cheek next to her cheek to warm it. I force my breathing to match hers and our faces rise and fall together for a while.

ACKNOWLEDGEMENTS

To my agent, Kate Burke: thank you for your energy and wisdom and skill. Thanks for giving me the chance.

To the team at Diane Banks Associates: thank you for your encouragement and warmth.

To my editor, Jenny Parrott: thank you for being whip-smart and sensitive and generous. Thanks for making this real.

To the team at Oneworld and Point Blank: thank you for being so dedicated and passionate. I could not ask for a more excellent publisher.

To all the bloggers and booksellers and reviewers and tweeters: thank you for your enthusiasm and time. Readers benefit so much from your recommendations and spirit. I am one of them. Thank you.

To the York Festival of Writing: thank you for teaching me things. Thank you for putting hundreds of writers in a room each year. Thanks to Julie Cohen and Shelley Harris for being stars.

To Claire McGowan: thank you for being a very early reader. Thank you for your encouragement and for your wise, succinct comments. You helped me.

To Hayley Webster: thank you for positive feedback years ago on a day I needed it most.

To Paddy Kelly: thank you for reading an early version of the book and for being so positive and kind.

To @DeafGirly: thank you so much for your expert feedback. In some ways your opinion matters to me more than anyone else's. I am very grateful.

To the Swedish nature: thank you for being wild. Thank you for being an inspiration.

To my family: thank you for letting me play alone for hours as a child. Thank you for letting me read. Thank you for not enrolling me in countless clubs. Thank you for allowing me to be bored. It was a special gift.

To my friends: apologies if I've missed barbecues and parties due to rewriting. Thank you for being wonderful (and patient).

To my sister: thank you for saying 'do you mind if I just wait for the movie.'

To my wife and son: Thank you. Love you. Always.

Red Snow is the hotly anticipated sequel to *Dark Pines*, featuring Tuva Moodyson, the relentless deaf reporter who has a knack for sniffing out secrets in small town Sweden.

Read ahead and discover the case that's going to make her wish she'd left arctic Gavrik long ago . . .

RED SNOW

WILL DEAN

1

There's a Volvo down in the ditch and I'd say it's been there a while.

I touch the brakes and my truck comes to a stop nice and easy, studded tyres biting into ice and bringing me to a silent standstill. It's all silent up here. White and utterly, utterly silent.

The display on my dash reads minus nineteen Celsius. I pull on my hat and move the earflaps so they don't mess with my hearing aids and then I turn up the heat and leave the engine idling and open my door and step down.

The Volvo looks like an ice cube, all straight lines and sparkling crystals, no signs of life, not a colour or a feature to look at. It's leaning down hard to the right so I'm roughly level with the driver's side window. I knock. My gloved knuckle sounds dull on the frosted glass so I rub my hand over the window but it's blasted solid with ice.

I step back, cold air burning my dried-out cheeks. Need more creams, better creams, prescription winter creams. My mobile has no reception here so I look around and then head back to my pick-up and grab my scraper, one from a collection of three, you can never be too careful, from my Hilux door well.

As I scrape the Volvo window the noise hits my aids like the sound of scaffolding poles being chewed by a log chipper. I start to get through, jagged ice shards spraying this way and that. And then I see his face.

I scrape harder. Faster,

'Can you hear me?' I yell. 'Are you okay?'

But he is not okay.

I can see the frost on his moustache and the solid ice flows running down from each nostril. He is dead still.

I keep scraping and pull the door handle but it's either locked or frozen solid or both. My breath looks nervous in front of my face, clouds of vapour between me and him, between my cheap mascara and his crystallised eye lashes. I've seen enough death these past six months, more than enough. I knock on the glass again and strain at the door handle. And then his eyes snap open.

I pull back, my thick rubber soles losing purchase on the shiny white beneath.

He doesn't move. He just looks.

'Are you okay?' I ask.

He stares at me. His body is perfectly still, his head unmoving, but his grey-blue eyes are on me, searching, asking questions. And then he sniffs and shakes his head and nods a kind of passive-aggressive 'thanks but I got this' dismissal which is frankly ridiculous.

'My name's Tuva Moodyson. Let me drive you into Gavrik. Let me call someone for you.'

The frozen snot in his moustache creaks and splinters and he mouths 'I'm fine' and I can read his lips pretty well, over twenty years of practice.

I pull on his door handle, my neck getting hot, and then it starts to give so I pull harder and the ice cracks and the door swings up a little. It's heavy at this angle.

'You trying to snap my cables?' he says.

'Sorry?'

'It's about minus twenty out here I'd say and you just yanked my door open like it's a treasure chest. Best way to break a door handle cable.'

'You want to warm up in my truck?' I say. 'I can call breakdown?'

He looks out toward my truck like he's deciding if it's a suitable vehicle to save his life and I look at him and at the layers of clothes he's entombed himself in: a jacket that must contain five or six others judging by its bulk, and blankets over his knees and thick ski gloves and I can see three hats, all different colours.

He coughs and spits and then says, 'I'll come over just to warm up, just for a minute.'

Well, thanks for doing me that favour mister Värmland charm champion.

I help him out and he's smaller than me, half a head smaller, and he's about fifty-five. There's a pair of nail scissors on the passenger seat next to a carrier bag full of canisters, and there's a bag of dry dog food in the footwell. He locks his Volvo like there are gangs of Swedes out here just waiting to steal his broken down piece of shit car, and then he trudges over to my pick-up truck.

'Japanese?' he says, opening the passenger side.

I nod and climb in.

'Ten minutes and I'll be out your hair,' he says.

'What's your name?'

He coughs. 'Andersson.'

'Well, Mr Andersson, I'm Tuva Moodyson, nice to meet you.'

We look out of the windscreen for a while, side by side, no talking, just staring at the white of Garvik Kommun. Looks like one of those lucky blanks you get in a game of scrabble.

'You that one that writes stories in the newspaper?' he says.

'I am.'

'Best be heading back to my car now.'

'If you go out there again you're gonna end up dead. Let me drive you into town, your car will be fine.'

He looks at me like I'm nine years old.

'I've driven more tough winters than you've had hot lunches.'

What the hell does that even mean?

'And I can tell you,' he says, rubbing his nose on his coat sleeve. 'This ain't nothing. Minus twenty, maybe twenty-two, it ain't nothing. Anyhows, I texted my middle boy three hours ago, told him my location, and when he's done up at the pulp mill he'll come pick me up. You think I ain't spent time in ditches in winter?'

'Fine. Go,' I say, pausing for him to think. 'But I'll call the police and then Constable Thord'll have to come by and pick you up. How about we save him the bother.'

Mr Andersson sighs and chews his lower lip. The ice on his face is thawing, and now he just looks flushed and gaunt and a little tired.

'You gonna be the one driving?' he says.

I sigh-laugh.

He sniffs and wipes the thawed snot from his moustache whiskers. 'Guess I don't got much choice.'

I start the engine and turn on both heated seats. As we pass his frozen Volvo he looks mournfully out the window like he's leaving the love of his life on some movie railway platform.

'Why don't you buy Swedish?' he asks.

'You don't like my Hilux?'

'Ain't Swedish.'

'But it goes.'

We drive on and then he starts squirming in his seat like he's dropped something.

'My seat hot?' he says.

'You want me to switch it down a notch?'

'Want you to switch the damn thing off cos I feel like I peed my pants over here.' He looks disgusted. 'Goddam Japanese think of everything.'

Okay, so I've got a racist bore for a passenger but it's only twenty minutes into Gavrik town. It's never the cute funny smart people who need picking up, now is it?

'Where do you want dropping off, Mr Andersson? Where do you live?'

'Just drop me by the factory.'

'You work there?'

'Could say that. Senior Janitor. Thirty-three years next June.'

I pull a lever and spray my windscreen and the smell of chemical antifreeze wafts back through the heating vents.

'How many janitors they got up there?' I ask.

'Just got me.'

'You get free liquorice?'

'I ain't got none so don't go asking. I'm the janitor and that's it.'

I drive up to an intersection where the road cuts a cross-country ski trail marked with plastic yellow sticks and they look like toothpicks driven into a perfect wedding cake. The air is still and the sky's a hanging world of snow and it is heavy, just waiting to dump.

'You did the Medusa story, eh?'

I nod.

He shakes his head.

'You just about ruined this place, you know that? Good few people be quite pleased to see you run out of town, I'm just saying what I heard.'

I get this bullshit from time to time. As the sole full-time reporter here in Gavrik, I get blamed for bad news even though I'm just the one writing it.

'I'd say it was a job well done,' I say.

'Well, you would, you done it.'

'You'd rather elk hunters were still getting shot out in the woods?'

He goes quiet for a while and I switch the heat from leg/face to windscreen.

'All I know is we lost some hard-won reputation,' he says. 'And thank God we still got the factory and the Mill to keep some stability. That's all I'm saying and now I done said it.'

As I get closer to town, the streets get a little clearer, more snowploughing here, more yard shovelling, and the municipal lighting's coming on. 3pm and the streetlights are coming on. Welcome to February.

'Suppose you were just doing your job like anyone but we're a small town and we're cut off from everywhere else so we've learned to stick together. I got eight grandkiddies to worry about. You'd know if you were from these parts.'

I drive on.

The twin chimneys of the factory, the largest employer in town, loom ahead of me. It's the biggest building around here save for the ICA Maxi supermarket. Two brick verticals back-dropped by a white sheet.

'Say, you hear me pretty good for a deaf person, don't mind me saying.'

'I can hear you just fine.'

'You using them hearing aid contraptions?'

I feel his eyes on my head, his gaze boring into me.

'I am.'

'I'll be needing them myself pretty soon, sixty-one this coming spring.'

I drive past the ice hockey rink and on between the supermarket and McDonalds, the two gateposts of Gavrik, and up along Storgatan, the main street in town. I head past the haberdashery and the gun shop and my office with its lame-ass Christmas decorations still in the window, and on toward the cop shop, and then I pull up next to the Grimberg liquorice factory established 1839 or so it says on the gates.

'This okay?' I ask.

He gets out without saying a word and I look around and there are five or six people scattered about all looking up to the sky. This doesn't happen, especially in February. A hunched figure in a brown coat slips on the ice as he walks away. I try to look up through the windscreen but it's frosted at the top so I open my door and climb out onto the gritted salted pavement. I can hear mutterings and I can sense others joining us from Eriksgatan.

They're looking up at the right chimney, the one I've never seen smoke coming out of. There's a man, or I think it's a man, a figure in a suit climbing the ladder that's bolted to the side of the chimney and he's climbing higher and higher past the masts and phone antennas bolted to the bricks. He's in a hurry. No hat or gloves. I look up and the sky is blinding white, dazzling, and the pale clouds are moving fast overhead, the wind picking up, and as I stare up it's like an optical illusion, like the chimneys are toppling over onto me. And then the man jumps.